A
HISTORY OF THOUGHT AND PRACTICE
IN
EDUCATIONAL ADMINISTRATION

A
HISTORY OF THOUGHT AND PRACTICE IN
EDUCATIONAL ADMINISTRATION

Roald F. Campbell
Thomas Fleming
L. Jackson Newell
John W. Bennion

Teachers College, Columbia University
New York and London

Published by Teachers College Press, 1234 Amsterdam Avenue,
New York, N.Y. 10027

Library of Congress Cataloging-in-Publication Data

A History of thought and practice in educational administration.

  Bibliography: p. 215
  Includes index.
  1. School management and organization—United States—History—20th century.
2. Universities and colleges—United States—Administration—History—20th century.
I. Campbell, Roald Fay, 1905–
LB2805.H56 1987   371.2′00973   87-1871
ISBN 0-8077-2844-6
ISBN 0-8077-2843-8 (pbk.)

Manufactured in the United States of America

92 91 90 89   2 3 4 5 6

To
Margaret, Fiona, Linda, and Sylvia

CONTENTS

Preface

WE ARE CONVINCED that to understand a field fully—its thought and practice—one must know how it took shape. Some elements of the history of educational administration have been written about, but there is no broad account of how the field evolved. This volume attempts to fill that void.

As an area of academic study and practical concern, educational administration is made up of elements of two broader fields of inquiry and practice: education and management. The administration of educational enterprises is closely tied to the more general field of education. All organized societies have made deliberate efforts to teach the young. These efforts, frequently institutionalized in schools and colleges, have commanded the attention of many scholars. Such accounts have long helped us to understand the nature of schools and schooling, but have given scant attention to their administration. Thus, a more thorough treatment of educational administration from a historical perspective is in order.

Educational administration is also part of the general field of management. *Management*, as the term is used in the business world, means much the same as the term *administration* does when it is applied to government and many other organizations. Over time, some scholars have dealt with the history of management thought and practice, frequently assuming that management, regardless of institutional setting, is based on common elements. While there is some merit to the generic view of administration, such an approach ignores the characteristics of administration peculiar to each type of institution. For this reason also, a more specific treatment of the history of educational administration is warranted.

Although this book deals specifically with the evolution of educational administration, to some extent our treatment of the field is circumscribed. Our coverage of educational administration, for example, focuses almost entirely on the twentieth century, since the first definitive training program for educational administrators was not established until the early years of this century at Teachers College, Columbia University.

We recognize that schools, colleges, and other formal organizations designed to foster teaching and learning existed for centuries prior to 1900, and that, in one way or another, these organizations had to be administered. Before this century, however, the administration of schools was hardly differentiated from teaching. Or, particularly in early rural schools, much of the administration was performed by laypeople who served as members of school committees and, later, school boards. With administrative duties performed by teachers or laypeople, educational administration was not generally recognized as a specialized field of practice or thought.

Our treatment of educational administration is also defined by place. We have chosen to focus on the history of educational administration in the United States, principally because the literature of the field—journal articles, textbooks, research monographs—for practitioners and scholars is essentially an American literature, generally published in the United States. In recent years, to be sure, there has been an increasing body of scholarship produced in other countries, particularly Canada, Australia, and Great Britain. At one point, we considered including these countries in our treatment, but we found that statements about administrative practice are not meaningful unless they are related to the broader history and culture of a nation. Thus, while we found we could deal with administrative practices in the United States, we were not confident we could do justice to those of other countries. For this reason, we have not addressed international developments in practice, although we believe that this study may have relevance to Canadians, who, as North Americans, share some of our historical and cultural characteristics.

Apart from the introductory and concluding chapters, this book has two major sections. Chapters 2 through 6 deal with administrative thought as it has evolved over this century. Within these chapters, four major views of administration are set forth. While we did not follow precisely any of the classifications offered by other scholars in educational administration or the general field of management, we are indebted to the major contributors in these areas of study.

We have tried to define and focus on four broad views that have characterized administrative thought and practice in public schools and higher education. We hope that these views have validity for other scholars and practitioners in the field, and that they prove to be a useful way to organize the history of administrative thought and practice. Finally, we recognize that categorizations of this kind are always a matter of judgment and that others may see the history of the field somewhat differently.

It also seems worth reporting that the major views of administration around which this volume is built have been tested in several settings over the past decade. In faculty seminars, graduate student seminars, and two prior publications, one or more of the authors has used the four views set forth here as a basis for instruction and writing. In each of these instances our framework has seemed to provide a useful way to treat the major approaches to administrative thought. These views recognize the necessity of balancing the needs of the individual with the mission of the organization. Indeed, balancing these two themes may be the persistent task for those who study and work in organizations, a theme we pursue in Chapter 6.

Chapters 7, 8, and 9 deal with the evolution of administrative practice in public schools and universities. These chapters include, for example, discussions of administrative study and practice in public schools, the evolution of administrative developments in higher education, and an examination of graduate study in educational administration. The volume concludes with Chapter 10, which reflects upon the history of knowledge and practice in the field.

In this joint endeavor, full use was made of the special competence of each author. Roald Campbell initiated and coordinated the project and took the lead on Chapters 5, 6, and 10. Thomas Fleming fashioned Chapters 2, 3, and 4; Jackson Newell forged Chapters 1, 8, and 9; and Chapter 7 was framed by John Bennion. At several retreats in Salt Lake City and Victoria, British Columbia, we met to revise and integrate the manuscript. Chapter drafts were discussed at length by all four authors and reworked collaboratively. In the process, we educated each other.

We extend thanks to the many professors, practitioners, and graduate students who responded to our ideas about this history and offered suggestions concerning the text. And we owe a special debt of gratitude to Ann Blanchard, Joyce Gorrell, and Janet Felker for their able assistance in preparing the manuscript.

This book should be of interest to several groups. Graduate students preparing to become educational administrators will find that this historical treatment illuminates ideas they encounter in other aspects of their programs. Practitioners in schools and colleges will find that it helps explain the current nature of their work and the context in which it occurs. Trustees, school board members, and government officials who deal with professional educational leaders may discover in its pages some clarification of the field and some insights concerning the men and women who work in it. The ever-growing body of laypeople who are becoming participants in educational policy making may find in this work explanations of ideas and institutions that may help them in their tasks. Finally, we hope that this volume will serve our colleagues who study and teach in this field and who, like us, spend much of their time trying to understand the relationship between thought and practice.

ROALD F. CAMPBELL
THOMAS FLEMING
L. JACKSON NEWELL
JOHN W. BENNION

Salt Lake City
January, 1987

A
HISTORY OF THOUGHT AND PRACTICE
IN
EDUCATIONAL ADMINISTRATION

1

INTRODUCTION:
THE NATURE OF THE FIELD

Let us then admit that there are two histories: the actual series of events that once occurred; and the ideal series that we affirm and hold in memory. The first is absolute and unchanged—it was what it was whatever we do or say about it; the second is relative—always changing in response to the increase or refinement of knowledge.

Normally the memory of Mr. Everyman, when he awakens in the morning, reaches out into the country of the past and of distant places and simultaneously recreates his little world of endeavor, pulls together as it were things said and done in his yesterdays, and coordinates them with his present perceptions and with things to be said and done in his tomorrows. Without this historical knowledge, his memory of things said and done, his to-day would be aimless and his to-morrow without significance.

—Carl L. Becker, *Everyman His Own Historian*

EDUCATIONAL ADMINISTRATION HAS BEEN A DISTINCT FIELD of study and practice since the early years of this century. In the mid-1980s, there were half a million men and women serving in administrative positions in American educational institutions, a figure that corresponded roughly with the number of physicians practicing in the United States. Whether these educational leaders, and the knowledge and values that defined their work, constituted a distinct profession, or simply a managerial class within the larger profession of education, remained an open question. As the end of its first century approaches, however, educational administration is at least a sizable professional specialization.

Preoccupied with the tasks of establishing and defining a new professional field, scholars and practitioners of educational administration have rarely displayed a significant awareness of the origins and development of their work. With notable exceptions like Raymond Callahan (1972) and David Tyack and Elisabeth Hansot (1982), scholars have seldom devoted specific or sustained attention to the history of administrative affairs in schools and colleges. Whatever the reasons, those affiliated with the field of educational administration in the late 1980s continue to have some confusion about their professional iden-

1

tity and intellectual roots. It seemed appropriate, therefore, to examine our heritage in thought and practice.

PURPOSE AND SIGNIFICANCE

Education, in its larger sense, is as old as the human race. Even schooling—systematic instruction provided by an organization designed for that purpose—goes back thousands of years. Administration has also been practiced for millennia. Whether building roads or temples for the Inca, or constructing pyramids for the pharaoh, ancient civilizations faced management problems comparable to the operation of a modern corporation or government bureau. Only in this century, however, have educational institutions become so large and complex as to make their administration a distinct area of practice and study. Educational administration, then, exists at the confluence of two professions, each replete with its own literature, traditions, and values. One cannot examine the evolution of educational administration without considering important milestones in the separate histories of education and administration. Both of these legacies will be taken into account as their synthesis is described in this book.

For several reasons, study and practice in educational administration have developed especially rapidly in the United States. Here education has been funded cooperatively by local, state, and federal governments, and it is overseen independently by private citizens elected or appointed to state and local school boards. This tradition of local lay control, however compromised since mid-century, is more than an evolutionary quirk; it remains a manifestation of western liberal idealism which seeks to protect the educational process from those who would use it for political indoctrination. Another factor that spurred attention to administration in education, especially around the turn of the century, was the national aim to assimilate millions of European immigrants and prepare them (and millions of rural American citizens) to assume roles in an emerging industrial nation. Indeed, educational leaders became key players in the formation of a new socio-economic order. A combination of circumstances placed them near the center of the stage. America's schools and colleges, then, set apart from other public and private institutions, faced unique challenges and constructed distinct patterns of governance which gradually commanded the attention of scholars.

Americans have also attempted to educate more people for a greater number of years than has any other society in history. The number of individuals holding leadership or administrative positions in schools and colleges is enormous. There are approximately 100,000 principals and school superintendents and over 10,000 college and university presidents and vice presidents. Many of these leaders are served by numerous professional assistants. Further, about 2,500 professors specialize in the study of educational administration and higher education and offer instruction to prospective managers of educational enterprises.

Because of the importance of the tradition of local control and the massive scale of education in the United States, educational administration emerged early as a distinct professional field in this country. As the literature has passed beyond America's borders, however, and as practitioners of educational management have multiplied elsewhere, scholarly activity and formal preparation in educational administration have become more common in other countries, especially Canada, Australia, and Great Britain.

NATURE OF THIS WORK

Unlike medicine, where formal training is more tightly controlled and professional identities are more precisely defined, educational administrators pursue their work with a variety of academic and professional degrees and certificates—usually earned over a period of years extending into mid-life. They also work in a great variety of institutions, both public and private, with vastly different purposes. It is important, therefore, to describe the boundaries of educational administration as it is treated in this volume.

Emphasis on Thought and Practice

Any assessment of the development of educational administration must reckon with at least three important elements: (1) thought about administration, (2) administrative practice, and (3) professional preparation of administrators for schools and colleges. These elements cannot be treated in isolation from each other, nor can they be separated from the evolution of educational institutions generally or from the profound changes taking place in American society in the twentieth century. These historical factors are important because they provide an understanding of the context within which educational administration has developed.

Of the three elements that make up the field of educational administration—scholarship, practice, and graduate programs—this book is concerned especially with the first two. Scholarly literature and theory, as they have expanded upon the conventional wisdom about the administration of education, are the focus of the early chapters. The development of administrative practice in schools and colleges is the chief concern of the later chapters. While graduate programs for educational administrators have become an important element of this profession and have provided an impetus for the expansion of knowledge within the field, they came into the picture relatively late. Since graduate programs represent a major intersection of theory and practice, however, they are treated in some depth in Chapter 9.

Educational administration means different things to different people. For some, the management of public schools comes to mind. But this field also includes the study and practice of administration in a wider range of institutions concerned with education and educational policy, including colleges and universities, government agencies at state and federal levels, and private foundations. Those who serve in administrative positions in schools, for instance, face quite different problems and maintain identities quite distinct from those of university administrators. The same is true of scholars who study leadership behavior in these two settings. Each group has developed its own journals, publishing houses, and professional societies. Without ignoring the important variations among such groups, a broader view of educational administration has been taken in this volume—one that is inclusive of these significant specialities. What was traditionally called school administration, however, will dominate these pages. There are two reasons for this: First, scholarly interest in school administration goes back to the first decade of this century and, second, far more practitioners and scholars are concerned with school administration than are devoted to administrative affairs in other educational settings.

Pioneering scholars Ellwood P. Cubberley and George D. Strayer, often credited with initiating the formal study of school administration, received their doctorates from Teachers College, Columbia University, in 1905. Their degrees were in education, with an emphasis in administration. Cubberley, after brief sojourns as a college president and school superintendent, distinguished himself in the fields of school administration and the history of education at Stanford University (Sears & Henderson, 1957). On the other edge of the continent, Strayer pursued his research and teaching, including his notable school surveys, at Teachers College. Subsequent decades witnessed a growing number of professors in the new field of school administration. Until the 1950s, however, most came from the ranks of school administrators and, by their own reports, taught by anecdote and prescription.

After World War II, when the social sciences began to come their own, the theoretical literature in educational administr began to grow, as evidenced by the publication in 1957 of *Administrative Behavior in Education*, written by 18 professors and edited by Roald Campbell and Russell Gregg. The 1964 Yearbook of the National Society for the Study of Education, edited by Daniel Griffiths, was another notable event. Scholarship advanced in the 1960s and 1970s, nurtured by a mature group of academic leaders that included not only those mentioned above, but also Francis Chase at the University of Chicago, Truman Pierce at George Peabody College, Roy Hall at the University of Texas, and John Ramseyer at The Ohio State University. These leaders drew upon prewar experience and responded to postwar conditions in a way that stimulated and supported a new generation of scholars led by Andrew Halpin, Jacob Getzels, Daniel Griffiths, and other important contributors who are noted in succeeding chapters (Cunningham, Hack, & Nystrand, 1977).

The academic study of higher education, like school administration, grew out of other disciplines and fields. Between the world wars, a few professors shifted their focus from school administration to the management of colleges and universities. More frequently, however, professors who pioneered the study of higher education were educated in the academic disciplines or in established applied fields. Few identified themselves as professors of higher education. Rather, they saw themselves as professors of political science or psychology, for example, who shared a common research interest in higher education. Professors of higher education *per se* were not found in American universities until mid-century or later. They did not have a professional society until the Association of Professors of Higher Education was formed in the early 1970s. Those in the academic field of higher education have eschewed the term "administration," preferring to take a broader view of the study of colleges and universities.

An Applied Field

Educational administration is an applied field rather than an academic discipline. It does not draw upon a single body of literature nor use a single set of scholarly tools. Whereas academic disciplines may concentrate on "pure" research—knowledge for its own sake, without regard for immediate utility—an applied field must maintain a vital concern not only with the extension of knowledge but also with the improvement of practice. Similarly, whereas academic disciplines may confine their attention to single dimensions of a given phenomenon, an applied field must be concerned with problems in their totality—drawing upon the methods of many disciplines. Educational administration, once confined primarily to leadership in educational institutions, now includes many agencies that are quite remote from the classroom.

Educational administration is one of many applied administrative fields. Related to it are public administration, business management, military leadership, and hospital administration. Although each of these fields has its own unique characteristics, stemming from the nature and values of the institutions in which administration is practiced, they also have much in common. Each must reckon with the distinctive values and purposes of a given profession, and each has problems associated with the particular blend of public and professional accountability for which its leaders are responsible. Historically, however, they have traded ideas rather freely, despite their different technical and academic language.

Turning to relationships within the field of educational administration, scholars and practitioners must be considered complementary elements of a common profession. Practitioners are concerned most with the goals and the work of a particular organization. They focus on the pragmatic, on "what will work," and their views tend to be dominated by immediate problems. Scholars, on the other hand, enjoy the luxury of time and distance. Less pressed by nettlesome interruptions and administrative deadlines, they are at liberty to take the long view and to consider ideas that may have little immediate utility. Scholars and practitioners are often the subject of each other's humor—and even disdain. Yet each is essential to the health of the profession as a whole. The scholar must continually urge practitioners to step back from their work to consider the appropriateness of their goals and the effectiveness of their procedures. Administrators, for their part, must constantly urge scholars to test their ideas in the crucible of practice. Ironically, if either succeeds in winning the other over, both are the poorer for it. The complementarity of their roles has been an important feature in the emergence of educational administration (Campbell & Newell, 1973).

EDUCATION, ADMINISTRATION, AND THE LARGER SOCIETY

Major movements in the field of educational administration, like those in education more generally, reflect deeper societal trends. The rise of the great corporations, the traumas of two world wars and the great depression, and the social upheavals of the 1960s and 1970s, to mention only a few of the monumental events in the larger society, have done much to shape thinking about the relationship between individuals and institutions.

The Dawn of a New Century

In the summer of 1893, Frederick Jackson Turner presented a paper at the annual meeting of the American Historical Association in Chicago. "The Significance of the Frontier in American History" was both an insightful analysis of forces that shaped the national character and the beginning of a new era of American studies. Turner (1947) postulated that the "existence of an area of free land, its continuous recession, and the advance of American settlement westward, explain American development" (p. 1). Values and institutions, he believed, reflected the continuous adaptations required of a people engaged in settling a wilderness and forging social, economic, and political institutions in a rough and open environment. The availability of free land rendered obsolete the property qualifications associated with the right to vote. Clearly, the frontier had a democratizing influence on emerging American society.

From Jefferson's Northwest Ordinances of 1787 until the early twentieth century, the influence of the American frontier revealed itself in national policy. Among the more notable events, the Morrill Acts of 1862 and 1890 and the Hatch Act of 1887 granted federal support for education and extension work in agriculture, home economics, and mechanical arts. As America approached the twentieth century, education no longer served a privileged few; it had begun to serve the interests of the people and the needs of a growing nation.

Even as the frontier vanished as an identifiable band across the hemisphere, industrial development was sweeping the eastern states and bringing a transformation of its own. Historian Arthur M. Schlesinger, Sr. characterized the resulting growth of cities as a force greater than the frontier in democratizing American life and shaping our social institutions (1933, 1941). Whatever the merits of these competing theories, immigrants, many of them from southern Europe, steamed across the Atlantic and settled not so often on the western frontier as in the burgeoning cities on the eastern seaboard. By the turn of the century, business was king, great corporations had taken shape, and America faced problems of social and economic justice with an uncertain hand. Some saw in the vast development of the business elite an expression of social Darwinism—a natural evolution of society that was both positive and appropriate. Others, especially the reformers of the progressive era, were concerned by the growing distance between rich and poor and the helplessness of common laborers before corporate monoliths. Forging an uneasy alliance between labor and agriculture, the progressives attempted to challenge established centers of power in both politics and education.

Cubberley at Stanford and other members of the so-called "educational trust" believed that education should foster the development of the middle class (Tyack & Hansot, 1981, p. 11). Schools were to inspire "southern European immigrants" with a loyalty to business and the work ethic—and they were to do this efficiently, with industrial management techniques. Cubberley and his colleagues sought with some success to professionalize educational leadership and transform the American school in the image of a business enterprise. In politics, municipal reformers sought to end "bossism" and usher in a new era of city governance based on professional rather than political leadership.

It was in this setting that conscious scholarly attention was first given to the study and practice of managing educational institutions. Tyack and Hansot (1981) wrote that by the turn of the century "leadership in American public education had gravitated from the part-time educational evangelist of the mid-nineteenth century to a new breed of professional managers, who made education a life-long career and who reshaped the schools according to the canons of business efficiency and scientific expertise" (p. 9). Social progress, the educators of the new century believed, could be managed toward "even nobler ends" by the application of management principles to school organizations (Cubberley, 1919; Cremin, 1964).

The transformation in educational administration was a fundamental one; schooling was too important to be left to teacher-managers. Leadership and control, it was then believed, must be centralized and placed in the hands of those who had the specific training, skills, and vision to advance societal purposes. This was no job for the amateur. The reformers of this era sought educational salvation through centralized, rational control. Cubberley, for one, contended that the genius of American civilization was centered in its philosophy of education—the schools had been harnessed to serve societal ends.

Democracy and Education

As Cubberley personified one era, John Dewey was the harbinger of another. Though the roots of the progressive education movement extend back into the eighteenth century, with Jean Jacques Rousseau (1762) and Friedrich Froebel (1826), it remained for John Dewey in his

1916 volume, *Democracy in Education*, to make the movement a tangible force in American educational institutions. Dewey's educational philosophy joined the aims of industrial and agricultural training with a new democratic social vision and new techniques of instruction. Learning was to be linked with living, and individual differences were to be respected and built upon. Moderating the role of authority in education would prepare students to participate fully in a free society, thinking creatively by habit and disciplining themselves as necessary.

Nearly half a century was to pass before Cremin provided the first serious treatment of the relationship between the progressive movements in American politics and education. His 1961 book, *The Transformation of the School: Progressivism in American Education, 1876–1957*, traced the fortunes of the progressive education movement until its decline in the 1950s. Cremin contended that John Dewey and other educational progressives in the early decades of this century caused a shift among educators from a preoccupation with content to a lasting concern for the human condition and for democratic values in the schools. But it did not all happen at once, especially in administration.

The coincidence of the progressive education movement, for which Dewey was the leading exponent, and the First World War, a war the Allies waged "to make the world safe for democracy," was to have substantial influence on education and administration. The brutality of the battlefield, and the excessive demands for industrial production in a wartime economy, loomed large in the public mind. For some, news from the trenches of the Western Front, and management practices in the workplace, seemed strangely at odds with the idealistic purposes for which they believed the war was being fought. Even so, the immediate press in management thought was to discover new ways to enhance management coordination from the top down. Educators, however, not being directly responsible for the production of war materials, became increasingly sensitive to the need to teach and model democratic principles in the schoolhouse. Dewey's work, of course, provided a strong philosophical, if controversial, rationale for this movement and encouraged professors of educational administration and leading practitioners to think and speak about democratic administration in the years following World War I.

Judging from the rhetoric of the time, progressive education and democratic administration were advocated for the schools throughout the 1930s and 1940s and into the 1950s. By responding to the ideas of Dewey, Counts, and others, educators led the larger society in the movement toward institutional democracy (Fleming, 1982).

Two threats to the American and Western European social fabric were to temper educational and administrative ideals in the 1930s. The deepening economic depression left eleven million unemployed and over six thousand banks closed in the United States. The larger social and human development aims that had become an integral part of education in the preceding decade were now regarded by some as cultural luxuries. For them, education and employment were to be tightly linked from grade school to university. But as Franklin Roosevelt's New Deal took form, the federal government expanded in vision and size. The soft underbelly of the new industrial society had been exposed and government responded by taking a more active role in the interests of social justice. By the end of the 1930s, Nazi storm troopers were sweeping across Europe, adding to the sense of bewilderment and malaise experienced by Americans as they emerged from the Depression.

Although his work was not generally discovered by professors of educational administration until the 1950s, Chester I. Barnard's *The Functions of the Executive* appeared in 1938. Reflecting upon his long experience as a business executive, Barnard concluded that neither scientific nor democratic management would suffice alone; good administration, he said, required a graceful balance of individual and institutional needs. Barnard also recognized that organizational crises or national emergencies would occasionally force democratic idealism into retreat. Chapter 6 describes how Andrew Halpin and Jacob Getzels, among others, later built upon Barnard's work to relate personal and institutional considerations to administration in education.

With the mobilization of sixteen million citizens for military service, and the conversion of a sluggish peacetime economy to the demands of a second global war, political and economic leaders faced organizational tasks of unprecedented magnitude in the early 1940s. Scholars were enlisted to study leadership and organization, and training programs for military and civilian leaders were hastily launched. The effects on educational administration, although not immediate, were far-reaching. Idealism about educational purposes, however, rose to heights unknown since the 1920s, as Americans again considered the humanistic values for which they fought. Near war's end, Harvard University's Committee on the Objectives of General Education in a Free Society initiated a movement in higher education by releasing its recommendations in *General Education in a Free Society* (1945), while the Educational Policies Commission, representing a variety of school organizations led by the National Education Association, issued *The Purposes of Education in American Democracy* (1938). Education was not to serve economic ends alone, these reports insisted; it was also to preserve the culture and nurture such fundamental societal values as self-discipline, sacrifice, and consensus.

Crucial Decades

Historian Eric Goldman (1960) characterized America at the end of World War II as "a nation accustomed to the categorical yes and no, to war and peace, and prosperity or depression, [that] found itself in the nagging realm of maybe" (p. 14). Foreshadowing what was to come, Franklin Roosevelt had kept a picture of Woodrow Wilson hanging in the meeting room of the war cabinet as a reminder of the tortuous changes that inevitably come in the wake of war. Major adjustments did come, and Americans made the transition to peacetime amidst a jumble of hardship and prosperity, responsibility and dissipation. Atomic weapons, race relations, and superpower responsibilities were the stuff of congressional debates and barroom discussions. The war had precipitated many changes: Revolutions in medicine gradually transformed the quality of life and skewed population curves; blacks and other minorities who experienced parity with whites while in uniform would not forget the taste of equality; and women, propelled by circumstances of war to serve as factory forewomen and business managers, acquired new confidence in their abilities and developed new aspirations in the workforce—setting in motion sweeping changes in the social fabric. Unknowingly, a packed national agenda for the coming decades had been established. Sometimes confidently, sometimes chaotically, America's schools and colleges responded to the larger turbulence and grappled with their responsibility to serve a changing society. What Jackie Robinson began to accomplish in a Brooklyn Dodger baseball uniform in 1947, as the first black American in major league baseball, was to be a task of much greater magnitude—and importance—in the schoolhouse and on the campus.

By the late 1940s, farm workers, factory laborers, and other blue collar people began also to ride the new tide of prosperity. The G.I. Bill of Rights was no small part of this movement for upward mobility. By 1947, four million veterans were enrolled in institutions of higher learning, preparing to establish their own business or improve the family farm. Colleges and universities experienced staggering increases in enrollments, and men who had survived Guadalcanal or Utah Beach brought a new realism and seriousness to campus life. They were older, they were impatient, and they did not need housemothers. The application of knowledge, long a purpose of land-grant colleges, was now seen to be of wider interest and greater importance throughout higher education. The enormous cost of underwriting this vast investment was eventually repaid to the Federal treasury in full—in the form of increased tax receipts resulting from the added earning power of educated veterans. More significant, but harder to calculate, were the social and cultural benefits accruing to the nation and its people.

The public schools were also rocked by developments of the postwar years. As G.I.'s were returning to school, they were also reunited with their wives and sweethearts. Postwar children surged into the elementary schools in the early 1950s, requiring an enormous number of new teachers and thousands of new schools. The resulting boom in teacher education programs stimulated scholars and scholarship, and demands for more and better administrators raised important questions about what they should know and how they should be prepared.

By the mid-1950s, three related developments precipitated major changes in educational administration. The problems of postwar readjustment gave the social sciences new status in American universities. Sociologists and psychologists, for example, were recognized as never before for their knowledge of societal change and their ability to help understand and resolve social problems. Federal funding for social science research, first provided in large amounts during the war, continued at high levels. Opportunities for professors in these disciplines mushroomed as they were called upon as consultants to government and industry. Professors and practitioners of educational administration also turned to the social sciences in their quest to understand and improve schools and colleges.

A second element that affected educational administration was the unanimous 1954 Supreme Court decision in *Brown* v. *Board of Education of Topeka.* "Separate but equal," a dictum that had guided U.S. racial policy in the schools since before the turn of the century, was declared inherently discriminatory. The Court's 1954 decision was extended to cover state colleges and universities in 1956. The decision to end legal segregation in the schools was historic, as was the process by which it was made. Reaching beyond the tradition of legal precedent, the justices sought evidence from social scientists concerning the effects of racial segregation upon students. Gunner Myrdal, Swedish sociologist, public servant, and author of *An American Dilemma* (1944), figured prominently in the decision. Many decades later, American educators are still grappling with the implications of this educational watershed. Legal and moral obligations have vied with interest group pressures in a protracted struggle to find ways to implement a simple but important principle. As the rights of women, the poor, and the handicapped also became major social issues, the schools were again frequently near the center of the conflict. The work of educational leaders was shifting increasingly from administering their institutions to managing important social and political conflicts. While this role was not new to superintendents and principals, it now claimed much more of their energy and time.

Third, as urbanization advanced, the reorganization and consolidation of school districts became a major factor in education. In 1947, when the National Commission on School District Reorganization made its survey, there were 104,000 local districts in the United States (Harris, 1960, p. 1195). By 1956 the number was down to 59,000, and by 1980 it had fallen below 16,000. As school districts grew in complexity, demands for efficiency rose. And as they increased in size and scope, the need to equalize educational opportunities became more evident. Again, those responsible for the administration of educational institutions accepted new duties and played a more prominent role in their communities.

These three postwar developments are intended to be illustrative rather than exhaustive. Certainly, other social changes would rock the field in the 1960s and 1970s, but they are the subject of a later chapter (see Chapter 7). The point is that the demand for new knowledge of educational administration far exceeded the inherited wisdom. By the 1950s, this gap had attracted the attention of many scholars, resulting in a wave of new research and theory. While further attention was given to the classical views of administration, a new awareness of the interrelationships between institutions and their larger environments, between administration and policy making, led to the "open systems" theory of administration. In Andrew Halpin's *Administrative Theory in Education,* Talcott Parsons (1958) anticipated the open systems view in describing three levels of organizational life: the technical system, the managerial system, and the community or institutional system.

ADVANCES IN THE ACADEMIC FIELD

Within the academic field of educational administration, cooperative effort was stimulated by a series of postwar developments. Walter D. Cocking called together a group of leading professors and practitioners in the summer of 1947. Their purpose was to take a measure of the field by considering the changing nature of administrative practice, the growing need for theory and research, and emerging demands on graduate programs. This group was soon formalized and expanded as the National Conference of Professors of Educational Administration (NCPEA). Since that time, an annual summer meeting of the conference has brought together professors of educational administration from across North America and sometimes from abroad. Loosely organized as professional associations go, NCPEA has nonetheless been an important mechanism for linking scholars scattered over a wide geographical area (Flesher & Knoblauch, 1957).

A few years later the Kellogg Foundation was instrumental in establishing the Cooperative Program in Educational Administration (CPEA). Nine institutions of higher learning, eight in the United States and one in Canada, were given resources to establish centers in their colleges of education to improve graduate programs and increase collaboration with practitioners. For the most part, research was not the major purpose—although scholarship was advanced in many ways at each of the centers.

By the late 1950s the Kellogg Foundation was interested in weaning the participating universities from its support. To do this, it seemed appropriate to consider the formation of a consortium of the CPEA institutions—and the inclusion of others. In 1956, representatives of thirty-three universities gathered to organize the University Council for Education Administration (UCEA). Located temporarily at Columbia University at first, the central office of UCEA was moved to Ohio State University in 1959. Kellogg provided substantial initial funding to launch the Council, whose major purposes were to improve the training of school administrators, stimulate and coordinate research, and distribute materials resulting from research and training activities. A partnership of doctoral granting educational administration programs in leading American and Canadian universities, UCEA has sponsored conferences and workshops devoted to the extension of knowledge about educational administration. In 1965, it launched the *Educational Administration Quarterly* and *Educational Administration Abstracts*. UCEA expanded to fifty-nine member universities by the early 1970s, before the consortium and the movement it represented began to drift.

For the academic field as well as for UCEA, the late 1970s and early 1980s were a period of reexamination. The reorientation of UCEA in the mid-1980s, including the launching of a National Commission of Excellence in Educational Administration in 1985, aided by grants from Danforth and several other foundations, suggested a reconsideration of approaches to both study and practice in the field. At the same time, with the sponsorship of the American Educational Research Association (AERA), Norman Boyan (1987) was editing a massive codification of scholarship entitled *The Handbook of Research on Educational Administration* which revealed a high level of quantity and quality of research in the field and documented the increasing fragmentation of scholarly endeavor. Whether looking ahead or taking stock, leaders in this professional field in the mid-1980s were seriously assessing what they knew and how they knew it and were devoting fresh attention to actual and potential relationships between the practice and the study of educational administration.

In the 1980s, educational administration, like education generally, was in a period of serious introspection and of scrutiny by parents, students, public commentators, and government leaders. Students' performance on standardized achievement tests had regressed in recent years, colleges of education had failed to attract their share of the most promising undergraduates, and scarce tax revenues had caused legislators to ask hard questions of educational leaders. Culturally, more freedom and less social restraint had allowed students, particularly in the secondary schools, to act in ways that sometimes impoverished the educational environment. Teachers, frequently faced with unruly or indifferent students, became disillusioned, and administrators became weary of the many conflicting demands placed on them from within their schools and communities. At the same time, educational leaders and public officials, constantly reminded of economic and military competition from abroad and changing technologies at home, had difficulty distinguishing between the social and personal ends of education. Schools were pressed to be "more effective," but criteria for effectiveness were often simplistic and unduly prescriptive.

As an act of faith, professors, practitioners, and the general public had long believed that leadership influenced the quality of education in schools and colleges. This relationship, however, was no longer taken for granted; it became a matter of spirited debate and an agenda for research. Although empirical studies reported by Leithwood and Montgomery (1982) and Bossert and his associates (1982) provided new evidence about the effects of leadership on schools, ties between administrative behavior and student achievement remained obscure. As practitioners and scholars increasingly felt pressure to demonstrate such relationships, the need for fresh perspectives from which to view the field and its purposes became more critical.

The questions professors of educational administration asked and responded to changed in the 1980s, as did their methods of inquiry. What began as the promulgation of scholarly ideas for the improvement of administrative practice became a reciprocal relationship that included examining practice for ideas. The three-decade reign of traditional positivistic social science methodology used to conduct research was challenged by a widening circle of scholars who explored alternate paradigms, searched for meaning in events, sought to understand administrative values (by asking what ought to be as well as what was), or advocated the study of administrative behavior and organizational life without the prejudice of preexisting theories. As professors asked penetrating questions about their own methods of research, additional evidence surfaced of a maturing professional group, one willing to endure the tremors caused by plumbing its own depths.

Because the field of educational administrative has entered an era of challenge, imposed from within as well as from without, it seems especially timely and important that its members understand, consider, and build upon their professional heritage. Succeeding chapters of this book trace the history of thought and practice in educational administration and explore the evolving relationship between the two in American schools and universities.

PART I

THE EVOLUTION
OF
ADMINISTRATIVE THOUGHT

2

SCIENTIFIC MANAGEMENT IN INDUSTRY AND EDUCATION

SINCE 1900, THE STUDY AND PRACTICE of educational administration has been influenced by several major bodies of administrative thought originating outside of education. Generally, these approaches to management study, or ideologies of organizing, as they are sometimes termed, have been products of industrial and social science research into human behavior in the workplace and elsewhere. One of the earliest approaches to shape educational thought about administration in the twentieth century was scientific management, a view of organizing that made its presence felt in educational administration from the late-nineteenth century to the time of the Great Depression. This chapter examines historically how this approach to management study came about, how it influenced educators in the first quarter of this century, and how it shaped the way school leaders thought about administering the nation's schools.

IN THE SHADOW OF THE FACTORY: INDUSTRIAL STUDY IN THE LATE-NINETEENTH CENTURY

Although scattered attempts to introduce systematic procedures to manufacturing industries may be traced as far back as the 1830s, when the American factory system was in its infancy in the New England states, it was not until the 1850s that industrial operations became a subject of more general study. Industrial conditions in the United States changed dramatically after 1850 and the second half of the nineteenth century was marked by unparalleled developments in transportation, communications, technical invention, and the further evolution of mass production techniques in the manufacturing sector. The growth of large industries and the emergence of the modern corporation as the dominant image of the business firm by the 1870s convinced industrial leaders that new forms of administrative organization were required to tighten and centralize control over what, in some instances, had become unmanageably complex and highly diverse enterprises. As business historian Alfred Chandler noted in his discussion of late-nineteenth-century industrial developments, "one of the basic challenges facing industrialists was how to fashion the structures essential for the efficient administration of newly-won business empires" (1962, p. 37).

The search for more appropriate methods of organization in the decades after the Civil War was initially directed toward efforts to define lines of authority, improve organizational communications, and otherwise rationalize industrial operations as a whole. With the assistance of engineers, more and better types of information were provided to supervisory personnel held responsible for planning and coordinating industrial activities, improved systems of cost accounting were introduced, and data were routinely collected to evaluate and forecast production rates. Despite such management innovations, it was nevertheless acknowledged by the turn of the century that neither structural refinement nor technical sophistication could, by itself, completely ensure high productivity or smoothness of operations.

If for no other reason than the tremendous growth in the labor force, attention might naturally have shifted to the significance of the human element in the social, economic, and technical revolution that was taking place in Victorian America. There were, of course, other factors involved. Interest in the human factor was generally promoted by a late-nineteenth-century scientific and intellectual interest in such subjects as psychology, naturalism, and human social organization. As cities and factories grew, the attitudes and behaviors of working people, in particular, were topics of interest to reform-minded members of the clergy and temperance leaders and to the industrial and commercial leaders who now found themselves in control of vast business empires.

In some instances, expansion of the workforce in the manufacturing industries accentuated management-labor tension and industrial strife. A rise in the number of manufacturing establishments from 252,000 in 1869 to 512,000 in 1899 and the growth in the ranks of factory workers from 2.1 to 5.3 million over the same thirty-year period were frequently punctuated by violent confrontations between industrialists and their employees (Derber, 1970, p. 30). In addition, high levels of absenteeism and voluntary employee turnover generally disrupted industrial operations and forced factory operators to continually hire and train new workers (Baritz, 1960, p. 3).

Given the radical industrial change of the post-1870 era, it was not surprising that labor resisted the structural and technical adjustments sought by corporate managers. As labor historian David Montgomery observed (1976, p. 486) in discussing factory life during this period: "Working people clung to their traditional, spasmodic, task-oriented styles of work and to a social code which was less tightly disciplined . . . and less exploitive than that which industrialization was forcing upon them." Certainly, attempts by industrial managers to improve efficiency, "speed up" production, and impose order in the workplace were often frustrated by the autonomous attitudes held by labor. Unions of skilled workers fought vigorously for the right to decide how and when work would be done.

From the standpoint of management, the uncooperativeness of workers and their reluctance to surrender whatever knowledge or jurisdiction they enjoyed with respect to their craft seemed to thwart administrative efforts to organize production on a systematic basis. "Employers were being forced," industrial historian Reinhard Bendix observed, "to concern themselves with labor as a problem rather than solve it by simply dismissing the worker who would not do" (1956, p. 266). Plagued by work stoppages, chronic labor shortages, worker indifference, and industrial sabotage, factory operators became receptive to the introduction of new management techniques that promised to motivate workers and impose greater discipline and control in the workplace.

Frederick Taylor
and the Search for Rational Systems

The opportunity for employers to revise outdated and wasteful industrial practices, and to reduce their dependence on labor, was presented toward the end of the nineteenth century in a concept of administration known as scientific management. This new approach to industrial organization became largely associated with the work of one man, Frederick Taylor, a mechanical engineer whose own experiences in industry led him to standardize the production processes that would later become known as scientific management, or "the Taylor system."

Taylor first outlined his notions about industrial reorganization in a paper read before the American Society of Mechanical Engineers in 1895. Entitled "A Piece-Rate System: Being a Step Toward Partial Solution of the Labor Problem," this paper not only reflected the interest in worker-incentive schemes that was becoming popular in the engineering community but, more significantly, outlined a set of ideas that pointed toward the development of a "science of work" (Derber, 1970, pp. 70-71). In his presentation, Taylor sharply criticized the disorganized character of traditional production practices, especially the tendency among employers to pay standard wages to members of various occupational classes and to distribute profits or savings on a collective basis to such groups. From his own experience in the steel industry, Taylor was convinced that industrial supervisors required new ways to measure and control work and that incentive systems functioned best when they rewarded individual rather than group performance. In line with these beliefs, he recommended a more exact method of rate fixing through time studies of specific job operations, and the application of a differential rate system for piece work by which workers could earn higher prices per piece if the work was completed to certain standard specifications in the shortest time possible. Furthermore, he advised that employees should be paid individually for what they produced, thus rewarding those who exhibited greater skills and effort.

Time, Motion, and the Science of Work

In the decade following the publication of his 1895 discussion on differential rates and time study, Taylor emerged as the most important industrial engineer of his generation. His reputation as the leading exponent of scientific management had been secured in several ways. Hundreds of factories across the country had adopted elements of his scientific management system or were using metal-cutting processes he had patented. His ideas about reorganization and efficiency had also been widely circulated and applied throughout business and industry by his disciples H. L. Gantt, Harrington Emerson, Carl Barth, Horace K. Hathaway, and Sandford E. Thompson. In addition, the publication of a paper on shop management in 1903 and its presentation before the American Society of Mechanical Engineers, together with lectures he gave at Harvard's Graduate School of Business and other institutions, further cemented Taylor's position as the high priest of efficiency.

It was not, however, until 1910, when the Interstate Commerce Commission was investigating an Eastern Railway proposal for a freight rate increase, that Taylor's work received widespread public attention. The enormous publicity generated by these congressional hearings and Taylor's subsequent lionization in a series of articles in the *American Magazine*, authored by its reform-minded editor, Stannard Baker, made Taylor's name a household word and scie management the topic of countless articles in the popular press (Callahan, 1962, pp. 21–22).

In response to his new-found notoriety and to increasing professional pressures for lectures and speeches, Taylor published *The Principles of Scientific Management* in 1911, a work that became his most famous treatise on industrial organization. Within a few years of its publication, it had been translated into almost a dozen languages and served as a guidebook for factory reorganization throughout the world. Inside the covers of this "progressive manifesto," as one historian described it (Nelson, 1980, p. 170), Taylor outlined the origins of his approach to management, the scientific procedures supporting it, and its potential for creating a new and more harmonious industrial state.

"In the past," Taylor wrote in the introduction to *The Principles of Scientific Management*, "the man has been first; in the future, the system must be first" (p. 7). This brief but sweeping statement captured the essence of the change Taylor sought to bring about in American industry. The emergence of large, complex, and highly differentiated industrial operations, Taylor believed, had not been accompanied by the development of new management structures necessary for efficient operations. Traditional forms of control, authority, and communication, as well as existing methods to measure productivity, had proven ineffective in dealing with modern industrial problems, he maintained, and, as a result, American industry was marked by disorganization, strife, and inefficiency. In Taylor's view, two primary and interrelated problems undermined industrial progress. One stemmed from the attitudes and behaviors of workers, their indifference, and their indolence, or what Taylor referred to as "systematic soldiering." This soldiering was a ubiquitous fact of industrial life, as Taylor observed: "So universal is soldiering . . . that hardly a competent workman can be found in a large establishment, whether he works by the day or on piece work . . . or under any of the ordinary systems, who does not devote a considerable part of his time to studying just how slow he can work and still convince his employer that he is going at a good pace" (p. 21).

In Taylor's view, the second major problem retarding industrial performance was an absence of effective supervisory procedures and uniform production standards and a lack of integration between the human and technical systems of industry. Managers, he suggested, failed to manage because they had not developed the control structures necessary to bring order and discipline to the workplace. Like their workers, they operated according to vague rules-of-thumb which inevitably resulted in employee soldiering and the "ignorance of the management as to what really constitutes a proper day's work for a workman" (Taylor, 1911, p. 53). Production rates and the overall operating efficiency of many companies were thus ultimately determined by worker attitudes and not by the designs of managers, Taylor concluded (pp. 48–49). Although such untenable situations could be overcome through scientific management, the successful implementation of such a system required, Taylor advised (p. 131), no less than "a complete revolution in the mental attitudes and the habits of all those engaged in the management, as well [as those] of the workmen."

The revolution proposed by Taylor, a revolution that in his view could double the productivity of the average man engaged in industrial work, comprised several elements or stages. First, Taylor observed, it was necessary to identify "one best method" of execution for every job by observing how competent workers performed certain tasks. Their actions could then be analyzed through time and motion studies, reduced to a series of simple movements, and reassembled in a way that eliminated inefficient motions of men and machines. "Perhaps the most prominent single element in modern scientific management is the task idea," Taylor wrote, according to which "the work by every workman is fully planned out by the management at least one day in advance, and each man receives in most cases complete written instructions, describing in detail the task which he is to accomplish, as well as the means to be used in doing the work" (p. 39). As various tasks throughout the production process were thus organized, they could then be joined so the activities of individual production units conformed to the pattern of factory operations as a whole.

Taylor, of course, realized that the scientific analysis of work processes would not alone lead to increases in production and that employees must be convinced that the adoption of new methods was in their interest. Taylor further knew from exhaustive experiments he conducted on worker performance that improvements in worker effort would not be sustained without adequate financial incentives. "It is absolutely necessary," he concluded, "when workmen are daily given a task which calls for a high rate of speed on their part, that they should also be insured the necessary high rate of pay whenever they are successful. This involves not only fixing for each man his daily task, but also paying him a large bonus or premium, each time that he succeeds in doing his task in the given time" (p. 121). Together, an appropriate reward system and the adoption of scientific principles, he maintained, would in all likelihood eliminate management-labor antagonism over the issue of productivity. In the new industrial world he envisioned, cooperation would replace conflict as scientific management secured "the maximum prosperity for the employer, coupled with the maximum prosperity for each employee" (p. 9). Ultimately, Taylor believed, the yardstick of science would finally, and impartially, measure what was possible in industry and how it should be done.

Taylor also sought to change the work of industrial supervisors and managers. At the shop floor level, for example, he recommended that foremen be charged with specific duties. Instead of appointing single foremen with broad powers, as it was commonplace to do, he proposed hiring several "functional" foremen to supervise discrete parts of factory operations such as work routing, discipline, speed of production, machine operations, and employees' wages. In Taylor's view, this supervisory system ensured greater control over production processes and employee behavior and, at the same time, improved communications among production workers, senior management, and their staffs. Implicit in this change was the notion that foremen should represent the interests of management and not those of workers, as they had done for so long.

Taylor further recognized that the effective use of scientific methods in industry rested ultimately on administrators themselves. Without their willingness to adopt new operating procedures and to decide how work should be done, Taylor knew that his proposals for industrial reform would fail. In instances where scientific management proved effective, he wrote, managers perform certain tasks:

> First. They develop a science for each element of a man's work, which replaces the old rule-of-thumb method.
>
> Second. They scientifically select and then train, teach, and develop the workman, whereas in the past he chose his own work and trained himself as best he could.
>
> Third. They heartily cooperate with the men so as to insure all the work being done in accordance with the principles of the science which has been developed.
>
> Fourth. There is an almost equal division of the work and the responsibility between the management and the workmen. The man-

agement takes over all work for which they are better fitted than the workmen, while in the past all of the work and the greater part of the responsibility were thrown upon the men. (p. 37)

More than Efficiency: Taylorism's Other Agenda

Taylor's ideas found immediate favor with industrialists and business leaders, for several reasons. Apart from the lure of efficiency, Taylor's scientific principles appealed to owners and managers of industrial firms on a deeper level because they promised to bring order and continuity to an industrial sector beset by problems of growth and change. In the wake of the massive social and economic upheaval that marked the closing decades of the nineteenth century, scientific management seemed to offer a way of bringing logic and organization to production processes while, at the same time, it tilted the pendulum of authority for industrial decision making clearly to management's side. Furthermore, by prescribing new ways to fit workers to their tasks and by standardizing on-the-job employee behavior through closer supervision and detailed work instructions, industrial managers could more directly exert control and authority over what was perceived to be a recalcitrant workforce.

Scientific management, as Taylor envisioned it, involved more than simply matching men to machines or dividing work assignments into their smallest components. Its meaning ran deeper than that. Taylor had, in effect, furnished a way for managers to eliminate their traditional dependence on the craft knowledge held by workers, thereby allowing managers to impose unilateral control over all aspects of industrial operations. For better or worse, Taylor's methods promised to transform radically the nature of social relationships in industry. In the words of sociologist Daniel Bell (1956, p. 7), Taylor had proposed nothing less than a new "social physics" whose laws would now define the nature of social behavior in the industrial workplace. Needless to say, the import of this dramatic change was not lost on industrial leaders, many of whom were pleased with Taylor's new organizational hierarchy and the way it reduced labor's influence over production matters. In light of the fact that union membership increased almost five-fold in the seven-year period from 1897 to 1904 (from 450,000 workers to 2 million), it is not surprising that industrial operators were keen to embrace a form of organization that offered to keep workers in check (Derber, 1970, p. 115).

Taylor's system no doubt also appealed to industrial managers and corporate leaders because it was purportedly "scientific" in nature and thus, by definition, impartial in its aims. By framing ideas for efficiency and reorganization in scientific terms, Taylor and other efficiency experts sought to promulgate the notion that their management approach was neutral in intent and not something designed solely to strengthen the hand of industrial administrators. Such a strategy left the impression that scientific study, and not the desire of managers to reduce costs or meet higher production targets, was chiefly responsible for speedier assembly lines, stricter forms of discipline, and new expectations for extra effort on the part of workers. The inference was simple: It was the stopwatch, not the supervisor who held it, that determined levels of worker performance. For managers, this was indeed a convenient myth and one to be seized upon and promoted. Scientific study had ruled what requirements for the "one best system" should be, and managers and workers alike were obliged to conform to the dictates of this new system. When presented in this fashion, Taylor's scientific principles depersonalized changes occurring in the workplace and helped managers deflect the blame for restructuring work away from themselves and toward some abstract scientific guidelines. This was an attractive idea to industrial operators who sought to avoid conflict with labor whenever it was in their interest.

Not surprisingly, Taylor's influence was not confined to industry. Publicity given to his accomplishments at the Interstate Commerce hearings, the popular success of *The Principles of Scientific Management*, and his appearance before the Hoxie Commission investigating scientific management practices in 1914 ensured that Taylor's reputation would rise above that of an innovative engineer or successful industrial manager. Like Henry Ford and Herbert Hoover, who were also catapulted into prominence during the early years of the new century because of their engineering expertise, Taylor became renowned in his time as a technician-philosopher whose ideas about human industry transcended his own field of specialization. Widespread public interest in Taylor and his ideas eventually led Americans to apply his efficiency principles more broadly to the foundations of national life—to the home, the church, and, as this discussion will now show, the public school.

CHANGES IN SOCIETY AND EDUCATION

It is not surprising that American educators, many of whom saw themselves as forward-looking and reform-minded, were drawn to Taylor's ideas at this time. For school administrators, particularly, Taylor's principles of scientific management held special appeal. The schools, like other public institutions in the early 1900s, had become engulfed in the storm of social criticism and political reform known as progressivism that was reshaping the nation. Part of this was due to the meteoric growth of public schooling after 1870 and to the fact that such development had presented school leaders with unprecedented organizational difficulties. Swelling school populations, great expansions in educational services and in the curriculum at all levels, a boom in school construction, an increasingly diverse educational clientele, and the supervision of an enormously enlarged teaching body were all factors posing new and onerous problems for school managers in the first years of the new century.

Naturally, this rapid growth had been paralleled by escalating educational costs. These costs had become a source of concern to many business and community leaders who began to complain vigorously about the outmoded and wasteful practices they saw in school operations. Besieged by this strong public demand for efficiency, or what is now called educational accountability, school administrators turned to Taylor's methods in the interests of their own professional survival.

The educational climate that welcomed Taylor's ideas after 1910 had been conditioned not only by social forces outside schools, but by other forces within education itself, most notably the emergence of a scientific movement in educational study during the first decade of the twentieth century. For this reason, the discussion at hand will examine how this scientific movement shaped educational thought prior to the advent of Taylor's influence and how it prepared the way for the eventual adoption of scientific management techniques, before turning to the story of scientific management in school administration.

Thorndike and the Science of Education

Among other things, the turn of the century was marked by the beginning of a great intellectual awakening in American education. Interest in educational research and scholarship blossomed early in the new century as education became recognized as a distinct field of study and as social scientists and educators began to investigate assorted theoretical and practical questions about children's learning and human understanding in general. This new enthusiasm for educational study was prompted by several developments. Public schooling's rapid growth in the latter years of the nineteenth century had made education a topic of national discussion and had led to public and scholarly speculation about educational beliefs and practices. At the same time, the establishment of numerous public and private universities, and other institutions for advanced study in the post-1870 period, provided new settings for educational inquiry and encouraged more careful and sustained study of pedagogical issues. In part, the increasing attention given to educational theory and practice after 1900 was also a result of the intellectual curiosity and excitement that characterized American social thought in the first two decades of the century. The spirit of inquiry that coursed through the halls and laboratories of the nation's leading universities and schools of education in the early 1900s was indicative of the faith in scientific study that became a hallmark of American reform at this time.

The emergence of what is now referred to as the "scientific movement" or the "measurement movement" in education may be traced at least as far back as the 1880s when James McKeen Cattell, a psychologist then at the University of Pennsylvania, began to investigate the nature of learning. However, it was not until the first years of the new century that the movement to establish a "science of education" really took form. A seminal figure in its development was Edward Thorndike, a psychologist who had studied at Harvard with the great philosopher-psychologist William James before undertaking doctoral study in animal behavior at Columbia University under the direction of Cattell, who had by then joined the Columbia faculty. After securing a position at Columbia's Teachers College, the citadel of educational knowledge at that time and for many years thereafter, Thorndike began a long and distinguished career in research and scholarship which yielded numerous monographs and articles on such diverse topics as mental capacity, the psychology of individual differences, teaching methods, pupil attrition, and adult learning.

Thorndike's work, perhaps more than any other single factor, imbued the scientific movement in education with its psychological and statistical character. Human behavior could be studied objectively, Thorndike claimed (1904, p. v): "The facts of human nature [could] be made the material for quantitative science." Traditional approaches to educational study, he observed, had failed in this regard. As noted in his 1903 study, *Human Learning*: "It is the vice or the misfortune of thinkers about education to have chosen the methods of philosophy or of popular thought instead of those of science" (Curti, 1959, p. 460). It was precisely this vice or misfortune he sought to correct.

In 1902, Thorndike offered a course in the application of "psychological and statistical methods to education" at Teachers College, a course that would later be recognized as a landmark event in American educational history. It was significant for several reasons. It was likely the first course offered to students of education to stress quantitative research and the use of scientific procedures (Sears, 1924, p. 125). Also, in taking as its focus the "measurement of physical, mental, and moral qualities, including the abilities involved in the school subjects, and rates of progress in various functions," Thorndike's course outlined what would be the emphasis and content of educational research for at least the next three decades (Sears, 1924, p. 134). In fact, in teaching this course, Thorndike had taken a decisive step in providing the investigative tools and methods that would shape the nature of study and research in all areas of education for generations to come. From this time on, neither the educational theorist nor the practitioner would be able to look at the world of the school in the same way.

Testing, Testing:
The Measurement of Movement Takes Form

Shortly after Thorndike's pioneering efforts at Columbia, the psychological and quantitative cast of the educational science movement was reinforced with the introduction of intelligence testing in American schools. Although interest in determining mental capacity had begun to develop in the latter part of the nineteenth century, it was not until 1908, when Henry Goddard applied a measurement scale to evaluate the abilities of youngsters at a New Jersey school for subnormal children, that intelligence testing became a part of educational practice in the United States. Goddard, a former student of eminent psychologist G. S. Hall, had translated and adapted this scale from the work of Alfred Binet and Theodore Simon, two French psychologists who had studied the learning of retarded children. Less than a decade after Goddard's initial use of Binet and Simon's scale, intelligence testing had become a mainstay of American education and was applied to all levels of schooling from elementary grades to universities. Over the same period, Binet and Simon's tests were also modified several times by American psychologists; the most famous revision was undoubtedly the Stanford-Binet revision of 1916 prepared by Stanford's Lewis Terman.

Intelligence testing was generally welcomed by psychologists, educators, and the public-at-large because it was believed that such tests might help reveal "laws of intellectual development," or in some other way advance the cause of science in education. To school administrators, however, intelligence testing held a special practical appeal because it offered a much-needed system of classifying pupils in the nation's schools. The increasingly heterogeneous nature of urban school systems had presented turn-of-the-century educational leaders with vexing problems in social bookkeeping. Also, school administrators were quick to realize that by testing populations of individual schools or entire systems, they could obtain statistically descriptive information that would allow them to sort and compare pupils according to their intellectual potential. Using such tests, it now seemed possible to identify what the "average" range of abilities was at certain age-levels and what "normal," "subnormal," and "above normal" represented in quantitative scores. Equipped with the power to discriminate in this manner, administrators could more easily place pupils in programs that did not exceed or insult their intellectual capacities.

The publication in 1907 of Thorndike's study, *The Elimination of Pupils from School*, and Leonard Ayres' volume, *Laggards in our Schools*, in 1913, illustrated how proponents of educational science utilized their new-found statistical techniques, and suggested the growing consciousness of educators regarding problems of instructional efficiency in schools.

To a large extent, this concern with efficiency similarly underlay the increasing interest in evaluating "educational products" at this time. Efforts to measure pupil performance in basic school subjects had begun prior to the turn of the century in the spelling tests of Joseph Rice, a physician-turned-educator; however, Rice's work in test development was not generally well received when it first appeared in the 1890s. Nevertheless, the idea did not remain out of favor for long. By 1908, for example, C. W. Stone, under Thorndike's direction, had completed one of the first major investigations of children's arithmetical abilities. Around the same time, another of Thorndike's students, M. B. Hillegas, developed similar kinds of achievement tests to measure pupil skills in English composition. And, in 1910, Thorndike himself published a handwriting scale. At a time of increasing educational concern about efficiency, such tests and scales, to be sure, were quickly recognized as having other than strict instructional uses.

Two other prominent members of the test construction fraternity in the era prior to the Great Depression were S. A. Courtis, supervisor of research for the Detroit school system, and Leonard Ayres of the Russell Sage Foundation. Ayres' spelling tests and the arithmetic tests designed by Courtis in 1909 were widely used by educators throughout the country for years; indeed, Courtis' influence was such that in one year alone he distributed more than 450,000 tests to teachers and administrators in 42 states (Courtis, 1916, p. 91).

By the end of the first decade of the new century, the measurement of instructional efficiency had emerged as one of the most obvious manifestations of the scientific movement in education. Although psychology would continue to provide the greatest theoretical or disciplinary influence on the direction that educational science would take, much of the movement's energy had become focused on the practical use of statistical techniques to gather and analyze information about pupils and to compare the educational products of schools and school systems. Methods of educational science, in effect, had become recognized as essential administrative tools—a development that had significant implications for the study and practice of school administration.

In terms of the intellectual development of educational administration, all of this suggests that the scientific movement in education accustomed educators to make use of "scientific" elements in administration and to accept a quantitative approach to school administration even before Taylor's scientific management became popular outside industry. In other words, in the years prior to 1910–1911, when Taylor's efficiency methods and principles first became widely discussed and publicized throughout American society, both school administrators and professors of education had already begun to acknowledge the need for precise forms of measurement, the importance of routinely collecting and analyzing information, and the use of other scientific procedures that would in time become intimately associated with Taylor's management system.

Salvation Through Science:
School Leaders Look to Industry

The manner in which Taylor's principles of scientific management became diffused in educational circles has been chronicled at length in Raymond Callahan's 1962 study, *Education and the Cult of Efficiency*. In that volume, Callahan examined how social forces outside the schools shaped the administration of public education from the turn of the century to the beginning of the Great Depression and how these forces changed the way school leaders viewed themselves and the nature of the work they performed. Two factors, Callahan concluded, were chiefly responsible for transforming the self-image of school administrators in this period. One of these was the ideological dominance of business and industrial thought in American society in the pre-1929 era, a dominance epitomized in Taylor's doctrine of efficiency and its influence on all areas of national life. The other was the "extreme vulnerability" of school administrators to public criticism and pressure, a vulnerability that inevitably caused them to forsake traditional educational values and to adopt the attitudes, ethics, and methods of corporate America (p. 52).

Once reform-conscious America discovered Taylor's efficiency methods, Callahan contended, it was just a matter of time before they were applied to education. And, indeed, circumstances existed to ensure that this would occur. By the time Taylor came to public attention, the schools were already under attack in various quarters for their inefficiency. Business and community spokespeople criticized teachers for their lack of efficiency and took schools to task for the impractical and antiquated curriculums they imparted. In the popular press, journalists likewise voiced disapproval about educational inefficiency and inquired why massive investments in public schooling produced such poor educational results. Even within the educational world, critics expressed uneasiness about school costs and the quality of educational "products" being turned out. This criticism only intensified, Callahan suggested (p. 47), after Taylor's rise to public notice.

Because school leaders were unable to stem the rising tide of adverse public opinion alone, Callahan claims, they were obliged to look outside their own ranks for assistance. This they did in the years after 1910 by embracing Taylor's efficiency methods and by adopting the attitudes and values of the business community. Ultimately, Callahan argued, this "capitulation" on the part of educators to business and industrial influences and to the doctrine of scientific management led school leaders to place business considerations before educational objectives in managing the nation's schools. Eventually, this development led to what he, not altogether clearly, described as "an American tragedy in education." To Callahan, the key element of this tragedy lay in the fact that school administrators no longer saw themselves as guardians of knowledge or as educational leaders, but as somewhat anti-intellectual business managers, unsympathetic to the higher purposes of learning and no less concerned with shallow measures of productivity and efficiency than their commercial and industrial counterparts. This unfortunate development, Callahan further noted, was not simply due to the flawed character of this new generation of school leaders, but owed equally to the influence of a cost-minded public that compelled school officials to become accountants rather than educators.

Questions have been raised about Callahan's conclusions, about how he defined the era of business efficiency, about his selection and use of evidence, and about the inferences he drew from this evidence. In particular, subsequent studies have challenged the notion that American educators became conscious of efficiency techniques only around the first decade of the twentieth century. In reviewing Callahan's book, Timothy Smith (1964, pp. 76–77), for example, suggested that educational interest in efficiency could be traced at least as far back as the

early 1880s, some three decades before Taylor reached national prominence. More recently, Barbara Berman's thoughtful reconsideration of
Callahan's thesis (1983, p. 316) argued convincingly that educational
interest in principles of business efficiency "did not emerge at the close
of the nineteenth century but was a basic tenet of common school
reform," and could be seen as early as the 1840s when school crusaders
employed business techniques "first to sell their new institution, and
then to alleviate problems encountered in its expansion."

Smith and Berman have likewise disputed Callahan's claim that
school superintendents were vulnerable to public pressures because of
a lack of tenure. In this respect, Berman has noted (p. 301) that prominent city school leaders of the late-Victorian era, such as Denver's
Gove, Wilmington's Harlan, Savannah's Baker, Louisville's Tingley,
Providence's Leach, and several others, all enjoyed reigns of twenty-
five years or more. Berman has further quarreled with Callahan's
contention that pre-1900 educational leaders were statesmen-like char-
acters divorced from business concerns and that ideas about business
efficiency philosophically conflicted with nineteenth-century educational thought. Her own study of nineteenth-century teacher-training
literature, she noted, revealed that "both acceptance of, and reservations concerning scientific efficiency—of which business efficiency
was only a special case—surfaced well before the twentieth century"
(p. 307).

Beyond this, as Tyack suggests (1974), there is the question of
motive or cause which, in retrospect, Callahan does not seem to have
treated in a fair or even-handed manner. Callahan does not, for example, acknowledge that late-nineteenth- and early-twentieth-century superintendents sorely needed whatever efficiency measures they could
find to deal with burgeoning school populations, increasingly complex
administration systems, and rapidly rising school costs. Nor does he
recognize that, in light of such developments, school managers might
have embraced Taylor's principles of efficiency for purely economic or
organizational, rather than political or ideological, reasons.

One further line of criticism involves the relationship Callahan
sought to establish between educational thought and practice in the
period from 1910 to the Great Crash of 1929. Although his citation of
speeches at annual meetings of the NEA and other professional bodies
illustrated that scientific management ideas were being voiced in educational circles, his work was less successful in connecting such endorse-
ments of efficiency engineering with actual developments taking place
in schools across America. As a result, serious questions remain regard-

ing whether these efficiency measures were more discussed than acted upon.

Nevertheless, if such cautions are observed, it is still useful to examine what leading exponents of scientific management in education had to say in the years prior to 1914. Their speeches and writings are revealing because they illustrate how ideas about managing derived from business and industrial studies were translated into educational terms, how educators sought to apply such ideas, and, last but not least, how school leaders viewed the organizational challenges they faced on the eve of the Great War.

Educational Experts on the Loose

Despite earlier attempts to promote scientific management notions in education, it was not until February 1913 that educators really began to formulate more complete statements about how Taylor's methods might actually be applied to administering the nation's schools. In that month, two of the most significant attempts to apply "the great panacea" to American education were made. One was found in a speech by Frank Spaulding, superintendent of schools for Newton, New Jersey, and a recognized leader among school administrators (Callahan, 1962, pp. 73–79). Speaking before the National Education Association's Department of Superintendence annual meeting in Philadelphia, Spaulding recounted his own recent efforts to utilize Taylor's management concepts in the Newton system and extolled at some length the advantages of this engineering approach.

Spaulding applied only certain parts of Taylor's system to his discussion of school administration. In particular, he focused attention on the importance of quantitative measurement and its use as a means of recording, analyzing, and comparing educational products and costs. Spaulding's somewhat selective interest in scientific management was directed largely toward applying Taylor's technique to budgeting, financial planning, and the control of educational expenditures. For whatever reasons, Spaulding did not propose that school operations be completely reorganized in line with the set of precepts developed by Taylor to rationalize industrial production.

Drawing on his own experiences in Newton, Spaulding argued that instructional cost was a key factor to control in searching for educational efficiency. Considerable savings could be made, he said, by increasing both the number of classes each teacher gave and the number of pupils in each class. In keeping with Taylor's view, Spaulding concluded that the school organization's overall efficiency was directly related to worker productivity and that, by regulating the work assignments of teachers, instructional expenditures could be adjusted. The most significant element of Spaulding's discussion was perhaps its broad emphasis on the business responsibilities of the school administrator, responsibilities that were increasingly becoming the domain of superintendents at that time as school boards gave their assent to the model of a unified superintendency. In short, what Spaulding proposed was that Taylor's efficiency engineering methods be used by school leaders to become business executives in their own right.

Also in February 1913, a more comprehensive attempt to apply Taylor's system to school management was made by Franklin Bobbitt, an instructor in educational administration at the University of Chicago. In a lengthy paper entitled "Some General Principles of Management Applied to the Problems of City School Systems," which was published as Part I of the *Twelfth Yearbook of the National Society for the Study of Education*, Bobbitt explored how Taylor's ideas could be used to address the administrative challenges facing America's urban schools. "At a time when much discussion is being given to the possibilities of 'scientific management' in the world of material production," Bobbitt wrote (p. 7), "it seems desirable that the principles of this more effective form of management be examined to ascertain the possibility of applying them to the problems of educational management and supervision." Because of its recent origin, the field of school administration was "rather backward," he explained (p. 8) and, therefore, school leaders could profit greatly from applying organizational principles that "appear to be most clearly conceived and to have been most fully and completely worked out by certain portions of the industrial and business world."

After all, management was management, Bobbitt proclaimed (p. 7), "whether the organization be for commerce or for manufacture, philanthropy or education, transportation or government, it is coming to appear that the fundamental tasks of management, direction and supervision are always about the same." And, taking his cue from Taylor, he summarized his view of what school administration should be and how educational work should be scientifically organized:

> In any organization, the directive and supervisory members must clearly define the ends toward which the organization strives. . . . Directors and supervisors must keep the workers supplied with detailed instructions as to the work to be done, the standards to be

reached, the methods to be employed, and the materials and appliances to be used. (pp. 7–8)

This description of managerial responsibility, of course, was in line with the supervisory role outlined in Taylor's volume on scientific management and suggested the extent of Bobbitt's conversion to the idea that schools should not be seen just as educational institutions, but as industrial plants where pupils represented the raw products to be processed, teachers were the workers, and school administrators served as the industrial managers who monitored the flow of the educational assembly line.

Bobbitt began his examination of problems in school management by pointing out that, if schools were to benefit from more cohesive and systematic organization, standards must be established. Past failures to develop suitable standards had led to "the greatest possible degree of individualistic freedom" which, in itself, undermined the best interests of the school organization and the public-at-large. As he put it:

> The result is, in city school systems, in normal schools, and in our universities, the relative autonomy of a very large number of small units—in other words, a low and primitive form of organization, direction, and management. All this stands in the way of accomplishing any large co-operative task. It results in a constitutional tendency to place the welfare of the worker above the welfare of the organization, and the welfare of both above the welfare of the total society of which school men and school institutions are but the agents. (p. 50)

Bobbitt undoubtedly understood that the net effect of standardization, as Taylor had foreseen, lay in the discipline, order, and unity of purpose it imposed on organizational members. Furthermore, by standardizing educational products or results, Bobbitt believed that administrators could get a firmer grip on the nature of production costs and how more efficient work methods could be introduced.

Certain educational benefits, Bobbitt advised, could also be obtained by imposing appropriate standards, particularly through standards that lent themselves to numerical description. Measurement scales and achievement tests of various kinds designed by Ayres, Courtis, Hillegas, and Thorndike had already proved their value in numerous ways, he noted. Such standards communicated educational objectives to teachers, showed them the strengths and weaknesses of their methods, and assisted them in evaluating pupil learning and their own progress toward their instructional goals. Standards similarly enabled principals to measure teacher efficiency and how pupils in their care compared with those in other schools, as well as pointed to areas in which remedial help for teachers and pupils was required.

The elements of managerial control implicit in Taylor's system also found favor with Bobbitt. "The new and revolutionary doctrine of scientific management," he observed (p. 52), "states in no uncertain terms that the management, the supervisory staff, has the largest share of the work in the determination of the proper methods. The burden of finding the best methods is too large and too complicated to be laid on the shoulders of the teachers." It was, therefore, the responsibility of school administrators to discover (p. 53) "the best methods of procedure in the performance of any particular educational task" and to provide such methods to teachers "for their guidance in securing a maximum product." "The worker," he wrote, "must be kept supplied with detailed instructions as to the work to be done" (p. 89). No doubt, Bobbitt intended that these methods would always be determined by school leaders. Like the shop managers who put Taylor's system into effect in sheet metal and steel-cutting factories, Bobbitt was conscious of the latent authority held by those in charge of craft knowledge. As he remarked later in his discussion: "Efficiency implies centralization of authority and definite direction by the supervisors of all processes performed" (p. 89).

Finally, Bobbitt outlined the importance of selecting and training educational workers according to the scientific guidelines Taylor had prescribed for industry. "Our profession," he wrote (p. 70), "must advance along the same road as that traversed by the best of the industrial world before we shall be able to place our workers with the same efficiency, justice, and certainty." Education, like industry, Bobbitt advised, faced similarly serious problems in selecting suitable workers for specific assignments and could profit from the methods Taylor pioneered. However, selecting teachers on the basis of desirable intellectual and personality traits was somewhat more difficult, he cautioned, than Taylor's task of identifying workers with certain physical attributes. "The problem is not so simple as the one of the factory girls," Bobbitt observed in referring to one of Taylor's studies of physical dexterity, "still our psychology is not quite so halting as to be unable to perform this task" (p. 64).

Taken together, Spaulding's speech and Bobbitt's paper suggested something of the strength and immediacy of Taylor's influence on the thinking of leading educators. Their addresses pointed out both how scientific management methods could assist school leaders in solving the internal organizational problems they faced and how educators could allay community fears and criticism about inefficiency in public education. Spaulding and Bobbitt also suggested that by adopting Taylor's principles, school administrators would be able to discuss problems and issues of educational management in ways that industrialists, businesspeople, and efficiency-conscious Americans could readily understand—to be sure, Bobbitt's metaphor of the school as a factory was much in keeping with the temper of the times. Moreover, in introducing a scientific element into educational administration through the incorporation of Taylor's notions, Spaulding and Bobbitt were no doubt cognizant of the respectability that science lent to the study and practice of school management. But, in their infatuation with efficiency methods, educational spokesmen such as Spaulding and Bobbitt, like many industrial managers at the time, failed to consider how dangerously simple some of Taylor's ideas were or how scientific management's philosophical assumptions might be at variance with certain educational values or the values of the American democratic creed.

The Ghosts of Efficiency

Whether or not one is entirely comfortable with Callahan's depiction of scientific management's effects, it is nevertheless apparent that, in the years following the endorsement of Taylor's principles by Spaulding, Bobbitt, and others, the efficiency movement influenced administrative thought and practice in education in at least several respects. For one, Taylor's influence led school administrators to emphasize (or overemphasize, as Callahan argued) the financial business elements of educational management (Callahan, 1962, pp. 65–178). An analysis of early twentieth-century college programs for school managers illustrates the great attention educators began to pay at that time to accounting procedures, budget preparation, all forms of record keeping, public relations, the publication of annual reports, and the adoption of other managerial trappings normally associated with the corporate world. This business emphasis in school operations, and indeed the tendency of school leaders to emulate the administrative practices of industrialists and businesspeople, helped produce a climate in which decisions about educational matters were, at times, made not always on the basis of pupil need or pedagogical value, but on the basis of cost and efficiency. The development of "platoon schools," as Callahan noted (pp. 126–147), was one obvious expression of administrative interest in delivering cost-effective educational services.

Taylor's doctrine of efficiency no doubt also encouraged to some extent the rise of management "experts" in education—individuals who were generally familiar with the intricacies of school finance and who consulted with school districts and state departments of education around the nation (Callahan, 1962, pp. 95–125). These self-styled "educational engineers" were usually professors of education at leading universities or, sometimes, well-known school superintendents. In the vanguard of this group in the years prior to the Wall Street Crash were individuals such as Stanford's Ellwood Cubberley, Paul Hanus of Harvard, Charles Judd of the University of Chicago, and George D. Strayer and Thorndike of Teachers College, to name but a few. Often, their work centered around designing pupil achievement tests and rating scales for teachers, as in the case of Ayres and Courtis, or they involved themselves, as Cubberley and Hanus did, with school survey work of various kinds.

As much as any administrative development in the pre-Depression era, school surveys reflected the enormous emphasis on measurement and efficiency in school management during the first three decades of the century. City schools from East Orange, New Jersey to Portland, Oregon were surveyed during those years and comprehensive studies of state systems were also undertaken. Overall, between 1911 and 1925, hundreds of school surveys of different kinds were commissioned. By 1924, the popularity of surveys prompted Cubberley (1924, p. 188) to remark that the "survey movement has rapidly developed into an important form of educational engineering. . . ." Moreover, the efficiency issue and the pressure of public discontent with school costs never seemed far from the surface of the reasons for such surveys, as Cubberley pointed out in describing his work at Salt Lake City:

> One of the problems presented at Salt Lake City was that of estimating the efficiency of the instruction given. This was made especially important by reason of the fact that there had been much criticism in the city, on the part of the businessmen, of the instruction in the so-called fundamental subjects in the school. (1916, p. 107)

Finally, another important way in which Taylor's scientific management shaped the practice of school administration may be seen in the creation of research agencies to assist school superintendents and their staffs implement efficiency measures and in other administrative changes. Largely as a result of Courtis' lobbying for greater cooperation between school officers and the professoriate in the development and use of standardized tests, research bureaus or "bureaus of research and efficiency," as they were often called, were established at centers for higher learning and in state departments of education throughout the nation, thus paralleling the rise of engineering and planning departments in industry. For example, research bureaus were organized at the University of Oklahoma in 1913, at Indiana University, Kansas State Normal School, and Iowa State University in 1914, and at the University of Minnesota and the Wisconsin State Department of Public Instruction in 1915 and 1916. The emphasis educators placed on efficiency and management research in the decade after Taylor's rise to prominence was manifested in the fact that in the years 1921 and 1922 alone, twenty-six such bureaus were founded (Monroe, 1950, p. 142). Like the industrial efficiency engineers who established planning and research departments to forecast and monitor production, educators in educational research bureaus also sought to rationalize production processes through, as one bureau director put it, "the herculean task of substituting fact for opinion in school practice" (Melcher, 1916, p. 120).

SUMMARY

The preceding discussion dealt largely with the immediate effects of scientific management on the study and practice of school administration. The impact of Taylor's ideas on educational thought, however, did not end when scientific management was supplanted by other views of administration after 1930. Taylor's ideas became part of the larger "classical" approach to administrative study in the late 1930s and 1940s, when they became linked with management principles advanced by other theorists such as Henri Fayol, Luther Gulick, Lyndall Urwick, and James Mooney. As such, they continue to be subjects of study for students of educational administration.

In a direct way, Taylor's concepts have continued to shape the character of school administration in the sense that scientific management's presence can still be seen in the practices of central offices throughout the country. The corporate model of administration, which emerged fully in the scientific management era, remains the model of administration on which school systems are generally based. Statistical techniques, measurement scales, and cost-accounting procedures introduced during that time are still used to some extent. School systems still strive for efficiency, only now the label management science is used rather than scientific management. Experts of various kinds still make their presence felt in educational circles, and school leaders, mindful of renewed public interest in school accountability and performance, continue to search for effective forms of management.

Finally, the embodiment of scientific management principles in school practices also helped shape the direction of educational thought about administration in the depression years and after. In reaction to scientific management's alleged dehumanizing of people and its enslavement of teachers and pupils to routine and to the autocratic and authoritarian behavior of some school leaders, there emerged a new view of school administration in the 1930s and 1940s, referred to initially as democratic administration and later as human relations.

3

DEMOCRATIC ADMINISTRATION
AND HUMAN RELATIONS

EDUCATIONAL INTEREST IN MANAGEMENT IDEAS derived from industrial practice did not cease when Taylor's influence on American society began to
wane in the late 1920s. Rather, industrial ideas about organization
continued to shape how educators thought about administration between the two great wars and after, especially in the post-1945 period,
when the study of school management was again influenced by a view
of administration originating outside of education. This new view,
known as the human relations approach, proved also to be immensely
appealing to educators and, like Taylor's scientific management,
changed educational thought about school organization and the roles of
school executives and teachers.

This chapter examines how the human relations approach developed in industrial and social science research, how it came to be an
important part of educational thought about administration, and how it
became intertwined with existing educational ideas about the need for
democratic practices in schools. As this chapter will illustrate, the
human relations view of school management was made up of two
interpenetrating bodies of ideas. The first was democratic administration, a philosophy of school administration originating shortly after
1900 and manifested in the work of John Dewey (Fleming, 1982). The
second arose after 1945, when notions about democratizing school
organizations became joined with human relations ideas drawn from
behavioral science and industrial studies pioneered by individuals such
as Kurt Lewin and Elton Mayo. The fusion of these two bodies of
thought in the 1940s was described first as "democratic human relations," and later as simply the "human relations" approach to school
administration. In the following discussion, special attention will be
paid to how this approach reflected intellectual and social changes
taking place inside and outside education and how it prompted educators to reexamine their understandings of school organization.

HUMAN RELATIONS STUDY IN INDUSTRY

Corporate Reform and the Human Element in Industry

Even before Taylor's death in 1915, scientific management practices had been sharply criticized in several quarters. Prior to the publication of Taylor's volume on the principles of scientific management in 1911, skilled and unskilled trades had registered their opposition to new production techniques that they claimed abused their rights. Labor leaders were especially alarmed by the way Taylor's methods allowed managers and foremen to "speed up" assembly lines and to manipulate hours of employment and piece-work rates. By the end of the first decade of the new century, workers often refused to participate in time and motion studies and in some instances boycotted companies using these methods.

Antipathy between trade unions and exponents of scientific management peaked in the years 1911 to 1914. In 1911, a strike by civilian union workers at the Watertown Arsenal, a federal installation in New York, led to a full-scale inquiry into "the Taylor and other systems of shop management" (Noble, 1977, p. 272). After lengthy congressional hearings, investigators concluded that scientific management practices were not in the best interests of employees and, as a result, bonus systems, piece-work rates, and, within two years, time and motion studies were prohibited in all federal government industrial yards. Throughout industrial circles, many had become suspicious that time and motion experts were really not as accurate as they claimed to be and that "scientific" estimates of potential production levels were frequently of a "best guess" variety.

Misgivings about the effects of scientific management were more broadly based than the particularistic reactions of certain business managers, workers, and labor leaders. Post-1900 American society was generally becoming more concerned with problems of human welfare and the rights of workers. Even in the latter years of the nineteenth century, socially conscious industrialists, academics, and other community leaders had begun to establish better health, safety, and educational programs in factories. In large part, such attempts at corporate reform were consonant with an emerging intellectual movement that emphasized the psychology of human behavior. Around 1910, Freudian ideas about clinical therapy were beginning to circulate in popular literature, and industrial psychologists such as Hugo Munsterberg, Walter Dill Scott, and Lillian Gilbreth were beginning to assist business and industry in solving manpower problems (Munsterberg, 1913; Scott,

1912; Spriegel, 1953). By the early 1920s, industrial administrators and the engineers and social scientists who advised them recognized that the "human element" in production could no longer be taken for granted or offset by new production processes. In a 1923 paper dealing with the social and psychological needs of workers. Elton Mayo, an Australian professor of industrial management at Harvard who would later direct the famous Western Electric studies, noted management's longstanding failure to appreciate the emotional and psychological adjustments that industrial organizations forced workers to make. "The problems of business," he observed in a thinly veiled reference to the efficiency engineers, "are not merely scientific, they are human" (Mayo, 1923, p. 120). By 1928, even Harlow Person, the managing director of the Taylor Society, acknowledged the possible effects of worker sentiment on productivity and the importance of social relations in factory life (Person, 1928). In fact, Person was one of the first management writers to use the term "human relations" to describe the social interactions and informal communications between managers and workers.

Mary Parker Follett:
The First Theorist of Human Relations

The first writer to formulate a comprehensive view of administration reflecting the post-1918 social and philosophical mood was Mary Parker Follett. Well-schooled in philosophy, history, and political science, she authored a number of theoretical studies that came to be recognized as major contributions to the study of general administration, including such works as *The New State* (1920), *Creative Experience* (1930), and *Dynamic Administration* (1940).

Follett was particularly concerned with improving industrial relations between managers and workers and with the general problems of personnel administration. Increases in organizational size and complexity had brought about special difficulties for administrators, she believed, most notably in coordinating differentiated work groups and in supervising large managerial units. In light of these changes, an organization's effectiveness, she advised, depended on the development of appropriate mechanisms to coordinate human resources (Pugh, Hickson, & Hinings, 1964, p. 48).

Follett's views differed markedly from much of the administrative thinking of her day. Not only was she one of the first theorists who attempted to enlarge the scope of management study from the problems of production units to a broader consideration of how organizations worked, but she also challenged what were then widely held ideas about the nature of administrative authority and leadership. She contended that if organizations wished to improve morale, communications, and, ultimately, productivity, they needed to restructure their power relationships and decentralize authority.

Not hierarchical rank, but the law of the situation, she believed, should determine who directed specific activities. "One person should not give orders to another person," Follett claimed, "but both should agree to take their orders from the situation" (Pugh, Hickson, & Hinings, 1964, p. 48). The task for those individuals formally charged with leadership and responsibility was therefore to elicit contributions from those around them to "create a group power rather than . . . a personal power." It was Follett's view that those affected by certain policies or decisions should be allowed to participate in their formulation. To Follett, the arbitrary use of executive power no longer had a place in industrial life; the notion of "power over" as a rule of management she sought to replace by the notion of "power with." In an effort to imbue the industrial environment with political principles drawn from the study of American government, Follett outlined what was perhaps the first major social philosophy of administration, a philosophy that would become intimately connected with the human relations view of management and with a broader social movement for democracy in the workplace.

The Hawthorne Investigations

Empirical support for the idea that organizational effectiveness was somehow related to the social and psychological climate of work groups was first presented in the mid-1930s when the results of the Hawthorne studies were published. Located in southwest Chicago, the Hawthorne factory was a major manufacturing and supply branch for the American Telephone and Telegraph Company and employed a staff of almost 30,000 workers in the late 1920s. Under the auspices of the National Research Council, a program of study had begun in 1924 at Western Electric's Hawthorne Works to explore the effects of illumination and other physical variables on worker productivity. By 1927, responsibility for the research project at Hawthorne had become a cooperative venture between the management of the factory and members of the Harvard Graduate School of Business, most notably Elton Mayo and Fritz Roethlisberger.

The most revealing of their experiments (Carey, 1967) involved a study of five young women employed to assemble telephone relays. For the purpose of the study, these individuals were transferred from their usual work stations on the factory floor to a special test room isolated from other employees. Here their work was directed by a researcher who had been counseled in techniques of friendly supervision. Without changing any other conditions, their performance was monitored and, after several months, it was apparent that their hourly output had increased. Gradually other changes were introduced into their work routines, including rest pauses, shorter hours of work, alternative assembly methods, and changes in humidity and illumination. Investigators also recorded off-the-job factors such as the time of meals and the number of hours that workers slept. Researchers, however, were unable to correlate changes in rates of output with variations in physical conditions.

After a year of testing, researchers concluded that the experimental group was responding to changes not accounted for in the research design. Further study led investigators to surmise that worker productivity was to some extent related to the special supervision and treatment given to workers by management. In singling out these workers from their peers, it seemed, researchers had unwittingly introduced another variable. The social and psychological satisfactions derived from management support and consideration, and the feeling of group membership and special status that employees obtained from their new working arrangements, were apparently the variables that Mayo and his associates had overlooked. In a 1941 *Reader's Digest* article, New Deal advocate Stuart Chase described the reaction of researchers when they learned what had taken place:

> The staff swooned at their desks. They had thought they were returning the girls to original conditions but found that those original conditions were gone forever. Because of some mysterious X which had thrust itself into the experiment, the experiment had changed under them, and the group they now had was not the group they had started with.
>
> This X wasn't in the production end of the factory. It was in the human end. It was an attitude, the way the girls felt about their work and their group. By asking their help and cooperation, the investigators had made the girls feel important. Their whole attitude had changed from that of separate cogs in a machine to that of a congenial group trying to help the company solve a problem. They had found stability, a place where they belonged, and work whose purpose they could clearly see. And so they worked faster and better than they ever had in their lives. (p. 17)

The inducement of positive change through the interaction of subjects in an experiment with those conducting it has since become labeled the "Hawthorne effect," in reference to the setting where the phenomenon was first identified. Indeed, this finding or "great *éclaircissement*," as Roethlisberger and Dickson put it, proved to be "an illumination quite different from what . . . [was] expected from the illumination studies" (1939, p. 568).

The conclusion by Hawthorne investigators that the quality and kind of interaction in the workplace significantly affected organizational morale and productivity marked the starting point of an emphasis in organizational research that would be widely recognized within a decade as the human relations approach. The key organizational dynamic constituting this approach, at least as Mayo and his colleagues defined it, was the conflict in goals and values between work groups ruled by "the logics of sentiment" and the production objectives of industrial administrators based on "the logics of management."

The inference underlying the results of the experimental work at Hawthorne was clear. If management failed to appreciate the nature of the human element and its ultimate expression in group productivity, then industry could not "make the most of men." It was this view that was propagated by human relations exponents through the publication of books such as Mayo's *The Human Problems of an Industrial Civilization* (1933), Roethlisberger and Dickson's *Management and the Worker* (1939), Roethlisberger's *Management and Morale* (1941), and Mayo's *The Social Problems of an Industrial Civilization* (1945).

Kurt Lewin and the Iowa Studies: Democracy Finds New Friends

Outside industry, the idea that the social climate of work groups was related to productivity found equally strong support toward the end of the 1930s in the work of Kurt Lewin and his associates at the University of Iowa's Child Welfare Research Station. Lewin, an internationally known figure in experimental psychology, had fled his post at the University of Berlin's Psychological Institute in 1933 when the anti-Semitic purges of the German academies began and had joined the migration of oppressed Jewish intellectuals to the United States.

Guided by Lewin, two graduate students, Ronald Lippitt and Ralph White, undertook a series of experiments in 1938 to examine how styles of leadership shaped group behavior (Anderson, 1963). The subjects chosen for these studies were children who met after school to make *papier mâché* masks and engage in other play activities. Initially, the researchers considered how two types of leadership styles enacted by adult leaders affected the behavior of the youngsters: An autocratic leader instructed the group in what to do and how to do it and generally dominated group activities in all respects; a democratic leader permitted group members to determine their own goals and methods. As the experiment progressed, researchers found that contrasts between the two groups became more pronounced and there appeared to be "far more quarreling and hostility in the autocratically-led group, and far more friendliness and group spirit in the one democratically-led" (Marrow, 1956, p. 125).

Intrigued by these results, they undertook a second and more carefully controlled investigation. The findings of this inquiry were even more remarkable. In an autocratic environment, the children seemed discontented, often aggressive, and lacking in initiative; on occasion, they destroyed their play materials. A laissez-faire atmosphere similarly produced problems for youngsters: Without direction of any kind, work was often unfinished and some group members appeared to be frustrated.

In contrast, democratically led groups seemed productive and socially satisfied; children working under democratic conditions appeared to demonstrate more originality and independence. Less hostility existed among members than in other groups. When the twenty children participating in this experiment were later polled, all but one expressed a preference for a democratically structured style of leadership (Marrow, 1956, p. 126).

Publication of Lippitt and White's work in 1939, and the results of similar leadership studies by the Iowa group in the following years, captured the public imagination (*New York Times*, 1940, pp. 6–7) and prompted popular and scholarly interest in the subject of leadership.

At a time when the nation was still recovering from the Depression and was increasingly apprehensive about the survival of democratic political systems in Europe and elsewhere, academic investigations that revealed democratic forms of organization to be superior to autocratic systems were noteworthy and much-welcomed events.

DEMOCRATIC ADMINISTRATION IN EDUCATION

The adoption of human relations ideas by educators after 1940 was brought about by a variety of social and intellectual forces, not the least of which was the already-established influence of an approach to school management known as democratic administration. Unlike the human relations approach that originated in industrial and social science research, the democratic view of school administration first evolved among educators in the early years of the twentieth century in response to several factors, including new social ideas, changes in the character of school organizations, and reactions on the part of some to autocratic and authoritarian supervisory practices in schools. In contrast to human relations, democratic administration was not based on empirical research that tested theoretical propositions about human behavior in work groups; rather, it was principally a "home grown" philosophy of school management that drew its strength from the ideas of educational reformers and was founded on a loosely integrated set of beliefs about democratic rights, individual welfare, and the need for cooperation in human enterprise (Fleming, 1982, pp. 53–202).

John Dewey
and the Democratic Conscience in Education

One of the earliest promoters of democratic administration in education, and perhaps its greatest exponent, was John Dewey, an individual who not only shaped modern pedagogical theory and practice but who also profoundly influenced the course of twentieth-century American social thought. Throughout a long and distinguished career in philosophy and education, Dewey remained absorbed in the study of democracy, not only as it pertained to the operation of educational institutions, but as it related to the broader character and direction of American life.

The great challenge to American democracy, as Dewey saw it, lay in extending the spirit of participation at the heart of the nation's political system to the economic world of men and women at work. Late nineteenth-century industrialization, he contended, had produced a class structure in which some individuals prospered and others were indentured to a life of industrial servitude. If America wished to remain democratic, he argued (Dewey, 1946, p. 260), the long-standing goal of political and social equality must be reflected in a participatory form of industrial government that would allow the benefits of production and decisions about work to be shared by all.

Dewey saw that the real change taking place in the workplaces of America had more to do with the social relations of work than with the kind of technical innovation that marked industrialization. He was particularly apprehensive about the introduction of scientific management methods in industry and the effects of Taylor's system on factory workers, most notably the quest by industrial engineers for efficiency and control at the expense of human values. "Much is said about scientific management of work," he observed, "it is a narrow view which restricts the science which secures efficiency of operations to movements of the muscles" (Dewey, 1916, p. 85).

Naturally, Dewey was no less concerned with the use of scientific management procedures in school administration. In his 1916 volume, *Democracy and Education*, he railed against the increasing popularity of scientific management techniques among school leaders and emphasized the need for educational managers to secure the consent of those they governed. Scientific management's preoccupation with efficiency did little to foster what he described as a "well-balanced social interest" and was therefore contrary to the proper ends of education. Under no circumstances, he believed, should the school "become an instrument of perpetuating unchanged the existing industrial order of society, instead of operating as a means of its transformation" (1916, p. 316).

Giving teachers opportunities for greater participation, Dewey contended, would change both the character of the school organization and the quality and kind of relationships between teachers and administrators. "In the degree to which the administrator achieves the integration of the educational phase of his work with the human and social relations into which he necessarily enters," Dewey wrote, "he will treat the school itself as a cooperative community" (1946, p. 64). For the educational leader, a cooperative approach to school management would also mean that "his leadership will be that of intellectual stimulation and direction, through give and take with others, not that of an aloof official imposing, authoritatively, educational ends and methods" (p. 64).

Although Dewey remained the spiritual godfather of democratic administration, there were numerous other spokesmen for the cause of democratic leadership within the educational professoriate during the first half of the twentieth century. Among the prominent professors who supported this approach to administration were individuals such as William F. Russell, Jesse Newlon, Paul Mort, and Ward Miller of Teachers College; Chicago's William Burton; Stanford's Grayson Kefauver and Jesse Sears; Ohio State's Boyd Bode; Arthur Moehlman of the University of Michigan; and Wilbur Yauch of Northern Illinois State Teachers College. During the 1930s and 1940s, in particular, democratic values in education (and other aspects of American life) were also greatly promoted by social reconstructionists such as George Counts, William Heard Kilpatrick, Harold Rugg, and others associated with Teachers College and by the social and philosophical group at the University of Illinois, including Archibald Anderson, Kenneth Benne, B. Othanel Smith, and William O. Stanley. Dewey and Childs expressed a view shared by many of these individuals when they advised that the school must "frankly face the fact that it will not contribute to the reconstruction of the social process until it seriously experiments with the reconstruction of its own procedures" (Kilpatrick, 1933, p. 210).

In the interwar years and after, democratic management in schools was also promoted by assorted professional bodies and through the publications of various departments and committees within the National Education Association (NEA). For example, in 1943, the NEA's Department of Elementary School Principals issued *Elementary Schools: The Frontline of Democracy*; in 1940, the NEA's Educational Policies Commission published *Learning the Ways of Democracy*, and in 1943, *Education and the People's Peace*; and the NEA's Department of Superintendence and Directors of Instruction focused on the need for democratic administrative procedures in its 1943 volume, *Cooperation: Principles and Practices*, and its 1943 volume, *Leadership at Work*. Influential studies with similar themes were also published during those years by the NEA's Association for Supervision and Curriculum Development.

In many respects, these individuals and organizations shared similar views about reforming the style and character of school administration. They generally agreed that educational leadership should be a non-coercive and less-directive process and that teacher involvement in many aspects of school decision making should be encouraged. As George Strayer, a proponent of scientific management before becoming an advocate of democratic administration, put it: "Participation by teachers is indispensable to the best development of the public schools" (Miller, 1942, p. 24). Supporters of democratic practices offered several reasons why such participation was necessary. First of all, there was a widely shared belief at the time that if teachers were treated in an autocratic and authoritarian manner by principals and superintendents, they would treat pupils accordingly. In line with this sentiment, A. S. Barr and William Burton advised in their 1926 textbook, *The Supervision of Instruction*, that supervision should be based on "democratic leadership in a group of co-workers to the end that the pupils of the school may make the largest possible growth in desirable ideals, interests, knowledge, powers, and skills" (p. 83).

A second and more practical motive behind the professoriate's endorsement of a democratic style of school management had to do with the day-to-day problems administrators faced as a result of the enormous growth in size and specialization of school organizations that had taken place since the late nineteenth century. Such developments and the bureaucratization they helped to promote brought with them communications problems, which had to do with span of control, and unprecedented problems related to the management of large school staffs. In short, structural changes within school systems compelled superintendents and other senior administrators to rely on the expertise of teachers and other staff members. It was, in effect, no longer advantageous for school leaders to maintain an autocratic or "top-down" style of management in light of the organizational developments that had occurred (Miller, 1942, p. 17).

Finally, in a closely related sense, democratic leadership promised to assist school administrators in securing the cooperation of their staffs by making them "members of the team." As Thomas Fleming noted in his history of school management during the interwar period and after, "the concept of democratic leadership suggested a way of repairing the damage that had been done to the social relations between administrative staff and teachers as school organizations had grown larger, more bureaucratic, more rule-bound, and more formal" (1982, p. 92).

Considering democratic administration's popularity among professors of school management by the late 1930s, it is not surprising that educators proved receptive to human relations ideas when they began to circulate outside industry in the 1940s and 1950s. After all, democratic administration and human relations appeared to be alike in a number of important respects. On the surface, both approaches seemed to be reactions against authoritarian administrative practices associated with scientific management: Both preached a doctrine of management by consensus; both described a new kind of organizational authority; both suggested a new role for managers in steering and facilitating the activities of work groups; and both were apparently concerned with issues of bureaucracy and organizational growth and the problem of worker alienation that size and specialization seemed to promote. Most important, human relations research seemed to confirm empirically what supporters of democratic administration had believed for some time: namely, that organizational morale and productivity could be enhanced by humanistic leadership practices.

School and Society after 1945

Educational interest in applying democratic and human relations ideas to problems of school administration was spurred by several developments taking place inside and outside schools at the end of World War II. The growing urban character of postwar American society, as well as improvements in transportation, had narrowed the distance between home and school for many Americans. More and more, schools were being sited in suburban areas to accommodate the educational needs of the nation's middle class who were increasingly abandoning the cities (Link & Catton, 1967, pp. 590–592). This development naturally facilitated community involvement in educational affairs. A trend toward administrative decentralization and the creation of more autonomous schools after 1945 also promoted direct interaction between school staff and the public, particularly with respect to curriculum planning and the evaluation of pupil progress (NEA, 1955, p. 209). The increasing membership in parent-teacher associations in the postwar years also illustrated new levels of public interest in education and the closer relationship that was being forged between educators and the communities they served (Griffiths, 1956, p. 117).

As teachers began to rate students in such intangible areas as citizenship, personal decorum, and their ability to mix with others and as report cards were issued in conjunction with individual teacher-parent conferences, school staffs were obliged (NEA, 1955, p. 209) to deal more often with the public about sensitive human issues. As a result of such contacts with parents and community members, educators sought new ways to deal effectively with public relations matters. For school administrators, the ability to work with others was particularly important. Unlike teachers, many school executives at this time still worked without the security of tenure, and their career success, if not professional survival, depended on their capacity to solicit support for the policies and programs they administered (Swift, 1971, p. 179). In short, the changing environment around the schools and the need for better public relations provided sound reasons for educators to adopt a view of management that promised to enhance their social and interpersonal skills.

Conditions inside school organizations in the post-1945 era also caused administrators to look to human relations. Staffing difficulties that had begun after 1941, when teachers left the classroom to join the armed forces or to be employed in wartime industry, became an acute administrative problem by the end of the war (Link & Catton, 1967, p. 653). Teacher shortages and the general high rate of attrition within the profession were aggravated by economic factors that made teaching an unattractive occupation (Hill, 1947, p. 124). To address such problems, school managers needed to gain public understanding and support and, at the same time, to improve morale among school staff. The tasks of balancing public and professional interests and of dealing with groups inside and outside schools were seen by postwar administrators as problems in achieving consensus among diverse elements, problems in creating an atmosphere in which change could take place, problems in communicating—in short, human relations problems.

The changing character of school populations in the late 1940s and early 1950s was another factor that encouraged educators to develop human relations skills. More students from different backgrounds were enrolled in public schools than ever before. Late-nineteenth-century and early-twentieth-century immigration had radically altered the complexion of American society. By 1930, only 58 percent of the total population was of white native-born stock; more than 32 percent of Americans were either foreign-born or came from families with one foreign-born parent (Moehlman, 1940, p. 71). Often, teachers and administrators were ill-prepared to deal with the heterogeneous clientele of metropolitan school districts (Cook & Cook, 1957, p. 135). Many teachers and school managers had been raised in small towns or rural areas where their social contacts had been largely limited to members of their own race, creed, and economic class (Cook & Cook, 1957, p. 135). Even for those educators familiar with urban culture, the increasing mobility of postwar society, the quickening pace of events, and the loosening of long-held values and traditions posed new and difficult problems, especially in the decade after the Supreme Court's landmark *Brown* v. *Board of Education* decision.

The conflict resolution skills associated with human relations were also seen by postwar educators as useful ways of dealing with other problems affecting schools, particularly public relations problems growing out of mid-century criticisms of schooling. Conservative opposition to progressive education and to the public school's emphasis on "life adjustment" skills rather than academic content emerged in the decade after 1945 and gained further momentum with the launching of the Soviet satellite in 1957. Books such as Mortimer Smith's *And Madly Teach: A Layman Looks at Public School Education* (1949), Albert Lynd's *Quackery in the Public Schools* (1953), Arthur Bestor's *Educational Wastelands* (1953), Hyman Rickover's *Education and Freedom* (1959), and James Koerner's *The Case for Basic Education* (1959) generally condemned public schooling for its alleged anti-intellectual tone, its dominance by professional educators, and its undemocratic methods in preparing and selecting pupils for careers.

In light of such criticisms, it is not surprising that professors of education recommended a form of management for schools that sought to employ strategies for cooperation borrowed from industrial research. The benefits of applying human relations ideas seemed clear. After all, studies published by Mayo, Roethlisberger, and others suggested that management's use of human relations techniques could help increase production, improve communication and morale, and generally smooth the troubled waters of interpersonal and intergroup conflict. What better way to address many of the difficulties that now faced the schools!

Human Relations Ideas
and the Literature of Educational Administration

One of the first educators to appreciate the changing view of administration that human relations research had brought about was Ralph Tyler, head of the Department of Education at the University of Chicago. In "Educational Adjustments Necessitated by Changing Ideological Concepts," an article published in 1941, Tyler noted the relevance of recent human relations research to school administrators and suggested that future research in educational management should be guided by Mayo and Roethlisberger's work at the Hawthorne plant.

Tyler's article was not the only educational writing published during the war years to suggest that professors of school management could profitably employ ideas derived from industrial study, although it was perhaps the first to cite the results of the Hawthorne experiments and to identify the intellectual direction that educational administration would take during the next two decades. Another early study of note was the American Association of School Administrators' (AASA) 1944 Yearbook, *Morale for a Free World—America and Not America Only*, a volume of almost 500 pages produced by the Commission on Education for Morale that featured a special chapter on "Human Relations in School Administration." Written as part of an effort to examine how public schools could improve morale in war and peace, this study drew its ideas from a number of social science writings on morale and group behavior, including Roethlisberger's *Management and Morale*. Two years later, in 1946, the influence of Roethlisberger and other Hawthorne researchers was again found in the National Society for the Study of Education's (NSSE) volume, *Changing Conceptions in Educational Administration*, a volume that clearly testified to the growing acceptance of human relations ideas among professors of education and others who were writing about school management in the early and mid-1940s.

After 1945, numerous educational monographs and articles appeared that disseminated human relations ideas in educational administration. Among these were *Supervision as Human Relations* (1953), written by Stanford's dean of education, John Bartky, Wayne State's Lloyd and Elaine Cooke's *School Problems in Human Relations* (1957), and Paul Mort and Donald Ross' influential study, *Principles of School Administration* (1957). The popularization of human relations was further bolstered in numerous articles found in the periodical literature of the time.

Of many postwar writings that applied the human relations view to school organizations, two major studies are particularly illustrative of the ways in which ideas from industry and the social sciences were adopted by those who studied and wrote about educational management: One of these is Wilbur Yauch's *Improving Human Relations in School Administration* (1949), and the other is Daniel Griffiths' *Human Relations in Educational Administration* (1956).

Wilbur Yauch's 1949 study, *Improving Human Relations in School Administration*, was the first full-length educational study to combine ethical generalizations from democratic administration with human relations research drawn from industry and to bring together the prescriptive approach to school management favored by educators throughout the 1920s and 1930s with a more objective appreciation of administrative problems. Conclusions reached by the Hawthorne researchers regarding the behavior of work groups in industry suggested to Yauch that parallel kinds of group forces were likely present in schools. "If spontaneous, almost unconscious, social organization arises from the relations of workers in industry," he wrote (p. 21), "it would seem inevitable that social organization of teachers in a school would develop just as naturally."

Accordingly, he advocated teacher involvement in all areas of administration, including staff participation in decisions concerning supervision, budget allocation, curriculum, general policy making, and teacher participation in clerical duties associated with operating a school. This meant that a principal's authority was to be no greater than that of other staff members. As Yauch put it: "The principal and the teacher meet on equal ground . . . each having equal authority in what is proper and what is not" (p. 114). Even though Yauch conceded that a principal was still obliged to serve as "school representative" and "executive of the superintendent," the principal's primary responsibility was to act as an "interpreter" or "executor of the group policy" and "coordinator of faculty activities."

Seven years after publication of Yauch's volume, another and more ambitious work appeared that also serves to illustrate the influence of the human relations approach on school management. This was Daniel Griffiths' 1956 textbook, *Human Relations in Educational Administration*, a volume that synthesized more than a quarter of a century of educational and social science thought about administration. In the words of its author (p. vii), it represented nothing less than an attempt "to bring together in one volume what is known about human relations and relate it to school administration."

Griffiths' book was designed to assist students of educational management appreciate the social aspects of their work. As Griffiths noted (p. 19): "The administrator needs to develop skills in relating himself and others to the social setting in which he is placed. These skills are integral parts of the behavior of the administrator and may be developed and improved by an understanding of the content of human relations and by constant practice."

Staff morale, Griffiths claimed, was a particularly troublesome problem for school administrators after World War II. The fact that postwar school systems were plagued by teacher absenteeism, tardiness, and attrition was evidence, he maintained, of low morale. Like other human relations advocates at this time, Griffiths believed that staff morale was related to the kind of leadership operating within schools; he pointed for support to the investigations conducted by Lewin's group and by human relations researchers at the National Training Laboratory at Bethel, Maine. "The development of morale in a school faculty is directly related to the degree in which the administrator can help individuals to achieve satisfaction in their work," he observed (p. 146). In making this statement, Griffiths, like Yauch and other writers of the period, depicted the school leader as someone whose chief responsibility was to facilitate the actions of others. In Griffiths' terms, the educational executive, while at times "an initiator," more frequently served as a "coordinator" of staff activities, a "helper" and "resource person" to others, and a "recognizer" of group talents. Above all, the school manager was a "social" individual, sensitive to the human needs of those around him (p. 252).

One striking contrast between *Human Relations in School Administration* and earlier writings on school management lay in the fact that Griffiths' work was considerably less prescriptive in character than much of what passed for educational scholarship on administration during the years 1918 to 1939. In contrast to such writings, Griffiths' study was not intended, as he wrote, to be a "cookbook" containing "lists of human relations rules and techniques" that could be applied widely to various situations (p. vii). Rather, *Human Relations in School Administration* sought to provide an intellectual basis for the study of school management using social science research and research drawn from other fields of professional study. As such, it signaled the beginning of a shift in educational interest from a practical application of human relations research to a concern with theoretically grounded understandings of human behavior derived from the social sciences, a change later characterized (Getzels, 1977, p. 9) as one in which educators began to conceive of administration as a "domain of study" rather than a "domain of action."

From Democratic Administration to Human Relations

To postwar educators who came to regard democratic administration and human relations as essentially the same body of ideas, evidence of their philosophical and intellectual congruence no doubt appeared straightforward enough.

Such apparent similarities, however, masked elemental differences between these two concepts of administration—differences attributable to the ideologies underlying each of these views. To Dewey and others who called for teacher participation in school affairs, democratic administration represented a way of bringing organizational practices in schools in line with long-standing political and social values, thereby endowing teachers with rights of organizational citizenship—rights that seemed to require greater definition and protection as school systems grew larger and more bureaucratic. If the spirit of American life was to be maintained, supporters of democratic administration argued, the paternalistic and sometimes-authoritarian practices of school executives had to be eradicated, and power, authority, and responsibility for educational policies and decisions had to be redistributed among school staffs. Only in this way, they proclaimed, could future generations of Americans be assured of institutions in which they might learn democratic beliefs and attitudes. To such individuals, securing the consent of the governed within schools took greater precedence over whatever organizational benefits might accrue to school leaders through the use of democratic procedures. If democratic management resulted in better communication and morale, or if it assisted administrators in capitalizing on the expertise and cooperation of school staffs, so much the better. Such ends, however, were less important than the primary goal of making schools laboratories for democracy and agencies for national regeneration.

In contrast, the human relations approach, as earlier shown, was born in industrial experiments designed to improve worker performance and generally to assist the cause of management. And even though early advocates of human relations in education such as Kenneth Benne, Wilbur Yauch, and others initially embraced human relations ideas because they promised to assist the cause of democratic leadership, the adoption of these ideas eventually led educators to focus more on solving administrative problems and tasks than on restructuring or democratizing schools.

By mid-century, the focus on democracy in schools and teacher participation was being cast aside by students of educational management in favor of other issues related to understanding the roles and responsibilities of school leaders. In short, the portrait of the socially conscious educational leader created by Dewey and others—a portrait popularized in countless writings on school management prior to Pearl Harbor—no longer occupied a central place in educational literature by the end of the 1950s. In its place, there emerged the portrait of school leaders as administrative functionaries, people who were not just morally chaste, as management critic Richard Sennett has described industrial managers (1979), but who also seemed to be ideologically neutral.

Instead of promoting the idea of educational and social change (as the social reconstructionists and proponents of democratic leadership had tried to do), human relations writers on school management generally seemed more concerned with understanding how group dynamics skills could assist administrators in dealing with public relations problems and problems related to staff morale. Their writings therefore addressed issues related more to "managing" and "administering" schools than loftier notions about what enlightened leadership should accomplish. No longer was there the same strong interest in "freeing the minds of men," and particularly members of the teaching profession, from "certain standardized patterns of working and living" that Clyde Campbell wrote about in advocating democratic practices in schools (1955, p. 32).

After mid-century, concepts of school leadership were no longer premised so much on philosophical worthiness as on how well school executives understood human behavior and the dynamics of interpersonal relationships. In human relations writings, development of skills in non-directive counseling, "feedback," conference decision making, and psychological testing was viewed as essential if administrators wished to be successful in promoting cooperation and harmony in the workplace, in improving staff morale, and in bringing about organizational changes that were controllable and predictable.

Several factors help explain why post-World War II professors of school management and other educators failed to see the inconsistencies that existed between democratic and human relations views of administration and why they failed to acknowledge an emerging body of criticism that pointed out the problems and limits of the human relations approach. One explanation is that educators were so swept along by the promise of human relations that they failed to perceive the narrowness of this view, its introspective focus, and its allegedly pro-management bias (Kerr, 1953; Tead, 1946). It may also be, as Andrew Halpin has charged in a commentary on educational administration, that educators have long been dazzled by new movements of any kind and failed to exercise sufficient caution in adopting fresh ideas from outside education (1958, pp. 13–15). Or, finally, the failure to distinguish between democratic administration and human relations may also be partially attributable to the unfamiliarity of educators with their own intellectual lineage and with the general field of management study at this time (Cohen, 1976).

SUMMARY

From the early to mid-1900s, teacher participation in school management emerged as a central theme in the study of educational administration, manifested first in concepts of democratic leadership and later in human relations ideas derived from industrial and social science research. During this time, professors of education and other students of school organization gradually shifted their attention from the technical concerns that dominated the scientific management of schools before 1930 to an investigation of human and social elements in organizational life. The early emphasis on task analysis and worker efficiency underlying Bobbitt and Spaulding's writings had, by the 1930s, been replaced by a new focus on the psychological and social character of the educational workplace.

In particular, the egalitarian and anti-authoritarian notions associated with democratic administration greatly appealed to educators, as they did to all Americans, not just because they were new management practices as such—although they were—but more importantly because they accommodated the democratic traditions of the national past. As historian David Potter observed (1962, pp. 216–217), participative forms of management—such as democratic administration and, to some extent, human relations—found ready acceptance because they were in accord with a long-standing American belief that leadership, however constituted, must always appear to be democratic in a democratic state.

On a more practical level, democratic and human relations views of administration were attractive to educators because they seemed to offer solutions to management problems resulting from the growing bureaucratization of schools and school systems. Growth in the size and specialization of educational organizations meant that school executives were increasingly dependent on staff expertise and teacher cooperation in managing school affairs. Democratic administration and human relations both seemed to offer ways of redistributing decision-making responsibility and of helping administrators work more effectively with teachers. They promised, in essence, to provide school administrators with the interpersonal skills and understanding seen as necessary to deal with management problems perceived at the time to be primarily human in nature—namely, problems of morale and alienation within school organizations and public relations problems with constituencies outside schools.

As part of this emphasis on the human factor, reducing interpersonal conflict became a central concern to human relations advocates. Generally, human relations writers in education and in business viewed conflict as something that should be suppressed for the good of the organization or as a "pathological case," as organizationalist Nicos Mouzelis described it (1968, p. 115). In fact, human relations writers in school administration refused to acknowledge that the goals of school managers and teachers were not always congruent or that sources of organizational conflict could be traced to natural tensions between bureaucratic and professional norms or perhaps to competing political, economic, or social values. Chapter 4 will show that this narrow view persisted until the 1960s, when educators began to examine the character and effects of school bureaucracy more closely.

4

RATIONALISM REDISCOVERED: BUREAUCRACY AND THE STUDY OF ADMINISTRATION

DESPITE THE TREMENDOUS INFLUENCE of human relations research on administrative study after 1945, students of management did not turn away completely from their earlier preoccupation with organizational structure or the rationality of "top-down" management. Granted, the Hawthorne investigations and other human relations inquiries had prompted industrial and social scientists to devote much of their attention to informal or social aspects of life in the workplace; nevertheless, this new emphasis on the attitudes and feelings of organizational members did not entirely extinguish long-standing interest in the so-called "formal" or "classical" approach to administrative study. Throughout the 1930s and 1940s, management theorists continued to explore the hierarchical character of large organizations in efforts to identify certain basic "principles of organization."

Publication of the influential 1937 volume, *Papers on the Science of Administration*, clearly illustrated that management study between the two world wars comprised diverse intellectual perspectives and that traditional concepts of administration postulated by Henri Fayol, James Mooney, and Luther Gulick coexisted quite comfortably with emerging human relations views advanced by L. J. Henderson, T. N. Whitehead, Elton Mayo, and Mary Parket Follett (Gulick & Urwick, 1937).

The study of formal organization was greatly encouraged after 1945 by several new developments, not the least of which was the translation into English of Max Weber's writings on bureaucracy. Although the German legal scholar and sociologist died in 1920, much of his work was not translated until the late 1940s and was therefore generally inaccessible to the academic community in the United States until that time. The release of various editions of Weber's work by British and American publishing houses in the postwar decade helped spur the growing fascination of sociologists and other scholars with the problems of bureaucracy and with the rise of a professional managerial class in industry, government, and education. Consequently, in the period from the mid-1940s to the mid-1970s, the study of bureaucracy became a central part of the vast postwar literature on administration.

This newfound interest in Weber's ideas—and the general phenomenon of bureaucracy—was not confined to sociologists or other social scientists. By the 1960s, students of educational administration had also begun to apply concepts of bureaucracy to the problems of school organization, much in the way that educators had applied scientific management and human relations ideas in earlier decades. In light of this development, this chapter will examine how ideas about bureaucratic administration began with Weber, evolved and eventually became incorporated into educational literature on administration, and came to influence the way in which administrative behavior in education was studied in the 1960s and 1970s.

Max Weber
and the Rules of Administrative Conduct

Because of his pioneering work in describing the character of bureaucratic administration, Max Weber has remained the most pivotal figure in the study of bureaucracy. For the past sixty years or so, his sociological writings on rational organization have provided the major theoretical source for scholarly discussion of this subject.

Weber's initial interest in bureaucratic administration was influenced in many ways by his own education and upbringing and by his understanding of the political, social, and economic forces that were transforming the structure of German society in the late-nineteenth century (Bendix, 1960). Born in 1863 into a cultured and well-to-do middle-class family, Weber witnessed Bismarck's unification of the disparate German principalities into a new federal state and the nation's dramatic rise as a world power.

Through his father, a lawyer and member of the national parliament, Weber met many of the leading politicians and government officials who were directing the course of the newly formed nation. His father's house, in fact, frequently served as an informal literary salon where distinguished professors, artists, businessmen, and other members of Germany's intelligentsia gathered to discuss matters of state and society. After completing a doctoral degree in law in 1889, Weber began a career in teaching and research, first at the University of Berlin and later at Heidelberg. At these two institutions, he quickly established a reputation, like his contemporary Freud, as one of the most important scholars of his generation, not merely in law but in the broader realms of history, economics, religious studies, politics, and sociology.

From studying history, Weber concluded that human social organization had been characterized in the past by two kinds of authority—charismatic leadership and traditional domination. A charismatic leader he defined as one who commanded the respect and obedience of followers on the strength of exceptional personal attributes. The authority of charismatic leaders, he noted, was sustained by the faith of their followers. Traditional domination was, on the other hand, a form of leadership in which a leader's right to command was derived from inherited position.

Charismatic leadership and traditional domination, Weber observed, had been supplanted in the modern age by a new form of social authority based on the right of law. This new form of authority, or "legal domination," as Weber termed it, found its organizational expression in bureaucratic administration. This legal or bureaucratic domination, he contended, was more rational than earlier forms of leadership because it gave authority to those whose training and competence qualified them to lead, or as sociologist Robert Dubin would later observe, "bureaucratic administration frees the organization from absolute rule by a single individual and from the dead hand of the past."

Bureaucracy, Weber suggested, was simply a natural and evolutionary response on the part of modern organizations to problems confronting them. As scientific and technical revolutions had transformed the character of the industrial workplace, managers had been forced to develop new systems to deal with problems caused by the greater specialization and division of labor and by the growth of larger offices and factories. Changes such as these had necessitated the development of comprehensive structures to control work, the creation of communication and coordination systems, and the establishment of codes of behavior for managers and their employees.

Bureaucratically led organizations had come to dominate the modern age, Weber maintained, because they proved to be the most effective means of carrying out administrative tasks. "The decisive reason for the advance of bureaucratic organization," he wrote (Gerth & Mills, 1948, p. 215), "has always been its purely technical superiority over any other form of organization. The fully-developed bureaucratic mechanism compares with other organizations exactly as does the machine with the non-mechanical modes of production."

Most of all, the great advantage of bureaucratic systems, as Weber saw it, lay in the fact that bureaucracies functioned in a more disciplined and orderly fashion than other organizations because they completely integrated administrative rules of conduct into the work process itself. Or, as Weber put it: "The discipline of officialdom refers to the attitude set of the official for precise obedience within his habitual activity, in public as well as in private organizations. This discipline increasingly becomes the basis for all order" (Gerth & Mills, 1948, p. 229).

In a collection of essays dealing with administration, political sociology, and other matters, Weber outlined the hallmarks of how a bureaucratic system functions:

> There is the principle of fixed and official jurisdictional areas, which are generally ordered by rules, that is, by laws or administrative regulations.
>
> The regular activities required for the purpose of the bureaucratically governed structure are distributed in a fixed way as official duties.
>
> Methodical provision is made for the regular and continuous fulfillment of these duties and for the execution of the corresponding rights; only persons who have the generally regulated qualifications to serve are employed.
>
> In principle, the modern organization of the civil service separates the bureau from the private domicile of the official, and in general, bureaucracy segregates the bureau from the sphere of private life. Public monies and equipment are divorced from the private property of the official.
>
> The principles of office hierarchy and of levels of graded authority mean a firmly ordered system of super [ordination] and subordination in which there is a supervision of the lower offices by the higher ones.
>
> The management of the modern office is based upon written documents, which are preserved in their original or draught form.
>
> The management of the office follows general rules, which are more or less stable, more or less exhaustive, and which can be learned. Knowledge of these rules represents a special technical learning which the officials possess. It involves jurisprudence, or administrative business management. (Gerth & Mills, 1948, p. 196)

In describing bureaucratic organization in this way, Weber was concerned with the legal and ethical, rather than the purely rational, import of bureaucracy—certainly as this form of organization pertained to the governance of society and to the survival of democracy in Germany.

In this respect, bureaucracy represented to Weber what public education represented to Jefferson—namely, a social structure that would foster and preserve democratic practices. In his own country, the advent of bureaucracy, he believed, had reduced differences among social clases and had helped replace the autocracy and absolutism once seen to be characteristic of Imperial Germany with a more just system of government administration. In addition, it had freed government officials from external political influences and kinship considerations. Bureaucracy's great value, at least to Weber, lay not in the fact that it was efficient but in that it was impartial.

Despite his optimism for the development of responsive and fair civic institutions, Weber was not unaware of the social dangers that excessive bureaucracy posed. He acknowledged, for example, that highly routinized and impersonal organizations were capable of stifling the creativity and freedom of individuals inside and outside them. For those inside bureaucracies, there was the threat of being socialized by bureaucratic procedures and rules. Rules, Weber recognized, integrated individuals into what he described as "the mechanism" (or what is today called "the system"), thereby constraining dissident organizational members from changing or overthrowing the organization's operating procedures.

For those outside bureaucracies, the threat was somewhat different. "The ruled, for their part," Weber wrote, "cannot dispense with or replace the bureaucratic apparatus of authority once it exists" (Gerth & Mills, 1948, p. 228). Also, this authority was largely derived from the way in which bureaucracies controlled information. "Every bureaucracy," he remarked, "seeks to increase the superiority of the professionally informed by keeping their knowledge and intentions secret. Bureaucratic administration always tends to be an administration of 'secret sessions': in so far as it can, it hides its knowledge and action from criticism" (Gerth & Mills, 1948, p. 233). And this, Weber charged, included keeping information from elected officials who were legally empowered to make policy. The people's representatives, Weber advised, were at times no match for professional bureaucrats: "The 'political master' finds himself in the position of the 'dilettante' who stands opposite the 'expert' . . . within the management of administration" (Gerth & Mills, 1948, p. 232).

In summary, then, Weber's essays on the rules governing "modern officialdom" represent a watershed in the history of administrative thought in that they provide the first theoretical study of the structure and rules identifying bureaucracy. His work, as management scientist Nicos Mouzelis described it (1968, p. 38), marked "the starting point and the main source of inspiration for many students of organization," and greatly influenced later sociologists to make systematic observations of this field. Indeed, Weber was the first scholar who tried to comprehend the character of bureaucratic systems and the social meaning of modern civilization's inexorable march toward bureaucracy.

Of course, in attempting to define rules of administrative conduct, Weber, like Taylor and other classical theorists, had assumed that authority should rightfully be distributed among individuals at the top of the organization, where, he believed, the greatest amount of specialized knowledge resided, and that rules could ensure the rational and impersonal behavior of organizational members. It was assumptions such as these that post-Weberian critics in sociology and education challenged when Weber's writings were translated into English and gained a wider audience in the years following the end of World War II.

WEBER RESURRECTED: HIS CRITICS AND DISCIPLES

The "discovery" and translation of Weber's work after 1945 by individuals such as H. H. Gerth and C. Wright Mills and its popularization by Talcott Parsons (Henderson & Parsons, 1947), Robert Merton (1959), and others represented an important turning point in organizational study, for several reasons. First, Weber's comprehensive view of rational administration provided a new focus for studying principles of organization and served as a countervailing force to the human relations emphasis on informal organization that had dominated administrative thought since the mid-1930s. In addition, Weber's concept of bureaucracy offered students of organization a broad sociological approach to understanding the great structural changes that were taking place in the organizational life of the United States. In this regard, bureaucracies appeared to be ideal subjects for scholarly study. As sociologists Peter Blau and Marshall Meyer noted (1971, p. 15), bureaucratic organizations were in themselves natural laboratories for social research because their formal nature and regulations offered controlled conditions for study and because such "controls have not been artificially introduced by the scientist but are an inherent part of the bureaucratic structure."

Since 1945, much of the organizational research in sociology and also in business and general administration has been deeply indebted to Weber's concept of bureaucracy and has tested his ideas in case studies that attempt to define what one writer (Mouzelis, 1968, p. 59) has described as the "inherent strains and dilemmas in bureaucratic organizations." In line with the rapid growth of public sector organizations during the postwar period, such studies have frequently focused on bureaucratic behavior in hospital management, welfare bureaus, military agencies, and educational institutions.

Altogether, these empirical investigations have produced a body of scholarship that has qualified Weber's characterization of bureaucracy in several important respects. In particular, postwar research has found reason to amend Weber's notions about such matters as the basis of dominance and authority, the rationality and efficiency of bureaucratic systems, the meaning of rules and their consequences, and the network of social relations underlying the administration of formal organizations.

Weber's concept of dominance, for example, has remained a topic of central interest to administrative theorists over the past three or four decades. As early as 1947, Talcott Parsons (Henderson & Parsons, p. 59) pointed out a serious problem associated with Weber's view of authority when he observed that Weber appeared to confuse two distinct types of authority—that which rested on the "incumbency of a legally-defined office," and that which was derived from "technical competence." This criticism was reiterated and elaborated on by Alvin Gouldner in his 1954 case study of a gypsum factory, *Patterns of Industrial Bureaucracy*.

In a later discussion (1960, p. 59), Parsons further criticized Weber for his failure to distinguish how the character and structure of administrative authority are shaped differently at different points throughout an organization. In his essay on administrative theory, Parsons wrote: "The theory of 'bureaucracy' has been so strongly influenced by the concept of 'line' authority that there has been a tendency to neglect the importance of what in some sense are qualitative breaks in the continuity of the line structure" (p. 59). In other words, Parsons charged that Weber had unduly limited his description of administrative functions to what was only one part of an organization's total system, the part Parsons defined as the "managerial" level. According to Parsons (p. 65), Weber's overall concept of bureaucracy was flawed because he had ignored the "institutional" or governance level above the professional managers, the "technical" level of staff and workers below them, and how the hierarchy of administrative authority was interrupted at these "two points of articulation."

In his 1964 study, *Modern Organizations*, Amitai Etzioni also observed flaws in Weber's notion of authority. Like Parsons, Etzioni argued (p. 85) that Weber's concept of bureaucracy wrongly assumed that "one major structure of authority (the line)" exists and that there is "always one center of authority where final decisions are made and conflicts can be resolved." Etzioni maintained that this is not true for professional organizations such as universities and hospitals, where two types of authority exist and where only the nonprofessional one is structured in a bureaucratic way. As he noted (p. 86): "The professionals who conduct the major goal activity do not form an authority structure in the regular sense of the term."

Etzioni likewise quarreled with distinctions Weber made among charismatic, traditional, and bureaucratic bases for leadership. In his view, such a classification was too strict and did not allow for the many mixed forms of authority that seem to exist in organizations. Organizations, he observed (pp. 52–53), frequently vacillate between charismatic and bureaucratic forms of dominance, and charismatic leaders may, on occasion, emerge from senior positions within the bureaucracy—and not from outside it, as Weber predicted.

Weber's depiction of bureaucratic authority was also challenged in Peter Blau's 1955 study, *The Dynamics of Bureaucracy*, a work based on case studies of a state employment agency and a federal law enforcement agency. In this volume, Blau claimed that, although strict hierarchical control may be desirable in Weber's view, it was virtually impossible to apply such a structure completely in a democratic culture like that of the United States. The formalism and strict rules described by Weber, Blau contended, conflicted with American ideals about equality and the individual's right to question authority.

Part of the criticism directed toward Weber's concept of authority stemmed from Weber's reliance on rules to prescribe and control the behavior of organizational members. In one of the earliest sociological writings to deal with Weber, Phillip Selznick (1948) emphasized that the value of bureaucratic rules is limited. Events occur within organizations, he noted, that may not be covered by rules, policy statements, or other kinds of operational procedures. Or, as Mouzelis would later write, rules "never succeed in completely controlling the situation and in directing the organizational activities toward their pre-defined goals" (1968, p. 59). Mouzelis also suggested (p. 60) that organizational members may not always comply with rules because "formal rules may be in conflict with informal rules or norms of conduct" and would thereby be resisted by workers.

In an extensive investigation into the use of rules and their role in the bureaucratization of an organization, Gouldner (1954) described how the appointment of a new industrial manager dramatically changed the character of social relations between supervisors and workers in a midwestern plant. In his investigation, Gouldner learned that before the arrival of the new manager "there were comparatively few rules in the plant, and fewer still [that] were strictly enforced" (p. 51). Because the new official was "sensitized to the rational and impersonal yardsticks which his superiors would use to evaluate his performance," he therefore imposed tight control over his own employees—and did so by ensuring that company rules were observed, especially as they related to reducing employee absenteeism and the workers' use of company property for their own ends (p. 72). This bureaucratic style of management, Gouldner found, provoked new problems and tensions in the factory and, on a deeper level, illustrated shortcomings in Weber's concept of rules and authority. Most notably, Gouldner charged (p. 21), Weber misunderstood the difference between "imposed and agreed-upon rules," or what Gouldner termed "punishment-centered" and "representative" rules.

Gouldner was not the only student of bureaucracy in the postwar era to conclude that rule enforcement can sometimes produce dysfunctions within organizations. In his 1959 study, *Social Theory and Social Structure*, Robert Merton likewise suggested problems that might emerge as a result of the way that rules were imposed. Merton argued (p. 197) that as individuals internalized bureaucratic norms they tended to interpret regulations more narrowly—that is, they hid behind rules in their own interest. This tendency, in turn, set minimum standards for behavior and reduced an organization's flexibility, its ability to solve problems, and, ultimately, its effectiveness in processing the demands of a changing environment.

Generally, then, postwar scholars in sociology concluded that, in practice, bureaucracies were dysfunctional in certain respects and not nearly as rational, efficient, or effective as Weber had theorized. Selznick, for example (1948), claimed that, within bureaucratic organizations, departmental sub-goals supplanted broader organizational goals in the minds of staff and that interdepartmental rivalry generated by the pursuit of special interests reduced the overall effectiveness of organizations. Selznick, as well as March and Simon (1958, p. 33), also noted problems resulting from delegation of authority to organizational sub-systems and the intra-organizational difficulties typically found in bureaucracies.

Finally, Weber's concept of bureaucracy was challenged by administrative theorists in another important regard—and this had to do with the character of social relations in the bureaucratic workplace. He assumed that equality and justice for all would be preserved, at least in public institutions, by bureaucratic officials who would act objectively in discharging their duties. Bureaucratic rules, Weber believed, would ensure the impersonal social behavior necessary for fairness and equality. In effect, he did not see that "irrational" human processes might be at variance with or might even undermine "rational" administrative structures.

That this phenomenon occurs in organizations was pointed out by writers and researchers in the decades after Weber's death (Roethlisberger & Dickson, 1939). Indeed, researchers learned that the "business" of organizations was not always conducted in a formal way, in line with a chain of command: Informal networks and informal arrangements existed that often prescribed how work would be done, how much work would be done, and which rules would be followed (Roethlisberger & Dickson, 1939, p. 568). Bureaucratic organizations, in short, did not prove to be as rational in their operations as Weber originally imagined.

Such criticism and refinements of the bureaucratic model, rather than detracting from Weber's stature, only added to it. Post-1945 studies of bureaucracy like those mentioned above continued to work within the general framework Weber set out. In keeping with the canons of scholarship, however, researchers tested Weber's concept of an ideal bureaucracy by undertaking case studies, by viewing his model in light of changing contextual factors, by seeking greater clarification and refinement of his ideas, and by searching for exceptions to the rules of administrative conduct he defined.

STUDYING SCHOOLS AS BUREAUCRACIES

Sociologists and students of general administration were not the only individuals to become interested in Weber's view of bureaucracy in the post-1945 era. Professors of educational administration and other scholars interested in school organization also turned to the study of bureaucracy, especially after 1960 when students of educational management began to work within the framework of general administration and began to employ behavioral science approaches to organizational study. What this meant was that, by the early 1960s, there was an extensive postwar literature on organizations, and particularly the sociological study of organizations, for educators to explore. Discussion about Weber's ideas constituted a central part of this literature; for the next two decades, the study of schools as bureaucracies would become an important theme in educational research in administration.

Rising educational interest in bureaucracy during the 1960s and 1970s may be illustrated in several ways. An analysis of the *Educational Index*, for example, shows that in the forty-year period between 1929 and 1969 only ten references to writings on bureaucracy were listed and that these writings were of a general nature, having little if anything to do with bureaucracy as an administrative concept. In contrast, in the decade from 1969 to 1979, a companion index, the *Current Index to Journals in Education*, listed references to 133 writings on bureaucracy, many of which specifically applied Weber's ideas to the study of school organizations.

Likewise, a review of widely used textbooks in educational administration since 1945 indicates that Weber's concept of bureaucracy was not included in discussions on the development of administrative thought until the late 1960s and early 1970s. For example, Roald Campbell, Edwin Bridges, John Corbally, Raphael Nystrand, and John Ramseyer's fourth edition of *Introduction to Educational Administration*, published in 1971, made no mention of Weber's contribution to administrative study. Since that time, however, textbooks and books of readings in educational administration have increasingly focused their attention on Weber's ideas and on the bureaucratic characteristics of educational organizations in general (Miller, Madden, & Kincheloe, 1972; Morphet, Johns, & Reller, 1967; and Milstein & Belasco, 1973).

This growing number of educational writings on bureaucracy, especially periodical literature, has been principally indebted to post-1945 sociological discussions of Weber's work. Educational writers, however, have typically limited the scope of their inquiry more than have their sociological counterparts. They have been concerned with particularistic applications of Weber's ideas to schools rather than with examining fundamental ideological issues pertaining to bureaucracy's meaning in a democratic society or with challenging Weber's characterization of an ideal bureaucracy. In general, studies of school bureaucracy have been pedestrian in character and have remained clustered around *three* major questions or issues: (1) Do schools conform to Weber's notion of a bureaucratic organization and, if so, to what extent? (2) What dimensions or characteristics describe educational bureaucracies, and can they be measured? and (3) What effects or dysfunctions result from organizing educational institutions along bureaucratic lines?

Not surprisingly, the first of these issues—the question of whether schools conform to Weber's concept of bureaucratic organizations—provided the focus for some early writings on school bureaucracy. One of the first students of educational administration to suggest that school organizations exhibited many of Weber's principles was Max Abbott (Carver & Sergiovanni, 1969, pp. 42–50). In his discussion, "Hierarchical Impediments to Innovation in Educational Organizations," Abbott outlined at some length why the school "can accurately be described as a highly developed bureaucracy":

> First, the school organization has clearly been influenced by the need for specialization and the factoring of tasks. The division of the school into elementary and secondary units; the establishment of science, mathematics, music, and other departments within a school; the introduction of guidance programs and psychological services; indeed, the separation of the administrative function from the teaching function, all represent responses to this need.
>
> Second, the school organization has developed a clearly defined and rigid hierarchy of authority. Although the term 'hierarchy' is seldom used in the lexicon of the educational administrator, the practices to which it refers are commonly prevalent.
>
> Third, the school organization has leaned heavily upon the use of general rules to control the behavior of members of the organization and to develop standards which would assure reasonable uniformity in the performance of tasks.
>
> Fourth, despite frequent proclamations regarding togetherness and democracy, the school organization has made extensive application of Weber's principle of impersonality on the basis of rational considerations rather than charismatic qualities or traditional imperatives. . . .
>
> Fifth, employment in the educational organization has been based upon technical competence and has constituted for most members a professional career. Promotions have been determined by seniority and by achievement; tenure has been provided; and fixed compensation and retirement benefits have been assured. (pp. 44–45)*

In "The School as a Formal Organization," educational sociologist Charles Bidwell (1965) offered a somewhat more guarded classification of educational organizations. In Bidwell's view (p. 974), schools displayed, "at least in rudimentary form," certain bureaucratic characteristics, including a functional division of labor, a definition of staff roles as offices, a hierarchical ordering of offices, and the conduct of operations in a routine manner according to rules of procedure.

In noting "the distinctive combination of bureaucracy and structural looseness" that characterized schools, Bidwell (p. 1012) was one of the first writers to suggest that educational organizations were not

---

*From Max Abbott, "Hierarchical Impediments to Innovation in Educational Organizations." In F. D. Carver and T. J. Sergiovanni (Eds.), *Organizations and Human Behavior.* New York: McGraw-Hill, 1969. Reproduced with permission.

bureaucracies of a "pure" type. Schools, he contended, differed from classical bureaucracies in several respects. For one thing, administrative practices varied considerably among schools and among the larger organizational systems to which they belonged. School organizations were also "de-bureaucratized," he observed, because they exhibited a certain "looseness" in the way their sub-units were coordinated. Moreover, unlike strict bureaucracies, school systems were not completely bound by regulations. Teachers, unlike bureaucrats, for example, enjoyed greater latitude and authority in making judgments about their clients and their work. Indeed, the affective rather than impersonal nature of relationships between teachers and pupils was decidedly unbureaucratic. As Bidwell put it, "the intrinsic nature of teaching runs counter to the bureaucratic principle of school organization" (p. 979).

In line with distinctions made earlier by Parsons and Gouldner, Ronald Corwin advised in 1965 that bureaucratic administration was not the sole source of authority in modern organizations (Carver & Sergiovanni, 1969, pp. 212–227). The emergence of professions—a historical development that paralleled the growth of the bureaucratic hierarchy—had given rise to the concept of professionalism as a new source of authority, which represented "a challenge to the traditional ideologies of control by laymen and their administrative representatives "(p. 214). As Corwin observed: "In a professional-employee society, the fundamental tension is not between the individual and the system, but between parts of the system—between the professional and the bureaucratic principles of organization" (pp. 213–214).

In educational organizations, Corwin claimed (p. 222), this tension was made evident in "a consistent pattern of conflict between teachers and administrators over the control of work," particularly matters relating to the degree to which teachers should be autonomous, who should select textbooks and teaching methods, and who should prescribe the curriculum.

Since Corwin's 1965 paper, the dualistic character of authority in educational organizations has been reiterated numerous times, most notably in articles by Isherwood and Hoy (1972), Martin (1975), Levine (1976), and Hansot (1975). Unfortunately, however, educational scholars have not sought to describe in any depth what actually occurs within schools when forms of bureaucratic authority conflict with those of technical competence or what this conflict means to educational organizations and to the clients they serve.

Instead, educational research and writing have often centered on a second and narrower area of interest having to do with defining and measuring bureaucracy in schools and with debating methodological procedures—sometimes to a degree that only medieval theologians might appreciate. In 1968, for example, in one of the lengthiest studies of school bureaucracy ever undertaken, James Anderson identified several independent measures of bureaucracy—rules, authority, conflict, impersonality, and goal displacement. Anderson also reported that the level of bureaucracy was positively related to the size of departments within schools and to the percentage of female teachers employed; that inverse relationships existed between the number of bureaucratic rules and the socio-economic level of the school community, the specificity of goals, teacher competence and status, and departmental routine; and that certain departments (most notably English and science) relied more heavily on rules than did others (pp. 159–173).

Two years later, in 1970, Keith Punch found that the level of bureaucracy in schools was closely associated with the administrative behavior of school leaders—in this case, the kind of leadership displayed by forty-eight elementary school principals in Ontario. As Punch observed: "The key factor in changing the level of *actual* bureaucratization is the administrative style of the principal" (p. 133). In contrast, Barrie Brennan's 1973 study of twenty Australian secondary school principals concluded (p. 176) that these administrators "rejected the relatively clearly defined role of the bureaucrat, and [that] their role performances suggest that they define their role in terms of being some sort of leader."

Methodological problems in defining the "dimensions" of bureaucracy in schools were further explored in two other studies—Punch's 1969 article, "Bureaucratic Structure in Schools: Toward Redefinition and Measurement," and Sousa and Hoy's 1981 "Bureaucratic Structure in Schools: A Refinement and Synthesis in Measurement." In the first of these, an analysis of relevant research and theory on bureaucracy led Punch to conclude: "Bureaucratic structure in schools is realistically conceptualized as a unitary, homogeneous variable only if restricted to the dimensions of hierarchy of authority, rules for incumbents, procedural specifications, and impersonality" (pp. 53–54).

The preoccupation of post-1960 educational researchers with statistical techniques to measure bureaucracy's dimensions in schools generally deflected interest away from examining bureaucracy's dysfunctional effects—a topic that was clearly of central interest to organizational sociologists after 1945. Nevertheless, students of educational administration expressed a modest amount of interest in dysfunctionalism, and this focus comprised the third, and final, strand in the literature on bureaucracy.

Writings on bureaucratic dysfunctionalism in education have generally been of two kinds—those pertaining to general organizational problems created by the bureaucratic administration of schools and those dealing with more specific effects of bureaucratic structures on individuals within educational organizations, especially on teachers. Regrettably, no educational studies attempted to describe bureaucratic dysfunctions as comprehensively as the case-study approaches used so effectively by Gouldner and Blau to describe bureaucratic dysfunctionalism in industrial and government organizations.

Criticisms of bureaucracy's negative effects in educational administration were perhaps first raised by Abbott and Corwin. Corwin observed (1965, pp. 215–216) that difficulties were bound to occur when bureaucratic and professional norms varied so appreciably and when administrators were charged with evaluating subordinates who were technically more proficient in certain tasks than they were themselves. Abbott, on the other hand, pointed out (1969, pp. 46–49) how bureaucratic organizations deterred change processes and impeded innovation. Bureaucracies, among other things, Abbott charged, stifled professional development and creativity, and hampered organizational communication.

Not everyone agreed, however, that bureaucratic organizations posed problems for those who worked in them. For example, Gerald Moeller's 1964 discussion, "Bureaucracy and Teachers' Sense of Power," concluded: "Certainly, bureaucracy as a rational and, hence, predictable form of organization, does *not* induce in teachers a feeling of powerlessness or alienation from the system" (p. 155). Instead, Moeller claimed: "Sense of power appears to be influenced by many diverse variables lying within the teacher himself, in his past, in his social groups, in his relations with his superiors, and in the organizational structure of his school" (pp. 155–156). Similarly, in 1970, Eddy found (p. 20) that "teachers were more satisfied with schools which they perceived to be more bureaucratic than the schools which they perceived to be less bureaucratic."

In contrast to Moeller and Eddy's findings, subsequent studies have detailed the deleterious rather than the benign effects of bureaucracy on teachers. Isherwood and Hoy's 1973 article, "Bureaucracy, Powerlessness, and Teacher Work Values," found (p. 135), among other things, that "professionally oriented teachers" experienced the greatest amount of powerlessness in "authoritarian" schools—authoritarian being roughly defined as bureaucratic. Miskel and Gerhardt's 1974 article on perceived bureaucracy and teacher conflict also pointed to bureaucracy's negative effects and, more importantly, stated that "heightening hierarchical differences increases teacher conflict with a concomitant decrease in job satisfaction" (p. 95).

Similarly, Gosine and Keith's 1970 study, "Bureaucracy, Teacher Personality Needs and Teacher Satisfaction," found (pp. 1–5) that teacher satisfaction in schools with a low degree of bureaucratization was significantly higher than that of teachers in highly bureaucratized schools. On the subject of the powerless dimension of alienation, Cox and Wood's 1980 article, "Organizational Structure and Professional Alienation: The Case of Public School Teachers," suggested (p. 6) that increasing alienation among teachers resulted from two factors— "greater professionalization of teaching and the concomitant rigidity of organizational structure of most school systems."

CONFLICTING CONCLUSIONS
OF BUREAUCRATIC STUDY

It is apparent that the three major lines of inquiry into school bureaucracy pursued by educators over the last two decades have produced conflicting conclusions. Taken as a whole, these studies suggest that bureaucracy may be defined and measured in numerous ways and that the level of bureaucracy in schools may be a product of numerous factors, including the organization's authority structure, its size, its rules, the exactness with which it frames its goals, the sexual composition and status of its staff, and the way in which its administrators behave and view the world.

Bureaucracy's dysfunctions have also been described in various ways. At different times, researchers have pointed to different problems with bureaucracy; there has been a notable lack of agreement, for example, on how bureaucracy affects schools staffs. However, major criticisms have been registered about the way bureaucratic organization inhibits professional development and change and how it fails to consider adequately the human element in the workplace.

Nevertheless, consensus exists that school organizations are to some degree bureaucratic. Consensus further exists that Weber's concept of bureaucratic authority is not an entirely appropriate model to explain the dual authority structures found in educational organizations. Overall, perhaps the most salient outcome of bureaucratic study in educational administration has been its illumination of the nature of organizational conflict in schools and of how conflict is related to the professional authority structure within educational organizations.

This new view of the competition for authority between teachers and administrators represented an important breakthrough in the history of administrative thought in education in that it marked a shift away from earlier and somewhat wishful thinking about the character of relationships between school managers and their staffs. Recognition that a natural and structural source of conflict exists between school administrators and teachers finally put to rest a long-held mythology that sought to downplay educational conflict by holding that teachers' and administrators' interests were congruent and that every member of the school was, in the words of the human relationists, "a part of the team." In one important respect, the emphasis of bureaucratic study on the competition for authority changed how students of educational administration thought about the character of school organization and illuminated tensions underlying authority and power relationships in the educational workplace that for too long had been overlooked.

Bureaucratic study in education during the 1960s and 1970s, however, also narrowed the scope of inquiry into school organizations. Much of the research on school bureaucracy was of a "low-risk, low-yield" nature and remained preoccupied with questions of measurement and definition. Such studies seemed at best only to provide a series of sometimes contradictory and highly limited findings. At worst, such investigations offered conclusions of questionable relevance and marginal interest to other scholars and practicing administrators.

Unlike the organizational sociologists who studied bureaucracy and from whose work educators learned of Weber, students of educational administration directed little attention to the meaning or philosophical import of bureaucracy in education. Educators generally seemed indifferent to how bureaucratic organization shaped the thought, behavior, and feelings of those who worked or studied in schools. Aside from research that dealt with teacher powerlessness or alienation as somewhat clinical concepts, educational theorists seemed largely unconcerned that the ideology of bureaucratic administration, like scientific management before it, seemed to emphasize structural and technical, rather than interpersonal, considerations. Nor did educators seek to explore how a form of management that prized discipline, order, rationality, efficiency, and predictability could impart a system of values that might be inappropriate for the administration of schools in a democratic culture. As in the case of previous approaches to management study, the study of school organizations as bureaucracies encouraged students of school administration to remain introspective and to look more at elements related to administrative mechanisms than to the way organizations responded to their environments or dealt with the human side of enterprise.

In fact, it now appears somewhat incongruous that such a narrow approach to administrative study should have occupied the attention of many educational scholars and social scientists in a period when American public institutions were being challenged by discontented constituencies outside them. Such an approach to administrative study, and the intellectual premises upon which it was based, had seemingly little relevance to school practitioners and other public officials besieged by increasing public demands for institutional reform and for greater citizen participation in decisions about social and educational policy. In emphasizing the internal structures of organization and the struggle for supremacy among insiders, bureaucratic study did little to address the clamor of minorities, women, and the young for representation within the system. Like other administrative ideologies before it, the use of bureaucratic theory in education and other areas of public administration ignored important questions dealing with community politics, the governance of public institutions, and the relationship between those who determine policy and those who carry it out. In short, while inquiry into bureaucracy provided educational theorists with new strategies by which to understand structural and power relationships within the formal organization that was the school, it provided little understanding for administrators of more troublesome educational problems in the 1960s and 1970s and did little to help public school administrators and others deal with social issues dividing American society during those decades.

SUMMARY

The incorporation of Weber's bureaucratic model into the study of educational administration has had important intellectual consequences for this applied field. The introduction of Weber's ideas, as well as those of later sociologists, fleshed out the scope of classical administrative theory in education and expanded the intellectual framework guiding educational inquiry into schools as complex organizations. Growing educational interest in bureaucracy after 1960 also brought educational researchers into more immediate contact with social scientists, especially sociologists, and generally drew educators closer to the orbit of study in general administration. Studying bureaucracy likewise shifted educational thought away from a major focus on human relations and the informal side of organizational life and reemphasized the importance of understanding the character of the school's formal organization. In doing this, it made students of educational administration more conscious of authority, more aware of rules in general, and more cognizant of organizational dysfunctions.

5

OPEN SYSTEMS:
ORGANIZATIONS AND THEIR ENVIRONMENTS

THE VIEWS OF ADMINISTRATION presented in Chapters 2, 3, and 4, though differing from each other in many respects, have one element in common: All three views perceived organizations as closed systems. In contrast, a view of administration has emerged in recent years that regards organizations as open systems. In this chapter consideration will be given to some of the social conditions that supported the emergence of the open-systems view, to movements in education that have contributed to such a view, to the work of the organizational theorists who have espoused open-systems ideas, and to some of the implications of this approach for organizational behavior.

SOCIAL CONDITIONS

As noted in preceding chapters, social and economic conditions have had at least some effect on administrative thought. Thus, it is no surprise to find that the social conditions of the 1950s and 1960s appear to be related to, and perhaps even to have helped produce, the open-systems approach to administration. Some of those conditions will be examined here.

For more than half a century following the U. S. Supreme Court Decision of *Plessy* v. *Ferguson* in 1896, which concerned railway facilities, the "separate but equal" doctrine was considered applicable to public schools. Separate school systems were maintained for whites and blacks in a number of states. This situation was challenged and finally reached the U. S. Supreme Court in 1954, in *Brown* v. *Board of Education of Topeka*. Events leading to the case began one bright September morning in 1950 when Linda Brown's father attempted unsuccessfully to enroll his seven-year-old daughter in the Sumner School, which was nearer their home and less hazardous to reach than the Monroe School, which required a walk through the railroad yard, and which Linda, with other blacks, previously attended. Similar cases, originating in South Carolina, Virginia, and Delaware, were considered with *Brown*. The Court posed the pertinent question:

> Does segregation of children in public schools solely on the basis of race, even though physical facilities and other "tangible" factors may be equal, deprive the children of the minority group of equal educational opportunities? We believe that it does.

In this instance, the Court spoke with unanimous voice and thus the long process of desegregating schools was begun.

In *Simple Justice*, a study that treats the history of the *Brown* v. *Board of Education* decision, writer and historian Richard Kluger (1977, p. 248) suggests that black-white relations in America have gone through three stages. First, black Americans were classified as property; second they were seen as marginal human beings; finally, only with the Supreme Court decision in 1954 was there a recognition that the quest for equality had really begun. While Kluger maintains that no single event can change the course of history, he contends that the Court's decision symbolized "the cresting wave of a tidal movement unleashed by the great economic earthquake of 1929." Kluger continues, "not until then did the nation seriously acknowledge that its most sacred obligation went beyond the protection of capital to the well-being of its citizens."

In 1979, educational historian Diane Ravitch noted the importance of this watershed event in American life:

> If *Brown* is defined in terms of equal access, it can be counted a great success. In the twenty-five years, which is a brief time by the historical clock, the major institutions in the United States have been transformed. A deeply entrenched caste system, embedded in law, custom, and daily usage, has been disrupted and nearly destroyed; certainly the legal and governmental supports for the racial caste system have been entirely eliminated. While the poison of racism persists, its incidence has substantially diminished. Whether one looks to the position of blacks in the media, the government, corporations, or higher education, the change of the past quarter century would have been unimaginable in 1954. (Bailey, p. 9)

In the decade after *Brown*, the Warren Court handed down a succession of decisions that followed the course set by the 1954 ruling. Public parks and recreation areas were finally opened to minorities, as were libraries, courtrooms, restaurants, and other public facilities. On the heels of this landmark decision, Congress passed the Civil Rights Act in 1964 and the Voting Rights Act in 1965, both of which are

discussed later. In *Brown* and subsequent court decisions and cor
sional legislation, American society granted basic human rights
major segment of the population that had previously been denied them.
The significance of what was happening to black Americans was not
lost on other minorities. Hispanics, Native Americans, women, and
other groups began to demand full rights of citizenship. Moreover,
Brown and the groundswell of civil rights legislation it initiated served as
a catalyst for what became known in the 1970s as the women's movement for equal rights. As already noted, however, both the civil rights
and women's rights movements were rooted in conditions that reached
at least as far back as the depression of the 1930s.

The *Brown* decision and the related legislation described above also
had immediate implications for state government. Legislative districts
were redrawn to conform with the "one-man one-vote" doctrine. The
implications for many school districts were even more drastic. Federal
intervention from the courts, Congress, and the federal agencies mushroomed. In particular, U. S. district courts, through use of the injunc-
tion, ordered many school districts to develop and implement desegregation programs. For example, in places like Boston and Cleveland,
judges became almost day-to-day directors of school districts. Local
boards of education suddenly found that the federal government was
no longer far away but an immediate presence in the environment of
their school districts.

The social revolution foreshadowed by the *Brown* decision was
marred by violence in the 1960s, particularly the assassinations of John
and Robert Kennedy and Martin Luther King, Jr. President Lyndon
Johnson was sensitive to the inequities in American society and was
determined to remedy them. Indeed, his leadership helped influence
Congress to pass the Civil Rights Act in 1964 and the Voting Rights Act
in 1965. Speaking in support of the Voting Rights Act at Howard
University, President Johnson said, "We seek not just legal equity but
human ability, not just equality as a right and a theory but equality as a
fact and equality as a result" (White, 1982, p. 109). What began as
equality of opportunity had become, at least in Johnson's view, equality
in result. The great differences between whites and blacks resulted
from the deprivation of blacks over centuries, and Johnson believed
these deprivations should be corrected by remedial legislation. The
Great Society programs dealing with poverty and education, for instance, were designed in large part to remedy some of these past
inequities.

The Great Society, however, soon ran into trouble. The war in
Vietnam, which Johnson had inherited and was determined to win,

brought about deep division in American society. Historian Theodore White characterized Vietnam as "the most mismanaged war in American history" (1982, p. 111). To many of the young, the war was illegal: Congress had voted neither a declaration of war nor a national emergency. In spite of this, young men were being drafted by executive order for a cause no one seemed able to explain. Tens of thousands of them were losing their lives in the questionable undertaking. As a decade, the 1960s began with racial turbulence and ended with the revolt of the young. White explained the youthful revolt this way:

> The student revolt—a revolt against the war, the draft, the killings in Asia—was one of the shortest-lived phenomena in American politics. It had begun in 1967; had boiled into violence at a dozen campuses; had reached its tragic ending in the Kent State killings of 1970. By 1971, however, "youth" had received its ultimate acknowledgement as full and equal citizens: a constitutional amendment, lowering the voting age in every state of the Union to eighteen. If a man was old enough to fight, ran the reasoning, he was old enough to vote. Swept by this logic, Congress passed, on March 23, and Richard Nixon— very reluctantly—signed this proposal. With record speed it had been ratified by July 1, 1971, as the Twenty-Sixth Amendment to the federal Constitution. (1982, p. 114)

Clearly, the 1960s brought changes in the social and cultural life of America. Minorities now were on the way to being recognized as full-fledged citizens, and the voice of youth was heard as never before. And then came what will likely be the most far-reaching social movement of the century—the emergence of women's rights. The women's rights movement has had a long history in the United States but it was not until 1920 that women enjoyed full rights in the voting booth. The 1970s and 1980s saw the fight for the Equal Rights Amendment and its subsequent defeat because it failed to pass in a few state legislatures. With or without constitutional provision, women also began to share equal status in the workplace, in education, and in the political life of the country.

Without doubt, these changes brought many American values and institutions into question. Traditional values gave way and were replaced by the emergence of new values (Getzels, Lipham, & Campbell, 1968, pp. 92-102). Sociologist Daniel Bell contends that the counterculture of the 1970s—which "appeared in the guise of an attack on the 'technocratic society'—was actually an attack on reason itself" (1976, p. 143).

In any case, rising concern with self and self-gratification helped place all social institutions under new scrutiny. Courts' decisions were scrutinized to see if justice was being done. The administration of welfare agencies was sometimes found to be chaotic. Schools were characterized as miseducative by such critics as Paul Goodman and Ivan Illich (Levine & Havighurst, 1971). Government itself was attacked for not being representative and, in some cases, for being oppressive. In public education this new skepticism often meant that school levy elections were defeated, that school board members and school super-intendents were replaced, and that new demands were made on schools from groups that heretofore had been silent. In one sense, the changes of the 1950s and 1960s, whether in legal terms as epitomized by *Brown*, in social terms as represented by the changed status of minorities in society, or in terms of changing social values and the growth of skepticism toward social institutions, all contributed toward forging a new cultural milieu within which school administrators had to work. As Ravitch observed, "the consensus that had undergirded American education for most of its history seemed to be dissipating" (1983, p. 316).

DEVELOPMENTS IN EDUCATION

The American educational system may be characterized as a sub-system of the larger society. Thus, it is not surprising to find movements in education that, over the last few decades, have tended to support an open-systems view of administration. Some of these developments will now be examined.

In and Out of the Organization

Only with the passage of the National Labor Relations Act in 1935 was a legal framework established for employer-employee relations in the private sector. It was not until 1959, more than two decades later, that the first bargaining law in the public sector was passed by the Wisconsin legislature. Anthony Cresswell and Michael Murphy (1980, p. 21) contend that World War II was the turning point in the development of "teacher militancy and collective bargaining as we know it today." By the mid-1960s, collective bargaining on the part of teacher groups was a widespread phenomenon across the country.

Cresswell and Murphy examined developments in collective negotiations from 1965 to 1976 and found that during that time the bargaining process had grown more formalized and that consultation had given way to both informal and formal negotiations. Also during that period, the National Education Association altered its position and became aggressive with respect to collective bargaining. Many states also passed legislation requiring local school districts to negotiate with teachers. In addition, the scope of bargaining tended to expand after 1945. While negotiations initially dealt mainly with welfare issues, as time went on curriculum and managerial issues often became matters for negotiation. In any case, the once closed door of the school administrator was pried open by teacher organizations in the post-war years.

Educational historians David Tyack and Elisabeth Hansot (1982) have divided the history of public school leadership in this country into two major periods. The first, 1820–1890, highlights the work of the public school crusaders, many of whom were laymen with public education as their cause. The second, 1890–1954, emphasizes the growth of the administrative progressives or professionals in educational administration. The professional managers of schools and school systems, influenced by both the political reformers and the business culture of the early part of this century, attempted to build what Tyack (1974) described in his work entitled *The One Best System*. In this process, the National Commission on School District Reorganization (1948) reported that school districts numbered over 100,000 in 1948. By 1980, there were about 16,000 districts. In each of these, administrative organizations, again largely patterned after business and frequently in the name of efficiency, were established. What began as a dispersed and simple enterprise largely under the auspices of lay leadership had, over time, developed into a complex bureaucratic structure under professional leadership.

In the last few decades, there have been sporadic efforts aimed at reducing or at least mediating the control that professionals exercise over the schools. Some of these efforts were benign in nature and were often reflected in activities of parent-teacher associations and similar organizations. Other efforts represented an indictment of professionals and an outright insistence on more lay control. For example, in 1968 James Koerner, one-time President of the Council for Basic Education, contended that public interest had "grown out of the frustrations of people who want to see reforms made but who see them constantly blocked by the rigidities of a well entrenched bureaucracy" (p. viii). Many professionals in education have not been immune to the need for public participation in the planning and operation of schools. In 1954, for instance, a number of professionals, joined by a few laypeople, including Roy Larsen, former editor of *Time*, prepared a yearbook for the National Society for the Study of Education, entitled *Citizen Co-operation for Better Public Schools* (Henry, 1954). While the yearbook reiterated the time-honored slogan that the schools "belong to the people," the emphasis was on cooperation on the part of laypeople and professionals.

The call for public participation has become more insistent, as illustrated in the very extensive literature on the subject. One example of that literature is a 1981 volume entitled *Communities and Their Schools*, under the editorship of Don Davies (1981). A key chapter in that treatment, written by the editor, is called "Citizen Participation in Decision Making in Schools." Davies describes specific forms of citizen participation, including the gathering of data about the quality of school programs and monitoring school operations.

The general movement for public participation has led to a number of definitive proposals, one of which has become known as family choice in education. One of the early programs devised to implement family choice was known as the voucher plan. While the idea may be as old as Adam Smith, conservative economist and Nobel prize winner Milton Friedman (1955, pp. 123–153) has often been given credit for designing the voucher plan. In simple terms, a voucher given to parents is intended to represent a pupil's share of the state's investment in schooling for a particular year and is redeemable in any approved school, public or private, that the parent decides to patronize. Friedman, a strong supporter of private enterprise, envisioned the voucher system as a way of making school services competitive and thus prompting schools to improve their services.

In the late 1960s, the Center for the Study of Public Policy at Harvard University, with a grant from the Office of Economic Opportunity (OEO)—a Great Society agency—developed a voucher program. The report was delivered to OEO in 1970 (Center for the Study of Public Policy, 1970). The Harvard group found that a voucher program is more easily formulated than implemented. Despite proffered funding by OEO, only one school district in the United States (Alum Rock, California) carried out such an experimental program (Warren, 1976, pp. 13–15). Results of that program were mixed, and with the withdrawal of federal funds the project was discontinued.

However, limited implementation of the voucher plan failed to extinguish the idea of family choice in education. Perhaps the most cogent argument for family choice was provided by lawyers John Coons and Stephen Sugarman:

> We will argue that the interests of children are best served in a decentralized policy giving maximum scope to free, chosen, communal relationships that are generally organized on a small scale. Systematic domination of education by large enterprise (public or private) ought, therefore, to be disfavored. This suggests to us the strengthening of the family's role in education and the growth of a teaching fraternity which is related to the family as professional to client rather than as master to servant. (1978, p. 2)

The argument presented by Coons and Sugarman for family choice in education was seen by many school people as a threat to the support of public education, which had required a century to achieve. Nonetheless, the advocacy of voucher plans and the argument for family choice seem to have had consequences among school people. First, many school districts appear to have reexamined their relationships with parents and in numerous cases attempted to establish better communication and develop ways by which parental wishes might be more fully taken into account. In some city school districts, this also led to the establishment of alternative schools under school district auspices and to open enrollment to allow parents and students to exercise some choice of schools. Some school districts also began to emphasize local school management as another way of augmenting parent participation in educational decision making.

But these measures on the part of the public schools have not dampened the interest in nonpublic schools as an alternative to public education or as a way of extending parental choice. The Reagan Administration gave this movement impetus by supporting legislation in Congress for tuition tax credits for parents with children in nonpublic schools. Organizations of public school people, both administrators and teachers, went on record as opposing tuition tax credit proposals. Indeed, in one of the few instances of joint action, the AFT and NEA joined in their opposition to tuition tax credit. A part of their resolution as it appeared in *Education Times* reads:

> The attempts to enact tuition tax credits schemes constitute an effort to undermine the financial support structure of the public schools of our nation. Such proposals are bad economic policy, improper public policy, harmful educational policy and violate the spirit and the letter of the United States Constitution. (1982, p. 2)

Regardless of the eventual outcomes of tuition tax credits, voucher plans, or similar arrangements, it seems clear that the movement for parental choice has become another element in the political and social environment with which school administrators must deal.

State and Federal Influence

The pervading influence of the *Brown* decision, not only in education but in the larger society as well, was noted earlier. At the federal level, in addition to desegregation legislation and court action, for instance, Title IX (Public Law 92–318), which was designed to end sex discrimination in schools and colleges, was passed by Congress in 1971–72 (Sandler, 1977, pp. 6–9). A major provision in Title IX reads, "No person in the United States shall, on the basis of sex, be excluded from participation in, or be denied the benefits of, or be subjected to discrimination under any educational program or activity receiving federal assistance." But the control inherent in this provision was extended when Congress amended Title VII of the Civil Rights Act to cover employment in *all* educational institutions, whether or not they received federal money.

Another example of the federal impact on public schools is found in Public Law 94–142, which was designed to improve the education of handicapped students and passed by Congress in 1975. This law stipulates that all handicapped children shall have "a free appropriate public education which emphasizes special education and related services designed to meet their unique needs. . . ." Moreover, this special education is to be provided "at no cost to the parents or guardians" whether in the classroom, in the home, or in a hospital. Both the U. S. Code and the regulations pertaining to Public Law 94–142 were very detailed, thus leaving little discretion to states or local districts. It was specified that each state should formulate a plan for the education of the handicapped and submit this to the federal agency. Moreover, each state was required, as part of the plan, to set up and work with an advisory council on special education. The law also stipulated that each student should receive an independent evaluation to determine his or her unique educational needs. Further, the law required that students be placed in the least restrictive environment for their instruction. The implementation of Public Law 94–142 was difficult, especially in districts with few handicapped students. As might be expected, the courts have been called on to adjudicate some situations. Even though attempts have been made to modify the regulations, Congress has not looked with favor on proposals to reduce the requirements of the law or to give states and local districts a greater voice in its interpretation.

Federal legislation, such as noted above, represented an extension of federal intrusion into the instructional programs of schools and school districts. In legal theory, state influence on school operation is long-standing: Public schooling consistently has been seen as a state function. In practice, states have historically been reluctant to impose extensive control on schools and school districts. Legislatures, state educational agencies, and state courts have left many decisions on school operation to local school districts. However, in recent decades state control over the operation of public education has increased. One reason may be that the financing of public education, in almost all states, requires that an ever larger proportion of funding come from state rather than local sources.

Still another factor that helps explain the greater state control over education is the federal legislation described above. Public Law 42-142 is a good example. For states to benefit from federal funds, additional state money must be provided to fund the programs. Moreover, the state, as noted above, must set up an advisory council on special education and give genuine consideration to the advice of the council in establishing and implementing state programs. Regardless of the merits of programs for the handicapped, state and federal influence on local school districts is pervasive today (Campbell et al. 1985, Chap. 2).

Interest Group Pressures

Interest groups are numerous and varied. They may have an educational orientation or a broader range of concerns, some of which relate to schools and their operation (Campbell et al., 1985, Chaps. 13–14). School-oriented groups include parent-teacher associations, teacher associations or unions, administrator associations, and school board associations. Interest groups with multiple concerns of which education is one include organizations related to race—blacks, Hispanics, and Native Americans; white ethnic groups; women's groups; religious groups; parents of the handicapped; and a number of taxpayer groups. Certain aspects of school programs have activated these groups in recent years. For example, one group has insisted that "creationism" be given equal place with the teaching of evolution in the schools; another group has resisted this notion with equal tenacity. One group has demanded that schools "return to the basics," while another group has advocated "open classrooms" and a more creative approach to education. Regardless of their demands, in recent years these groups have become more numerous, more vocal, and more insistent on having access to school decision makers.

There are first the "generalized norms" valid throughout the community either as codified into law or agreed upon as "good practice." The second type of control is the creation of some kind of interstitial organization between the managerial structure and the "public interest." In education, this interstitial arrangement may be represented in a board of education. The third type of control may involve the creation of some governmental structure to oversee the managerial and technical levels of the organization. In education, this structure takes the form of state education agencies charged with general supervision over the schools. Parsons noted that it is not only a matter of institutional control over management; management must depend upon the institutional level for legitimization and support. Particularly in his treatment of the relationships between the managerial and the institutional levels, he forecast the open-systems view of administration, a view that has specific implications for education.

External Factors

In 1965, in *A Framework for Political Analysis*, political scientist David Easton described the political system as a subsystem of the larger social order of the environment in which it existed. The environment obviously contained other subsystems such as the economic and the social systems. Easton developed a simple model. It had a box in the center, representing the political system set in the environment. The environment provided inputs of two kinds, demands and support, to the political system. These inputs were mediated by the political system and resulted in two kinds of outputs, decisions and actions. These outputs in turn became part of the environment and thus affected the next round of inputs for the political system. Easton called this conceptualization of the interaction between the political subsystem and the larger social system quite simply "systems analysis."

Today, the idea of this interaction between a subsystem and the larger social system seems quite obvious, but in 1965 it was not as obvious and represented something of a new and useful way to look at political behavior. While Easton's inputs and outputs are couched in very general terms, his use of such terms prompted others to provide more specific examples of such dimensions.

Easton's framework for political analysis has also been applied to organizational analysis, because organizations can be seen as political entities. In particular, public organizations such as schools can be seen as political subsystems in the larger social environment. Certainly, the environment provides inputs for public education. Demand inputs, for instance, may include citizen insistence that certain things be taught or not taught. Support inputs may include such items as tax revenues and moral approval of school programs or procedures. Schools and school systems obviously mediate these inputs and provide outputs to the environment. For instance, a decision to place more emphasis on the basics would be such an output. The feedback loop by which such an output affects the next round of inputs can also be visualized. Wirt and Kirst (1982) organized their entire book, *Schools in Conflict*, around Easton's notion of systems analysis.

The Easton framework is a useful component or precursor to the open-systems view of administration. Some who have worked with the concept in school situations, however, have encountered two kinds of problems (Campbell et al., 1985, pp. 487–488). One, as noted above, is the very general nature of the terms employed. Such investigators recognized the need for more precise descriptions of the environment of schools and school districts. A second problem involves the boundaries that separate the organization from its environment. In school situations, for instance, the board of education can in one sense be considered within the organization, while in another sense, certainly in Parsonian terms, the board is outside of the organization. Other contributors, noted below, have provided concepts that appear to complement Easton's view and have made the open-systems approach to administration more complete.

Organizational scholars Paul Lawrence and Jay Lorsch (1967) appear to have been among the first to treat extensively the relationship between an organization and its environment. Their volume, *Organization and Environment* (1967, p. lcv), examined six business organizations in an effort to understand "the organizational characteristics which allow firms to deal effectively with different kinds and rates of environmental change, and especially technological and market changes." They found three of these organizations—manufacturers of plastics, food, and containers—to be "high performing" organizations, and much of their analysis dealt with these organizations. They noted that conflicts were resolved differently in these three effective organizations. In the plastics organization, it was the integrating department that had the most influence. In the food organization, the research and marketing units had the most influence, while in the container organization, it was the sales and production departments that exerted the most influence. In each case, however, the organization seemed to be responding internally to the stresses found in the environment, regardless of whether they had to do with technical or market changes. It should be noted that Lawrence and Lorsch, in including both technological and market conditions, may have defined the environment more broadly than have some political scientists.

These differential responses of organizations to their respective environments led Lawrence and Lorsch to formulate their contingency theory of organizations. A partial statement of that theory follows:

> The more differentiated an organization, the more difficult it is to achieve integration. To overcome this problem, the effective organization has integrating devices consistent with the diversity of the environment. The more diverse the environment, and the more differentiated the organization, the more elaborate the integrating devices. (1967, p. 157)

While business and educational organizations differ in several respects, it seems that contingency theory, as a version of the open-systems approach to administration, may be useful as one way of viewing the operation of schools. Clearly, different schools have different environments. For instance, a school district in a central city under court order to desegregate its schools is in a quite different environment from a school district in an all white upper-middle-class suburb under no such constraint. At the very least, the contingency theory has made specific some ways by which organizations, viewed in an open-systems context, must modify their internal behavior in order to cope adequately with elements in their environment.

Loosely Coupled Systems

Organizational scholars Cohen and March (1974) described the American college presidency in a study entitled *Leadership and Ambiguity*. In this volume, the college president was portrayed as someone who faces four ambiguities: those of purpose, power, experience, and success. These four ambiguities might be restated in terms of four questions: What are the real goals of the organization? Just how powerful is the president? How does the president make inferences from his experience? When is the president successful? Anyone familiar with colleges and universities will recognize that there are no precise and generally accepted answers to any of these questions.

The ambiguities faced by college presidents caused Cohen and March (1974, p. 203) to conclude that "we confuse the issues of leadership by ignoring the basic ambiguity of leadership life. We require a plausible basic perspective for the leader of a loosely coupled, ambiguous organization." The concept of colleges as loosely coupled organizations prompted Cohen and March, perhaps with tongue in cheek, to characterize such institutions as "organized anarchies."

While depicting a college as an organized anarchy may seem a bit cavalier, there can be no denial that colleges are loosely coupled. It may also be useful to examine other organizations from this perspective. In particular, such a perspective provides additional understanding of public school organizations. To be sure, teachers in schools ordinarily do not exercise as much influence in their organizations as do professors in colleges, but schools as well as colleges have ambiguities of purpose and of administrative power. Moreover, frequently what happens in one part of a school organization affects, at least to some degree, other parts of the organization. In many respects schools can be seen appropriately as loosely coupled organizations.

It was social psychologist Karl Weick (1976) who explicated specifically the concept of educational organizations "as loosely coupled systems." Weick maintained that a concept such as 'loose coupling' served as a sensitizing device causing the "observer to notice and question things that had previously been taken for granted" (1976, p. 2). While he noted that the "concept of loose coupling need not be used normatively" (p. 4), Weick admitted that he felt "mildly affectionate . . . toward the concept." He then proceeded to list a number of functions and dysfunctions of such an approach to organizational behavior. For instance, he argued that loose coupling allows some proportion of the organization to persist, that it may be a good system for localized adaptation, that a breakdown in one part of the organization may be sealed off and not affect other parts of the organization, and that such a concept allows more room for self-determination on the part of organizational actors. In education, loose coupling might help to rationalize the concept of decentralization by placing more autonomy at the single-school level.

In 1981, sociologist Richard Scott sought to integrate the many views of organizations under three theoretical perspectives: rational systems, natural systems, and open systems. The chief concern of this chapter is with what Scott had to say about open systems. To begin with, he noted that, "Most theorists now pay lip service to the open systems perspective, which stresses the critical importance of organizational-environment connections, but few pursue the implications of these relations for the organization's internal structures and processes" (1981, p. xvi).

As examples of the open-systems view of administration, Scott selected four schools of thought. The first such school of thought looked to systems theory as a source of ideas and dealt with such matters as workflows, control systems, and planning mechanisms. Scott saw this group as pragmatic and applied and as trying to change and improve organizations from a managerial perspective. The second group selected by Scott consisted of the exponents of contingency theory and included Lawrence and Lorsch, whose work was alluded to above. Scott characterized the third group as those concerned with environmental approaches, particularly Darwin's natural selection model and the resource dependent model sometimes known as the political economy model. As the fourth group, Scott referred specifically to the work of Weick and other social psychologists who focused on processes in organizations.

At the end of his insightful chapter on open systems, Scott (1981) draws a number of conclusions, some of which are paraphrased here. The open-systems perspective developed late, gained adherents rapidly, and profoundly altered conceptions of organizations. The open-systems view stresses the complexity and variability of component parts— both individuals and subgroups—and the looseness of connections among them. Such a view shifts attention from structure to process in organizations. The interdependence of the organization and its environment is the major focus of the open-systems view. Scott concludes his description of open systems with these words:

> In general, it seems clear that the open systems perspective brings with it a much needed dimension to—if not a reorientation of— previously existing viewpoints. After the emergence of the open systems perspective, the old image of a closed, self-contained, self-sufficient system will be difficult to resurrect. The doors and windows of the organization have been opened, and we are more than ever aware of the vital flows and linkages that related the organization to other systems. Further we see more clearly than we did that organizations are processes as well as structures, and that some of these processes are not recurrent cycles but forces changing the existing structures. (1981, p. 120)

This thought may help educators accept the reality of multiple environmental forces playing upon the school.

FURTHER CONSIDERATION OF OPEN SYSTEMS

Some of the people whose contributions were discussed above might not admit that they have contributed to an open-systems approach to administration. Nevertheless, political theory as set forth by Easton, contingency theory as formulated by Lawrence and Lorsch, and the loose coupling first suggested by Cohen and March and later extended by Weick have provided useful elements to the larger concept referred to here as open systems. Because the open-systems approach to administration is somewhat recent, empirical evidence supporting such a view may appear to be sparse. Yet administrative scholars and practitioners alike seem to recognize that in earlier approaches to administration the relationships between organizations and their environments tended to be ignored or taken for granted and that the open-systems idea requires at least that these relationships be examined.

It seems difficult enough to get a fix on organizational behavior when organizations are viewed as closed systems, as they were by administrative scholars as different as Frederick Taylor, Elton Mayo, and Max Weber, discussed in Chapters 2, 3, and 4, respectively. Consideration of the environment, as required in the open-systems view, brings an array of additional factors to an already complicated arena of study about human behavior. Pessimists might conclude that in the open-systems view the variables are so many and their interrelationships so difficult to determine that scientific study is hopeless.

Others, however, see the open-systems view as a new opportunity. They agree with Wayne Hoy's (1982, p. 2) summary of theory and research in educational administration which holds that "closed system theories . . . are not adequate." If this is the case, scholars and practitioners are required to take more comprehensive views of organizational behavior. Since organizations exist in and are influenced by their environments, to treat them as closed systems is hardly defensible. Organizations are affected by factors within and without organizational boundaries. Indeed, some actors, such as students and school board members, tend to move fluidly in and out of organizations. In short, organizational boundaries are clearly more permeable than was once thought.

It is worthwhile to underscore the point that the open-systems view requires that additional organizational variables be examined, and to some extent this has been done. For instance, Pfeffer in *Power in Organizations* concludes:

> Power and politics are often part of organizations, and need to be understood as fundamental and important processes. Power and politics are basic processes which occur in many organizations much of the time, and are empirically researchable and analyzable using a set of conceptual tools which are already largely in place and which have constituted the subject matter of this book. Although ignoring these

Theme p399

topics may be favored, given the ideology and political purpos
served, it is time to begin incorporating the issues raised here ir
much more systematic and comprehensive way in both the research
and teaching in the field of organizations. (1981, p. 370)

In terms of educational research, Glenn Immegart and William
Boyd (1979, p. 275) say "that we can now begin to see the outlines of an
emerging synthesis in the field." They then suggest that the "approach
that appears most conducive to the new thrust is that of policy analysis" (1979, p. 277). Any such synthesis obviously involves consideration
of environmental or external variables as well as internal variables
affecting organizations.

Not all educational scholars agree that policymaking represents a
new synthesis for the field. Norman Boyan (1981, p. 12), for example,
contends that "the requirements do not exist for emergence of a new,
single, synthesizing paradigm to guide research across the entire territory or even within any of the several major specializations." Boyan
adds: "On one dimension, however, I do detect an unusual degree of
unanimity across the constituent specializations, namely, renewed determination to extract, compile, and synthesize reliable data about what
actually happens in and around schools and other educational organizations" (1981, p. 13).

If Boyan is correct, and he appears to be, there seems no way to
dispute the fact that schools as organizations respond to their environments in one way or another, whether at local, state, or national levels.
It seems, therefore, that those who study schools and those who direct
them are left with but one choice: External as well as internal factors
affecting schools must be scrutinized carefully. To be sure, problems
still persist in understanding more precisely what these variables are,
how they may be related, and to what extent they can be manipulated
by anyone who seeks certain outcomes from the schools.

SUMMARY

Forces in the larger society, such as the *Brown* decision, increased the
emphasis on civil rights, and the women's movement helped set the
stage for the open-systems view of administration. In education itself
there were also developments that tended to shape the open-systems
approach. These included the rise of collective bargaining, the increased
influence of state and federal governments, and the augmented pressure of interest groups. Administrative theorists soon took account of

these social and educational developments in their formulations of administrative theory, exemplified particularly in the "systems analysis" of Easton, the "loosely coupled systems" of Weick, and the more detailed treatment of open systems by Scott. In the last decade or so the open-systems view has provided a more accurate view of reality for both scholars and practitioners in educational administration.

6

THE PERSISTENT TASK: BALANCING THE INDIVIDUAL AND THE ORGANIZATION

Clichés

THE FOUR MAJOR ORGANIZATIONAL IDEOLOGIES so far considered have emerged roughly in historical sequence: scientific management, human relations, bureaucracy, and finally open systems. Important as it is to note the distinguishing characteristics of each of these four views of administration, for the purpose of this chapter the four views will be grouped in two broad categories. The first focuses on the organization and the second on the individual. The chapter will discuss how these two major concerns have persisted, consider more comprehensive organizational ideologies that have embraced both concerns, and note some recent thrusts and attempts to synthesize organizational thought.

EXPONENTS OF INDIVIDUAL *OR* ORGANIZATIONAL CONCERNS

One might assume that as each succeeding view of administrative thought became prominent the preceding view would have given way and even disappeared. Such has not been the case; instead, each of the four views has persisted. In particular, they have rotated around the two broad categories discussed here: the individual and the organization. Possible explanations of this persistence will be considered next.

Old Wine in New Bottles

The organizational approach, beginning with scientific management, deals with tasks that are to be done to make organizations more productive. For instance, Taylor and his followers believed that it was possible to analyze tasks performed by workers in order to determine which procedures would produce the maximum output with the minimum input of energy and resources. As shown, this engineering ap-

proach to organizations was modified by the human relations movement. It was not long, however, until the human relations view tended
to be pushed aside by the structural or bureaucratic approach to organizational behavior. The rhetoric had changed somewhat, but the emphasis was still on organizational efficiency.

The similarities between scientific management and the bureaucratic approach to organizations led Scott to include both of these views
as part of a larger rational systems approach. Scott observed:

> From the standpoint of the rational system perspective, the behavior
> of organizations is viewed as actions performed by purposeful and
> coordinated agents. The language employed connotes this image of
> rational calculation: such terms as *information, efficiency, optimization,
> implementation,* and *design* occur frequently. But another somewhat dif-
> ferent set of terms also occurs within this perspective; it indicates the
> cognitive limitations of the individual decision maker and the effects
> of the organizational context in which rational choices are made.
> These terms—*constraints, authority, rules, directives, jurisdiction, performance
> programs, coordination*—imply that the rationality of behavior within
> organizations takes place within clearly specified limits. (1981, p. 58)

While Scott may oversimplify, the point can be made that the bureaucratic perspective on organizations, with its emphases on rationality
and organizational efficiency, was in some ways closely related to scientific management.

Scott includes human relations as one school of thought in his
natural systems and views open systems as belonging to a separate
broad category. Even so, some similarities exist between the two approaches. For Mayo, one of the fathers of human relations, the engineering considerations were at least tempered by psychological considerations. Physical factors, such as illumination, and economic incentives
were found to be less important than previously thought, and psychological factors such as self-esteem and group solidarity were seen as
more important.

While these same considerations may not characterize precisely the
open-systems view, Scott has noted that the open-systems approach
"stresses the variability of the individual participants and subgroups. . . ."
"Moreover," to quote Scott (1981, p. 119) again, "it shifts attention"
from structure to process." In broad terms, both human relations and
open systems pay attention to the individual and group needs of people,
while scientific management and bureaucracy tend to focus more on
organizational work systems and rules determining the behavior of
workers and managers.

Collapsing organizational thought into two broad categories—one with a focus on the organization and the other on people—permits one to see how new formulations are often new more in dress than in substance. Scientific management has had a number of reincarnations, some of which will be noted. Thomas James (1969) was one of the first to call attention to this phenomenon. His Horace Mann Lecture in 1968 had the prescient title, *The New Cult of Efficiency and Education*. In obvious reference to the work of Raymond Callahan (1962), who had documented the influence of the scientific management movement on education early in the century, James saw a resurgence of the efficiency concept in education, which he suggested began as part of the 1946 Hoover report on efficiency in government. He thought the most influential publication was *The Economics of Defense in the Nuclear Age* written by Hitch and McKean in 1960. This document seems to have influenced President Johnson, who at a news conference in 1965 was reported to have said:

> This morning I have just concluded a breakfast meeting with the Cabinet and with the heads of federal agencies, and I am asking each of them to immediately begin to introduce a very new and very revolutionary system of planning and programming and budgeting throughout the vast federal government, so that through the tools of modern management the full promise of the finer life can be brought to every American at the lowest possible cost. (Knezevich, 1973, p. 14)

Shortly after this news conference, President Johnson directed Bulletin 66-3 of October 12, 1965 to the heads of all federal executive departments, and planning and programming and budgeting (PPBS) was on its way. The U. S. Office of Education was one of the agencies directed to implement PPBS in its allocation of monies to state and local educational agencies. Congress, too, gave some attention to this new formulation for, as James (1969, p .38) noted, PPBS approaches were "imbedded in the Elementary and Secondary Education Act of 1965." Some states, notably California, mandated that PPBS procedures be followed by their school districts. This mandate proved difficult to implement, but some of the ideas emanating from PPBS procedures, such as zero-based budgeting, have remained and are still frequently advocated.

Other approaches related to school planning and school costs also emerged: cost-benefit analysis, management by objectives, and the so-called accountability movement. In each case, the focus was on efficiency—the maximum result at the lowest cost. Without debating the relative merits of each of these ideas, we can say that they suggested a new cult of educational efficiency.

Peter Gronn (1982, pp. 17–35) has suggested that scientific management or Taylorism flourished in still another new dress during the late 1970s and early 1980s. In "Neo-Taylorism in Educational Administration," Gronn examined eight studies in educational administration, all of which were inspired by *The Nature of Administrative Work* (1973) by Henry Mintzberg. Setting aside for the moment the need to examine what administrators actually do, Gronn's major conclusion is as follows:

> First, the authors of the studies utilize methodologies which, put simply, are nothing more or less than latter-day replications of the motion and time studies conducted by F. W. Taylor and reported in *The Principles of Scientific Management*. Secondly, the authors' discourses exhibit the same overweening preoccupation with virtues like "efficiency" as is found in Taylor's original work. Finally, all these accounts seriously misconstrue the phenomenon they purport to explain. (1982, p. 18)

Perhaps Gronn's characterization was intended to be something of an indictment of the eight studies he examined and more generally of research in educational administration. Or, neo-Taylorism might still be a viable approach to administrative thought and administrative research. Willower (1982, p. 102), for instance, who pointed out certain weaknesses in Mintzberg's observation approaches, such as neglect of the emotional components of activities and the slighting of the social context within which activities occur, nevertheless saw the methodology as providing a general sense of the realities of administrative life. Whether or not Gronn was entirely accurate in his assessment of Mintzberg's type of studies, Gronn's analysis may serve as an example of how one view of organizations can reemerge and persist.

Still another new expression of scientific management is found in the work of Jacob Michaelsen, whose article, "The Political Economy of School District Administration," set forth the recently developed public choice model from economics. Michaelsen (1981, p. 99) contended that "all economic agents are assumed to act largely, if not solely, to advance their own welfare within whatever institutional arrangements they find themselves." This language is hauntingly similar to the economic incentives offered Mr. Schmidt, Taylor's (1911) "high priced man," early in the century. In sum, a number of instances have been noted in which scientific management, first advocated by Taylor and his associates early in this century, has in recent decades again captured the imaginations of politicians and organizational scholars.

The human relations view of educational administration or democratic administration, as it was often called in educational circles, prominent during the 1930s and 1940s has also had a number of recent reincarnations. This reemphasis on people as opposed to structural characteristics of organizations has perhaps been more forcefully set forth by Thomas Greenfield. In a number of journal articles and culminating in a response to certain of his critics, Greenfield (1980) set forth nine propositions, some of which are paraphrased here: Organizations are accomplished by people; organizations are expressed by will, intention, and values; facts do not exist except as they are called into existence by human action and interest; man acts and then judges the action; organizations are essentially arbitrary definitions of reality woven in symbols and expressed in language; there is no technology for achieving the purposes of organizations. Greenfield put it this way:

> They are the voices—some contemporary . . . and some ancient
> . . . these voices speak to us of ideas that have been largely ignored in
> the pursuit of a set of universal, objective, and "scientific" propositions about organizations. The consequence of this exclusion has led
> to a science of organizations that is no science, to a definition of
> organizations that excludes much of what we want to study in them,
> and to a failure of methodology and technique in the face of the moral
> and existential questions that are embedded in organizational life.
> (1980, pp. 27-28)

It seems very clear that Greenfield stresses personal meaning and individual values much more than he does corporate or collective purposes and structural characteristics of groups. His position seems much more compatible with the humanities than with the social sciences.

A more straightforward return to human concerns in administration is found in the work of William Ouchi (1981). With obvious reference to the work of Douglas McGregor (1960), who popularized "theory Y" as an earlier view of human relations in administration, Ouchi set forth his own position. His book, which has the interesting subtitle, "How American Business Can Meet the Japanese Challenge" (1981, p. 4), begins unabashedly by stating that the theory Z approach quite simply assumes "that involved workers are the key to increased productivity." For Ouchi, Japanese industry has exemplified theory Z; he suggests three key words as the essence of such business practice: trust, subtlety, and intimacy—all very human concepts. Ouchi goes further and maintains that "the most important characteristic of the Japanese organizations is lifetime employment" (1981, p. 15). He continues, "Probably the best known feature of Japanese organizations is their participative approach to decision-making" (p. 36).

In recognizing that Japanese culture is father to many of the business practices in Japan, Ouchi also suggests that a number of business firms in the United States have become what he calls type Z companies. In these companies, he notes that decision making is participative in nature, but the ultimate responsibility still resides in one individual. These companies also have a broad concern for the welfare of their workers. Egalitarianism seems to be a central feature of these organizations. The association between business firms with type Z characteristics and productivity, as observed by Ouchi, has not been lost on the world of business or the world of education.

This discussion cannot ignore a more popular book, *In Search of Excellence*, by organization writers Thomas Peters and Robert Waterman (1982). After examining forty-three "best-run" American companies, the authors set forth eight attributes that seem to distinguish these organizations. Some of these attributes are a bias for action, staying close to the customer, and productivity through people. The authors state their key position as follows:

> The clear starting point is acceptance of the limits of rationality. . . .
> Building on that, four prime elements of a new theory would include
> our observations on basic human needs in organizations: (1) people's
> need for meaning; (2) people's need for a modicum of control; (3) peo-
> ple's need for positive reinforcement, to think of themselves as
> winners in some sense; and (4) the degrees to which actions and
> behaviors shape attitudes and beliefs rather than vice versa. (1982,
> p. 102)

While Peters and Waterman attempt to establish a synthesis in organizational theory, their main thrust is a new interpretation of human relations. They acknowledge their indebtedness to Mayo for his insistence on "attention to employees" and to B. F. Skinner for his stress on "positive reinforcement." Strangely, Abraham Maslow and his formulation of basic human needs is not given specific mention, but the influence of such a concept seems apparent.

Ouchi, Greenfield, and Peters and Waterman have all revived, each in his own way, an interest in the human dimension of administration. In somewhat similar fashion—as noted by James, Gronn, and Willower—PPBS, cost-benefit analysis, management by objectives, accountability, and other formulations represent a resurgence of certain aspects of the organizational dimension. None of these new formulations duplicates precisely earlier expressions, but their essense seems to represent earlier ideas in new dress.

Different Elements of Reality

The recurrence of different views of organizations may also spring from attempts to deal with different aspects of reality. For example, the human relations view obviously places more emphasis on people as individuals—their needs, aspirations, and values. All organizations are peopled, and thus this emphasis on individuals clearly is seen as part of the reality of organizations. But organizations are more than individuals; they are collectivities of individuals. Collectivities have structures, roles, sanctions, and other identifiable characteristics, which also deal with the reality of organizations. Without engaging in a long discussion about reality, one can recognize that reality is a perceptual matter: Individual needs and group structures exist as concepts within one's mind. But a person must also act in terms of such concepts. Psychologists tend to deal more with the concepts related to individuals, while sociologists tend to give greater stress to those that are related to collectivities.

Among psychologists, Abraham Maslow, in *Motivation and Personality* (1954), has provided and continues to provide much of the rationale for the human relations view of administration. In his theory of human motivation, Maslow set forth what has now become his well-known hierarchy of basic human needs: physiological, safety, belongingness, esteem, and self-actualization needs. While Maslow acknowledged some exceptions, he maintained that these needs tend to appear in that order. In Maslow's words, a "person will *want* the more basic of two needs when deprived in both" (1954, p. 99). Since motivation of the members of any organization is important, it is not difficult to understand why these basic human needs, set out in such explicit detail, have become important guideposts to those who are concerned with organizations from a psychological position.

In shifting from a psychological to a sociological approach to organizations, a rather different set of concerns emerge. Scott (1981) put it as follows:

> Most analysts conceived of organizations as social structures created by individuals to support the collaborative pursuit of specified goals. Given this conception, all organizations confront a number of common problems. All must define (and redefine) their objectives; all must induce participants to contribute services; all must control and coordinate these contributions; resources must be garnered from the environment and products or services dispensed; participants must be selected, trained, and replaced; and some sort of working accommodation with the neighbors must be achieved. (1981, p. 9)

Such concerns as structures, group decisions, coordination, resources, and the environment must be taken into account. Indeed, psychologists and sociologists examine different aspects of reality when they study organizations.

Different Approaches to Administrative Functions

The two views of reality dealt with above tend to persist for still another reason. Each view seems to inform certain administrative functions and problems. Neither view tells the practicing administrator what to do, but each may give him or her some additional insight with respect to the functions to be performed and the problems that may be encountered.

Campbell and others (1983, Chap. 1) have set forth six major functions of administration, the first four of which are summarized as follows: (1) discern and influence the setting of goals and policies for the organization, (2) stimulate and direct the development of programs to achieve the goals, (3) establish and coordinate an organization to implement the program, and (4) procure and manage resources needed to support the program. To deal with the first function, the setting of goals for the organization, obviously requires value choices. In a school organization, these value choices require responses from teachers, parents, the board of education, and members of the community at large, as well as from school administrators. Here individuals as well as collectivities are involved. Goals for the school as an organization must somehow correspond in large measure to the values held by most of the individuals who participate in the goal-setting process. It seems quite clear that an understanding of individual motivation as well as collective behavior would be useful to an administrator seeking some agreement on a set of goals for the school.

In terms of the second function, the stimulation and direction of the development of a program designed to achieve the goals, the very words, stimulation and direction, tend to evoke different approaches to organizations. Stimulation is obviously much more people centered. Perhaps, to use Maslow's terminology, people in an organization respond best when organizational activity also helps fulfill some of their basic personal needs, such as the need for belonging and for esteem. The word direction has much more of a structural connotation. In an organization, certain role incumbents, in this case administrators, are expected to provide some direction. Indeed, most organizational members fault their administrators when they do not give direction. But this direction can easily go awry if it becomes domination or pressure. Thus, in terms of this function, useful understandings may stem from both the personal and the structural views of organizations.

The third function of administration deals with the establishment and coordination of an organization to implement the program. Any effort of this kind involves the selection of people to fill different positions in the organization, or, in structural terms, to establish differential role expectations for a number of people. The very concepts of role and role expectations can be informed by both views of administration. Perhaps this is most clearly exemplified in an attempt to achieve role compatibility for each person in an organization or to reduce role conflict on the part of organization members. Role conflict can derive from many sources, one of which is a sharp difference between role expectations and personal dispositions. For instance, appointment to a principalship ordinarily carries the expectation that the principal will appraise the performance of teachers. This expectation runs counter to the personal disposition of some people, so that their appointment to the principalship would probably result in much role conflict and inadequate performance.

The final function of administration explicated here has to do with the procurement and management of resources to support the program. For purposes of this discussion, resources will be limited to money. On first glance, money appears to involve *things* much more than people. But such a conclusion can be quite misleading. Money must be secured from the people of the local and larger community. Obviously, there are structural aspects involved in this revenue quest. There are, for instance, governmental bodies through which money is sought and established procedures by which it may be obtained. Each of these governmental bodies is in itself a collectivity with its own set of behaviors. In the request for money, the administrator must also cope with the individual values of the people of the community, particularly those who provide its leadership.

By shifting from consideration of administrative functions to actual administrative problems, one can be even more specific about how both the people view and the structural view of administration may inform the practice of administration. For example, an inservice education program for teachers would clearly involve the people approach, while the development of a program for transporting students in a large consolidated school district might make considerable use of the engineering approach. Consideration of such specific problems as well as the more general functions of administration suggests the continuing viability of both the organization and individual views of administration and hence their tendency to persist.

THEORISTS WITH A TWO-DIMENSIONAL VIEW

To this point, one-dimensional approaches to administration—whether organizational or individual—have been considered. The discussions have not included the contributions of those who had a more comprehensive approach to the field, namely, a two-dimensional view of administration. Some of their formulations will now be treated.

Organizational Theorists

In late 1937, Chester Barnard gave eight lectures at the Lowell Institute in Boston. These lectures, with some expansion, became the book, *The Functions of the Executive* (1938). Barnard was then President of New Jersey Telephone Company, a position he held for many years; he later became President of the Rockefeller Foundation. Barnard integrated the insights of an experienced executive with the concepts of organizational scholars. He was not intimidated by the scholars; rather he contended (1938, p. ix) that "rarely did they seem to sense the processes of coordination and decision that underlie a large part at least of the phenomena they described." At the same time, he was familiar with the work of sociologists, social psychologists, economists, political scientists, and historians, particularly as they dealt with organizations. Barnard recognized economic factors as important in understanding human behavior, but he felt that "Adam Smith and his successors depressed the interest in the specific social process . . . and greatly overemphasized economic interests" (1938, p. x). While Barnard took scholarly concepts into account, they had to make sense in terms of his own experience as an executive.

No single concept of administration, whether scientific management or human relations, was enough for Barnard. He recognized that people were subject to forces over which they had little control. At the same time, Barnard also insisted on giving attention to "those philosophies that grant freedom of choice and of will, that make of the individual an independent entity" (1938, p. 21). This duality was also present in his concept of authority, which recognized the authority of *position* and the authority of *leadership* (1938, p. 173).

For present purposes, Barnard's position with respect to what is required in a cooperating system is most significant:

> The persistence of cooperation depends upon two conditions: (a) its effectiveness; and (b) its efficiency. Effectiveness relates to the accomplishment of the cooperative purpose, which is social and nonper-

sonal in character. Efficiency relates to the satisfaction of individual motives, and is personal in character. The test of effectiveness is the accomplishment of a common purpose or purposes; effectiveness can be measured. The test of efficiency is the eliciting of sufficient individual wills to cooperate. (1938, p. 60)

In contending that the test of efficiency had to do with the willingness of individuals to cooperate, Barnard clearly departed from the usual economic interpretation of the word. In his concepts of effectiveness as nonpersonal and efficiency as personal, he combined, in a sense, concerns with productivity as stressed by Taylor and those of human relations as stressed by Mayo. In so doing, he seems to have been the first to ascribe not one, but two dimensions to administration.

Another two-dimensional view of organizations was offered by Chris Argyris in *Personality and Organization* (1957). Argyris was at that time a professor of industrial administration and Project Director of the Labor and Management Center at Yale University. The book was a product of some six years of effort and dealt with the central question of why people behave as they do in organizations. Major chapters in the book were devoted to the human personality and to the formal organization. He concluded that there was a basic incongruity between the characteristics of a healthy personality and the requirements of the formal organization. A key statement from Argyris follows:

If the analysis is correct, this inevitable incongruency increases as (1) the employees are of increasing maturity, (2) as the formal structure (based upon the above principles) is made more clear-cut and logically tight for maximum formal organizational effectiveness, (3) as one goes down the line of command, and (4) as the jobs become more and more mechanized (i.e., take on assembly line characteristics). (1957, p. 66)

He then considered how individuals and organizations responded to this basic incongruency between personal roles and organizational demands. Individuals, Argyris suggested, adapt in a number of ways, such as "leaving, working their way up the ladder, distorting their world through defense mechanisms, becoming apathetic and uninterested, reducing production, goldbricking, rate setting, and creating informal groups" (1957, p. 119). Argyris maintained that management responded by seeing the employees as at fault "for high turnover; high absence rates; low productivity, apathy, disinterest" (p. 162). Argyris contended that these practices by management tended only to exacerbate the problem.

Argyris next considered ways, such as job enlargement and reality leaderships, by which the incongruency between people and organizations could be reduced. Reality leadership was defined as leadership that takes account of situational factors in the organization. Argyris gave attention to ways by which personal and organizational imperatives could be made more congruent. His 1964 book, *Integrating the Individual and the Organization*, focused on that concern.

But Argyris' basic proposition continued to be ". . . a lack of congruency between the needs of healthy individuals and the demands of the formal organization" (1964, p. 233). This incongruency notwithstanding, Argyris recognized, as did Barnard before him, that an understanding of organizational behavior requires consideration of two major dimensions.

Comprehensive Views in Education

Even preceding the work of Argyris, Carroll Shartle (1956) and his colleagues organized the Personnel Research Board (PRB) at Ohio State University and began a decade or more of research on leadership. They were primarily concerned with the leadership behavior of people officially designated as leaders in formal organizations—whether military, business, or educational. The fact that leadership was removed from its more generic consideration and placed in organizational settings makes these studies pertinent to this consideration of organizational behavior in education.

Hemphill and Coons constructed the original instrument designed to measure leaders' behavior, the Leadership Behavior Description Questionnaire (LBDQ). The instrument was later adapted by Halpin and Winer (1952) for use with Air Force commanders. As a result of several studies, Halpin later described two major dimensions of leader behavior, initiating structure and consideration, as follows:

> Initiating Structure refers to the leader's behavior in delineating the relationship between himself and members of the work-group, and in endeavoring to establish well-defined patterns of organization, channels of communication, and methods of procedure. Consideration refers to behavior indicative of friendship, mutual trust, respect, and warmth in the relationship between the leader and the members of his staff. (1956, p. 4)

These two dimensions of leader behavior were derived from the work of a number of investigators. Halpin recognized some similarity between these dimensions and the two dimensions of goal achievement and group maintenance, characteristics found in group dynamics research summarized by social psychologists Cartwright and Zander (1953). Recognition was also given to the effectiveness and efficiency concepts of Barnard, referred to above. Halpin summarized the principal findings of the PRB studies; excerpts are shown below:

> The evidence indicates that Initiating Structure and Consideration are fundamental dimensions of leader behavior, and that the Leader Behavior Description Questionnaire provides a practical and useful technique for measuring the behavior of leaders on these two dimensions.
>
> There is, however, some tendency for superiors and subordinates to evaluate oppositely the contribution of the leader behavior dimensions to the effectiveness of leadership. Superiors are more concerned with the Initiating Structure aspects of the leader's behavior, whereas subordinates are more concerned with (or "interested in") the Consideration the leader extends to them as group members. . . .
>
> There is only a slight positive relationship between the way leaders believe they should behave and the way in which their group members describe them as behaving. . . . (1956, pp. 23–24)

With these findings as background, Halpin undertook a study of the leader behavior of school superintendents. Using the LBDQ, with slight modification, an attempt was made to secure a description of the actual leader behavior of 50 Ohio superintendents from the superintendents themselves, from members of their staffs, and from members of their boards of education. These descriptions were called the "LBDQ real." In addition, each of the respondents was asked to indicate for the items on the LBDQ how the superintendent *should* behave. These responses were termed the "LBDQ ideal." The 12 scores on each of the 50 superintendents were then analyzed.

Two of the findings are reported here. On the LBDQ real, staff members and board members did not agree in describing the behavior of a particular superintendent. Halpin stated the results as follows:

> On each leader behavior dimension, the staff respondents tend to agree in the description of their respective superintendents. Likewise, the board respondents tend to agree in the description of their respective superintendents. Although the staff and the board members each agree among themselves as a group in their description of the superintendent's leadership behavior, the two groups do not agree with each other. (1956, pp. 75–76)

However, on the LBDQ ideal, staff members and board members tended to agree on how a superintendent should behave. Thus, as Halpin continued, "These conceptions constitute general norms of how staff, boards, and superintendents believe a superintendent should behave" (1956, p. 77).

These and related findings led Halpin to conclude:

> The evidence from the present inquiry shows that effective leadership in the case of a school superintendent is characterized by high Initiation of Structure and high Consideration. These two dimensions of leader behavior represent fundamental and pertinent aspects of the superintendent's leadership skill. (1956, p. 85)

Thus, Halpin found that leaders of formal organizations, to be seen as effective, had to cope with two sets of expectations: one having to do with setting the tasks and procedures in the organization and the other with establishing supportive relationships with members of the organization. Like Barnard and Argyris, but from quite a different perspective, Halpin saw organizational behavior as two-dimensional.

Halpin's work was essentially empirical and not theoretical. It had still another distinction; it went beyond examining military and business leaders and actually dealt with leaders in educational settings. The adaptation of the LBDQ for use in educational settings and the established methodology surrounding its use as a research tool had other consequences. Literally hundreds of studies using the LBDQ were made of educational leaders. These studies dealt with other school superintendents, school principals, department chairpeople, and still other leaders in education. W. W. Charters, Jr. (1963, p. 786) contended that Halpin's work and other studies based on the LBDQ had "a severe methodological problem" in that "the various informants do not agree in their description of how the official behaves." This observation seems to ignore two possible explanations. First, as suggested by Halpin (1956, p. 81) himself, superintendents appeared to differentiate their role behavior in dealing with their boards and their staffs. Second, as noted by Abbott (1960) and other observers, role incumbents in an organization have differential or selective perceptions about the behavior of other role incumbents. Thus, the reservations of Charters notwithstanding, the initial study and subsequent developments have made Halpin's contribution significant in the history of educational administration.

Important as Halpin's contribution is to the field, some limitations in his leadership studies might be noted. Because his focus was essentially on leader behavior in organizations, much less attention was given to follower behavior in those organizations. Moreover, little, if any, explicit attention was given to the external environments of organizations. Nor was there any specific bridge between the dimensions of leader behavior and such administrative tasks as program direction, personnel selection, and budget determination, all of which leaders are expected to perform. But these limitations in no way reduce the contribution of Halpin's leadership studies, which clearly set forth two dimensions in leader behavior.

For about fifteen years, during the 1950s and 1960s, Jacob W. Getzels and his colleagues at the University of Chicago turned their attention to the study of educational administration. The initial publication by Getzels appeared in 1952 under the title "A Psycho-Sociological Framework for the Study of Educational Administration." Getzels noted that there was a systematic lack of research in educational administration due, he thought, to the dearth of theory in the field. He then posited administrative relationships as the basic unit for inquiry. He thought that three aspects of these relationships—the authority dimension, the scope of the relationship, and the affectivity dimension—were crucial. In these and the other concepts discussed, the beginning of a framework for the study of administration had been set forth.

By 1957, Getzels, now joined by a colleague, Egon Guba, set forth a more comprehensive model for the study of administration. Much the same formulation was presented by Getzels at the first theory conference of UCEA, organized jointly with the University of Chicago in 1957. A pertinent paragraph from Getzels' presentation follows:

> We conceive of the social system as involving two classes of phenomena which are at once conceptually independent and phenomenally interactive. There are first the institutions with certain roles and expectations that will fulfill the goals of the system. And there are second the individuals with certain personalities and need-dispositions inhabiting the system, whose observed interactions comprise what we generally call "social behavior." We shall assert that this social behavior may be understood as a function of these major elements: institution, role, and expectation, which together constitute what we shall call the nomothetic or normative dimension of activity in a social system; and individual, personality, and need-disposition, which together constitute the ideographic or personal dimension of activity in a social system. (1958, p. 152)

With time and the benefit of a number of studies based on the initial model, Getzels and his colleagues (1968) saw that there were still other determinants of behavior in a social system. These additional dimensions of the framework appear in *Educational Administration as a Social Process*, the most complete report of Getzels' work and the research emanating from it. One excerpt from that volume is shown below:

> In addition to these primary determinants of social behavior, a number of other relevant but more or less subsidiary factors must be considered . . . the central one being the cultural dimension with its component *values*. Both the institutional expectations and the individual dispositions have, at least to some extent, their source in and are related to the culture in which the system operates. (1968, p. 106)

The recognition of these additional dimensions of social behavior, particularly the cultural dimension, while important, did not influence greatly the initial thrust of the Getzels-Guba model. Research in the 1960s and 1970s, for the most part, was based on the conceptualization of the normative and personal dimensions.

This framework permitted a number of empirical derivations, some of which will be mentioned here. Possible sources of conflict in a social system were hypothesized. Getzels and his colleagues (1968, Chaps. 6–10) noted that conflict might ensue under a number of conditions: conflict between cultural values and institutional expectations, conflict between role expectations and personality dispositions, conflict between roles and within roles, conflict deriving from personality disorders, and conflict in the perception of role expectation. Each of these derivations provided a starting point for an empirical study, and a number of such studies were reported. Methodologies employed in these studies included opinion polling of large samples of the population, clinical interviews with small samples, personality assessment methods, phenomenological observations of actual behavior, and laboratory-type experiments. These studies tended to support "the importance of understanding the behavior of the *person* as well as the structure of the person's *role*, the ideosyncratic perceptual *process* as well as the normative institutional *prescription*. . . ." (Getzels et al., p. 400).

The Getzels-Guba framework dealt with the organization as a whole and in that sense was a more comprehensive view of administration than was found in the Halpin formulation. As with Halpin, however, the normative and personal dimensions focused on the internal behavior of the organization and said little about the impact of external factors. To be sure, a third dimension having to do with cultural factors was suggested but received little attention at the time. One other possible limitation of the Getzels-Guba framework might be noted:

Some found the formulation rather static; it seemed to accept organizations as they were without due regard for the dynamics in organizations that might effect change. Charters noted that those who sought to measure the nomothetic-ideographic-transactional leadership styles of school officials faced the same problem that confronted Halpin: "Parties providing the information about the official do not agree" (1963, p. 787). Again, this criticism appears to ignore the phenomenon of selective perception on the part of individuals in an organization. Despite any limitations of the Getzels-Guba model, Daniel Griffiths, among others, has called it "the most successful theory in educational administration" (1979, p. 50). Moreover, the dual dimension of administration was clearly set forth by conceptual and empirical work. The work of Barnard, Argyris, and Halpin had been extended.

RECENT THRUSTS AND ATTEMPTS AT SYNTHESIS

The persistence of concerns emphasizing the individual and those emphasizing the organization has been noted, and the work of a number of scholars who enunciated a two-dimensional view of administration has been discussed. Attention is now turned to some recent concepts and some writings that attempt a theoretical synthesis of the field.

New Conceptual Developments

As suggested earlier, the position of Greenfield was, in one sense, an example of the recurring emphasis on people as an approach to administration. But that is only part of the story. He also questioned the scientific or rational approach to administration and insisted that a more fruitful approach might be found in the humanities. Greenfield argued that scientific theories are too restrictive and that people ought to "let the data of organizational reality speak for themselves" and not be forced into some preconceived framework (1979, p. 187). Hoy places these matters in a broader social context:

> Open-system models of organizations began to supplant closed-system ones in the 1960s, and by the late 1970s, the transition virtually was complete. However, just as the human relations perspective underscored nonrational elements of organizational life that were neglected by the rational tradition of the classic models, a similar trend in organizational theory characterizes the newer, open-system theories. (1982, p. 7)

While others may demur, Hodgkinson (a Canadian as is Greenfield), in *Toward a Philosophy of Administration* (1978), drew a distinction between management and administration. Hodgkinson maintained that management is "more routine, definitive, programmatic," whereas administration deals "more with the formulation of purpose, the value-laden issues, and the human component of organizations" (1978, p. 5). As Hodgkinson put it:

> Among the chief of these [management and administration] must be the belief that being an administrator is more than being a technician and a politician, those dual faces of conventional professional managerial expertise. Secondly, there is the conviction that the realms of politics and administration, of policy and execution, are not so immaculately distinct as some received theory might lead us to believe. And thirdly, there is the intuition that to some significant extent administration is the disease for which, in a special sense, philosophy must be the cure. (1978, p. x)

For Hodgkinson, administration is philosophy in action. He makes a powerful case for the centrality of values in decision making, the essence of the administrative act. In his view, administration is more art than science.

Concern with emerging approaches to administration led to the organization of a seminar on research in educational administration at the University of Rochester in 1977. The major presentations of the seminar appeared later as the book, *Problem-Finding in Educational Administration*, referred to above. Glenn Immegart and William Boyd attempted to identify the lines of convergence that characterized the conference. A key conclusion is shown below:

> Of several promising approaches, however, the research approach that appears most conducive to the new thrust is that of educational policy analysis, that is, the study of the causes and consequences of policy differences at all levels of the educational infrastructure. . . . (1979, p. 276)

Norman Boyan was not quite convinced that policy analysis provided the basis for a new synthesis in educational administration. He thought that Immegart and Boyd "ask too much of policy analysis, an altogether worthy modality in its own limited right" (1981, p. 12).

Still another thrust can be found in the work of Michaelsen (1981). As noted above, Michaelsen has, in a sense, once again made a case for economic incentives, characteristic of the scientific management view of administration. But in addition, Michaelsen and others of like mind have attempted to look at the consequences of self-interest in governmental or nonprofit institutions. In addition to his statement, noted earlier, Michaelsen's description of the approach follows:

> What is new in this approach is the effort to trace out the consequences of self-interested action under the institutions of representative government in which decisions are necessarily taken collectively, including those of both elected and appointed officials. (1981, p. 99)

Willower did not find great merit in public choice theory. Excerpts from his appraisal of the formulation follow:

> The self-interest concept seems particularly limited when applied to behavior in schools. These organizations are focal points for community expectations and aspirations. This and their stewardship over children and youth, along with the moral dimension that entails, make for a setting that can evoke commitment to the welfare of others and a spirit of selflessness. . . . Actually, contrary to public choice theory, it appears that school personnel are quite sensitive to community standards and demands. (1982, pp. 19–20)

Willower's comments notwithstanding, the public choice approach to administrative behavior seems to represent another current thrust in the field.

"Corporate culture" has become a recent catch phrase in organizational literature. In one sense, the concept is as old as Barnard's (1938) concern with informal organization and Selnick's (1957) treatment of organizations as institutions. In another sense, a new emphasis has emerged: the growing conviction that organizational behavior should be studied by using anthropological approaches. Wolcott's (1978) study of the school principal is perhaps the classic example of such a study in education. Edgar Schein, in *Organizational Culture and Leadership*, has contributed to the burgeoning literature in this field. Schein defines organizational culture as follows:

> A pattern of basic assumptions—invented, discovered, or developed by a given group as it learns to cope with its problems of external adaptation and internal integration—that has worked well enough to be considered valid and, therefore, to be taught to new members as the correct way to perceive, think, and feel in relation to those problems. (1985, p. 9)

Hoy and Miskel, in their extensive discussion of organizational culture (1987, Chap. 8), suggest that it may be examined at different levels: tacit assumptions, shared values, and shared norms. The idea of organizational culture may, on one hand, be seen as having some affinity with loose coupling and thus affording individuals in an organization much freedom. On the other hand, if there are shared values and shared norms, members of an organization may find themselves under great pressure to conform and thus individual freedom may be reduced.

A number of newer developments in organizational thought have been discussed. These approaches make use of concepts found in phenomenology, philosophy, politics, economics, and anthropology.

Pluralism and Attempts at Synthesis

The preceding chapters demonstrate that concepts, typologies, and theories regarding organizations have been generated and applied to education with increasing frequency. As Scott noted, these approaches "seem often not to be evaluated or sorted out but simply added to a growing pile" (1981, p. xv). Scott attempted to lead the field out of this morass:

> My approach to injecting some order into the present scene is to make use of three general theoretical perspectives: one that views organizations as rational systems; a second that views them as natural systems; and a third that approaches them as open systems. More than one perspective is employed because I believe that no single existing perspective is adequate to comprehend the important features of organizations. (1981, p. xv)

In taking this position, Scott concluded that the various theories regarding organizations cannot be integrated into a single model. Instead, it is most useful to examine organizations from three perspectives.

Still, some scholars have attempted to synthesize a number of factors that seem to affect administrative behavior into a more comprehensive model. The Getzels-Guba model was discussed above as an example of a two-dimensional approach to administration. While the normative and personal dimensions received most attention at the time, early in his work Getzels posited biological and cultural dimensions to his model as well. These dimensions were not well developed, but at one point Getzels insisted that both the institution and the individual must be viewed in the context of the culture. More recently, Getzels (1978) dealt extensively with the third or cultural dimension of his model in "The Communities of Education." While the focus of the article was that of providing a more complete framework for understanding the behavior of children, its implications for administrative behavior were equally clear.

McPherson (1983) wrote an insightful paper entitled "The Evolution of the Getzels Model." McPherson's appraisal of Getzels' contribution is contained in the following:

> ... it is obvious that the revisions of the model in the early 1960s predicted rather than concurred with the shift from closed to open system perspectives. In its present state the model is comprehensive, encompassing the closed and open views of organizational life and behavior. . . . In the theoretical contribution of Getzels we see the linkages between the past and present of the field of educational administration and possibly the shape of a future paradigm whose absence is so greatly and generally deplored. (1983, pp. 13–14)

McPherson's observation that the initial Getzels-Guba model evolved over time into a more comprehensive social systems framework for viewing educational administration seems well founded.

Another example of an attempt to develop a synthesis of the theoretical work in educational administration was set forth by Wayne Hoy and Cecil Miskel (1987, Chap. 3). In their treatment of the school as a social system, they present an expanded model. Their reliance on the work of Getzels and Guba is acknowledged, but there are some interesting amplifications. With respect to the normative dimension, they suggest that bureaucratic expectations may be a better explanation than role expectations. Regarding the personal dimension, they contend that work motivation is the single most relevant set of needs. They also deal extensively with the nature of the work group and with organizational goals. In sum, Hoy and Miskel contend that in a

> social-systems model for schools, organizational behavior is determined by the interaction of at least four key elements—bureaucratic expectations, informal norms, individual needs and motives, and organizational goals. Moreover, all the elements and interactions within the system are constrained by important demands from the environment as the organization solves the imperative problems of adaptation, goal achievement, integration, and latency. In addition, internal and external feedback mechanisms reinforce appropriate organizational behavior. (pp. 82–83)

One can appreciate this effort to bring into relationship the many factors that seem to affect organizational behavior. Clearly, organizational behavior is a complex matter and thus many variables are involved. It may be, however, that an attempt to place all these variables in a single model makes the model too cumbersome to be useful. Parsimony, a desirable characteristic of any theory, may have been violated.

SUMMARY

This chapter began by grouping the four major views of administration into two broad categories: those dealing with organizations and those dealing with individuals. The stability of these two concerns suggests that each may capture some aspects of administrative behavior. Moreover, it seems that each view may inform certain kinds of administrative problems. It was then noted that some scholars found a single view of administration unacceptable. For them, there were at least two dimensions to organizational behavior. These formulations included the effectiveness and efficiency concepts of Barnard, the personal and organizational requirements of Argyris, the initiating structure and consideration constructs of Halpin, and the normative and personal dimensions of Getzels.

At this point, a number of recent thrusts in the field were discussed. These included an emphasis on phenomenology by Greenfield and others; a call by Hodgkinson to recognize the centrality of values in policy making; the suggestion by Boyd and Immegart that policy analysis represented a new synthesis for the field; an exposition of self-interest as the chief motivating power in organizations as set forth by Michaelsen; and the concept of organizational culture exemplified by the work of Wolcott.

Other scholars sensed a fragmentation in the field and sought to provide a synthesis. Noted were the efforts of Scott, Getzels, and Hoy and Miskel. All these attempts at new thought—whether an adaptation of an earlier view, a two-dimensional stance, a recent thrust, or a proposed synthesis—demonstrated a certain vitality in the field.

PART II

THE EVOLUTION
OF
ADMINISTRATIVE PRACTICE

7

EVOLVING ADMINISTRATIVE PRACTICES IN PUBLIC SCHOOLS

THE HISTORY OF EDUCATIONAL ADMINISTRATION is closely intertwined with the development of public education in general. This chapter will treat those aspects of educational history that are most pertinent to the development of administrative practices. The transition from lay to professional administration, professional developments in the field of educational administration, and administrative behavior in the schools, to the extent that it can be determined, will be examined. Since objective descriptions of administrative practices over the century are relatively scarce, the assumptions and beliefs that underlie administrative practices will, at times, also be noted.

FROM LAY TO PROFESSIONAL ADMINISTRATION

The contemporary American city or suburban school system with its complex organization, highly trained administrative specialists, and hierarchical authority structure is a stunning contrast to the early town meetings of residents. When schools first appeared in colonial New England, there were no professionally trained teachers or administrators and no lay school boards as they are known today. Schools were established and maintained by local communities to meet local needs. This tradition of local control continued when the U. S. Constitution left responsibility for education to the states. Although the early schools were typically established by local initiative, legal control of education eventually became a responsibility of the states. In colonial America, communities sometimes operated schools by virtue of enabling acts of colonial legislatures, but state leadership and control were not strongly felt until early in the nineteenth century (Brubacher, 1966, p. 547). State leadership emerged when agricultural life in small, isolated communities began to give way to the development of manufacturing and the rapid growth of towns and cities (Cubberley, 1928, p. 9).

Lay Administration

An early and characteristic example of the relationship between states and local communities was the Education Act, passed by the Massachusetts legislature in 1789, which required every town to provide an elementary school and the larger towns to support grammar schools (Callahan, 1975, p. 19). The law further required towns to certify teachers and authorized the establishment of special committees to regulate the schools.

Because early American communities were small and rural, the governance of public schools remained comfortably in the hands of town councils and their committees. The first American schools were small, ungraded, and staffed by teachers who were poorly paid and not highly educated themselves. Managing such schools was not a complicated or arduous task. During the colonial period, it was not uncommon for conflicts among community residents and school committees to erupt over such issues as where to place the schoolhouse or which teachers to hire and fire (Tyack, 1974, p. 17).

Throughout the seventeenth and eighteenth centuries, the rural one-room school was the typical pattern of school organization. However, as populations became more concentrated, schools grew in size and complexity. One-room schools became graded multi-room schools with several faculty members. The need thus arose for some coordination and internal management, and it became advisable to appoint one teacher as "head teacher" to coordinate the program.

The Principalship

The "head teacher" or principal, as the position was later called, was the first professional position in American schools to have administrative and supervisory responsibilities. Although those responsibilities remained limited in nature until the nineteenth century, the emergence of the principalship nevertheless represented a movement toward professional leadership and management in public education.

The early duties of head teachers or principals included keeping school attendance records, making reports to the lay school committee, attending to the maintenance of the school building, and coordinating the use of school equipment and supplies. Supervisory responsibilities typically involved classifying and promoting students when necessary

(Brubacher, 1966, p. 561). Later, principals often conducted what is now described as inservice training for teachers and became involved in curriculum development.

The principal's role was not accorded much status until city schools became large enough to require a full-time administrator. By the late nineteenth century, urban schools were often divided into departments, each with its own coordinator. Toward the end of the nineteenth century, organization by department gave way to a system of graded courses of study under a single head. By the turn of the twentieth century, the principalship in large cities was well established (National Education Association [NEA], 1928, p. 39).

Until the early years of the twentieth century, most principals were satisfied to attend to routine, clerical tasks. Opportunity for professional leadership was present but rarely seized. A turning point in the development of the principalship was the establishment of the Department of Secondary School Principals in 1916 and the Department of Elementary School Principals in 1920, both units of the NEA. These organizations encouraged scientific study of the principal's problems, and courses on the principalship were soon offered by colleges of education (Pierce, 1935, pp. 22–23).

The nineteenth century was a period of rapid urbanization in America. As people streamed into cities, the task of building and managing schools became far more difficult than it had been in small, rural communities. At first, the response was to increase the size of school committees, and in some cases to divide cities into wards and appoint ward committees to look after the schools. By 1900, there were school boards with as many as 500 members and, because boards of such size became unwieldy and ineffective, board members complained of the workload and the impossibility of discharging their responsibilities effectively (Reller, 1936, p. 17). It soon became untenable for part-time lay board members, regardless of their numbers, to manage large city school systems with rapidly increasing enrollments of immigrant children, many of whom came from non-English speaking countries.

Even as the need for full-time professional administrators to assist city school boards became compelling, it was difficult for lay boards to agree that such professionals should be hired. Opposing the establishment of district-wide professional administration were many teachers and principals who feared a loss of the prerogatives they had enjoyed. Reluctant board members were also concerned about a single leader being in control. Moreover, the tradition of lay control, firmly established by the mid-nineteenth century, did not easily give way to professional leadership and management (Reller, 1936, p. 20).

The District Superintendency

The first superintendents were appointed under various circumstances in response to the rapid growth and complexity of local school districts. Some were appointed in accordance with state legislation; others were selected by city councils, as in Providence in 1838 and Boston in 1851. Between 1837 and 1888, thirty city superintendencies were established (Gilland, 1935, p. 15). In studying the duties of newly appointed superintendents during that period, Gilland (1935, p. 71) found that the superintendents were expected to concern themselves primarily with educational rather than financial matters. Even after early boards appointed superintendents, they themselves remained large and heavily involved in administrative work. No distinction was made between the policy-making function of the boards and the administrative functions of superintendents. Frequently, the responsibilities of superintendents were limited to routine clerical duties and the coordination of instructional programs. In 1896, thirteen years after a superintendent had been appointed, Philadelphia had a central board of thirty-seven and over 400 elected members of ward boards (Griffiths, 1966, p. 11).

The first superintendents were not, for the most part, highly educated or professionally trained; there were no specific training programs for superintendents until the beginning of the twentieth century. A few of the early ones were educated in the liberal arts tradition and saw themselves as scholars or statesmen rather than business managers. Callahan (1966, p. 188) described the superintendents of the period between 1865 and 1920 as scholar-educators who were students of education, teachers of teachers, and educational leaders in the communities they served. Few early superintendents actually fulfilled the role of the scholarly educational leader. There were some exceptions, such as St. Louis' William T. Harris, who later became U. S. Commissioner of Education; Brooklyn's William Maxwell, who later became New York State Commissioner of Education; Boston's John Philbrick; and Cleveland's Lewis Jones. Such men were influential in dignifying and strengthening the leadership role of the superintendent in the late nineteenth century.

The State Superintendency

Although the states provided a legal framework for the establishment of schools, they did not give strong leadership in the formative period of public education. Nevertheless, the first school superintendency in the United States was at the state level. New York State, in 1812, was the first state to appoint a superintendent. The office was abolished in 1821 but reestablished in 1854 (American Association of School Administrators [AASA], 1951, p. 41). By 1850, all northern and many southern states had chief state school officers.

Duties of the early state superintendents typically included visiting local school districts, advising local authorities, and giving advice on proposed new programs (AASA, 1951, p. 42). State leadership and regulation evolved slowly over a long period of time, even though the Tenth Amendment to the U. S. Constitution was interpreted to mean that the states were legally responsible for organizing and regulating public schools. State constitutions assigned responsibility for public education to state government. As states became more involved in meeting their constitutional responsibilities, the role of chief state school officers expanded to include development of courses of study, codification of school law, supervision of finances, certification of teachers, statistical reporting, and initiating new school legislation. With few exceptions, however, state leadership in public education was not strong during the nineteenth century.

A handful of early chief state school officers became articulate and persuasive spokesmen for public education. They marshalled public support for education and lobbied legislatures in support of public schools, established teacher training programs, and provided leadership to teachers and administrators in local school districts. Largely through their efforts, the principles of universal, publicly financed education with state support took root in the nation and became a common pattern (Campbell et al., 1985, p. 53).

State school organizations emerged gradually. Developments within the office of the superintendent of public instruction in Illinois, for example, suggested the pattern of growth and specialization typical of many states. In 1907, the superintendent's office comprised three major divisions—country schools, law, and publicity. Five years later, new divisions were added—one to supervise high schools and one to collect educational statistics. Over the next two decades, the scope of the superintendent's office grew appreciably, and new personnel were recruited to administer programs in art, vocational and industrial education, home economics, and kindergartens and to issue textbooks. By 1934, the superintendent's staff consisted of fourteen professional educators and twenty other individuals in support positions. By the mid-1960s, three decades later, the number of people employed in the office

had risen to nearly 200 as departmental responsibilities for the development, coordination, and supervision of programs continued to grow
(Ferris, 1969, p. 359).

Clarifying the Roles
of School Boards and Superintendents

As indicated, lay school board members were slow to give up their
powers, prerogatives, and authority. The size of school boards continued to remain large and unwieldy. Between 1870 and 1898, the
number of pupils in schools more than doubled to over fifteen million.
The rapid increase was due to both population growth and compulsory
attendance laws enacted during that period. Fourteen million immigrants settled in cities between 1865 and 1900 (Callahan 1966, p. 32).
City school districts were plagued by inadequate physical facilities,
crowded classrooms, poorly trained teachers, and lack of resources.

It is not surprising that under such conditions, superintendents,
although not professionally trained at the time, became restless for
more authority to deal with the educational problems they faced. Then,
too, these early superintendents, as Tyack observed, saw their task "as
an evangelical enterprise, a search for an organizational means to
realize the goal of creating a 'redeemer nation'" (1976, p. 258).

School board members were sometimes inept, politically motivated, and subject to the temptation of giving favors in the awarding of
building contracts and the hiring of teachers. After observing conditions in public schools in thirty-six cities in 1892, Joseph M. Rice (1893,
p. 19), a pediatrician and school critic, argued that schools should be
taken out of the hands of politicians and turned over to competent
educators. He urged school boards to give superintendents autonomy
sufficient to improve conditions in the schools.

In February 1893, the "Committee of 15" was established by the
Department of Superintendents of the National Education Association
to examine, among other things, the organization of city school systems. The subcommittee on school organization was chaired by Andrew S. Draper, then superintendent of the Cleveland city schools. The
committee recommended that city school boards should be small, appointed by the mayor, and divorced from partisan politics. The Draper
report urged boards to legislate and give superintendents independent
authority to supervise and fire staff and exercise control over the
instructional program (Callahan, 1966, pp. 96–98). The report was
highly critical of school boards and urged that the independent power

of superintendents be secured by a law requiring five- to ten-year term contracts.

The Draper report precipitated a vigorous national debate on what the role of the superintendent should be. William G. Bruce, then editor of the *American School Board Journal*, led the opposition. In a critique of the report entitled "The Czar Movement," Bruce argued that school boards should retain both legislative and management functions (Callahan, 1966, p. 107). He portrayed Draper and his colleagues as despots who were trying to turn school boards into rubber stamps. A number of superintendents at the time joined the debate, arguing that superintendents needed more authority, prestige, and security to cope with the complex problems of urban school districts. Superintendents John Philbrick, Thomas Bicknell, Emerson White, William Maxwell, and the President of Columbia University, Nicholas Murray Butler, were leading proponents for strengthening the leadership role of superintendents. Although the issue was never fully resolved, the Draper report had an effect on many school boards. By the turn of the century, superintendents had gained considerable authority in the administration of school affairs. School boards retained legal control, but the trend to delegate administrative authority to superintendents was clearly established.

The Draper report reflected the progressive theme evident in business and public administration during this period. For the progressives, the ideal model for governance was the corporate model of management by trained professionals who were insulated from partisan political influence. Professional experts were thought by business leaders to be more appropriate than lay leadership for governing large, complex organizations such as corporations or city school districts. School districts were frequently compared with corporations: School boards were described as boards of directors, superintendents as executives, and teachers as workers. Tyack and Hansot concluded that "businessmen were active in the political movement to abolish ward school boards and to refashion urban systems on the corporate model" (1982, p. 108).

As a result of these and other changes, schools were buffered from partisan politics, and school boards were generally reduced in size. However, superintendents were not given legal status and power independent of school boards. School boards retained legal authority to govern local schools under state law and authority to hire and fire superintendents. This key relationship between school boards and superintendents continues to this day. The conventional wisdom has been that school boards should set policies and superintendents should implement board policies and manage the day-to-day affairs of school districts. In practice, however, this differentiation has been difficult to establish.

DEVELOPMENTS IN THE FIELD

Growth of Specialization

As cities grew in size and complexity, it was not uncommon for school boards to appoint two co-equal district superintendents, both of whom reported directly to the board. One was in charge of the educational program and the other was responsible for the financial affairs of the district. This pattern, however, has all but disappeared during the present century in favor of one chief executive officer responsible for all phases of a district's organization and operation. Superintendents were gradually given assistants to relieve them of certain tasks. Thus began, after the Civil War, the proliferation of specialized administrative roles in large school districts, most notably in such areas as curriculum, supervision, school business, staff personnel, pupil personnel services, public relations, building maintenance, and, more recently, data-processing services, federal relations, and negotiations-contract administration.

These specialized administrative roles were paralleled by the development of professional organizations, specialized literature in the form of textbooks and journals, and specialized certification requirements in many states. Beginning at the turn of the twentieth century, it became increasingly common for some school administrators to pursue careers as school business managers or curriculum supervisors. Specialist positions were found primarily in city and large suburban school districts. In small, rural districts, principals and superintendents assumed responsibility for all administrative activities. In larger districts, superintendents directed, coordinated, and evaluated the work of other administrative specialists in both line and staff positions. The growth of administration can be seen in the fact that today there are an estimated 51,000 central office administrators and supervisors. Additional administrative assistants, both generalists and specialists, are commonly found in large school buildings, particularly at the secondary level. By the mid-1970s, school administration had become a highly diversified profession.

Like superintendents and principals, most central office administrators began their careers as classroom teachers and were appointed to their first administrative position by age 30. In recent years, women have been better represented in central office positions than in the superintendency and principalship. It is estimated that today a little less than one-third of central office administrative positions are held by women. Generally, women are concentrated in lower-level central office positions (Kimbrough & Nunnery, 1983, p. 22).

As districts grew in student enrollment, central office administrators were added in one or more of the major administrative task areas, such as curriculum and business management. Sometimes, large districts were divided into areas and assistant superintendents assigned to administer and coordinate the day-to-day affairs of schools within each area. In large districts, second- and third-echelon administrators and supervisors were appointed to serve under the direction of assistant superintendents. The chief business officer of a large district, for example, often supervised a purchasing agent, a director of buildings and grounds, a transportation director, a food services director, and an accountant, while indirectly overseeing the work of a number of clerks and secretaries.

The emergence of an administrative hierarchy and specialized administrative roles in recent decades complicated the governance of school districts. No longer was the issue simply a matter of the relative roles and responsibilities of the superintendent and the school board. Issues concerning the relationship among line and staff positions, and between generalists and specialists inevitably arose in the decision-making process.

Impact of Collective Bargaining

Prior to the 1960s, teachers had little influence on school board or administrative decisions. Although the National Education Association (NEA) was organized in 1857, its policies and leadership were dominated by college presidents and school administrators until the 1960s (Cresswell et al., 1980, p. 60). A classroom teacher was not elected president of the NEA until 1928, and even as late as 1946 only three teachers had served as president (Cresswell et al., 1980, p. 61). For nearly a century, the NEA and teachers generally functioned under the assumptions that there was a common interest and bond among all educators and that the best way for educators to increase their personal welfare was to improve the quality of education. The NEA became an umbrella organization for virtually all associations of professional educators, including administrators, supervisors, and principals. The major concerns of the NEA and its many departments at the time were to raise professional standards, promote public support, and increase the quality of public education.

The only serious competitor of the NEA for teacher allegiance was the American Federation of Teachers (AFT), which was organized in 1916 by teachers in Chicago and Gary, Indiana who felt that the NEA was not sufficiently concerned with teacher welfare issues. Prior to that time, the Chicago Teachers' Federation was formed and was affiliated with the Chicago Federation of Labor until it was prohibited from doing so by the Chicago Board of Education. From the outset, the AFT was union oriented and maintained close ties with the American Federation of Labor (AFL). The platform of the AFT called for the right of teachers to organize and affiliate with labor, voiced the need to make teachers' salaries commensurate with the important work teachers do, and urged that adequate pension programs for teachers be established (Cresswell et al., 1980, pp. 74-75). The AFT appealed mainly to teachers in large cities, where the labor movement was strong. The first collective bargaining contract was won by an AFT affiliate in Cicero, Illinois in 1944. However, the AFT did not become a major force until its New York City affiliate, the United Federation of Teachers (UFT), won exclusive representation rights for New York City's 40,000 teachers in 1961.

Until the early 1960s, the NEA prided itself on its professional orientation and denounced the labor methods of the AFT as unworthy of a true profession. The stunning 1960 victory of the UFT in New York City, however, was a turning point for the NEA. The attitude of teachers was changing. Militancy was on the rise. The UFT won large salary increases and other concessions on class size and policy-making prerogatives in the three years following its assumption of power. The AFT soon won exclusive bargaining rights in a number of other major cities. Clearly there was a new movement underway in the teaching profession, and the NEA responded. Over a period of several years, the NEA became an advocate of collective negotiations, grievance procedures, and "withdrawal of services," if necessary. By 1968, the NEA had essentially adopted the labor-oriented philosophy of the AFT. The growing militancy of the NEA slowly broke up the coalition of professional organizations, such as the American Association of School Administrators (AASA) and the Association for Supervision and Curriculum Development (ASCD), under the NEA umbrella. By 1975, all departments whose members were not classroom teachers had become independent organizations.

In public education, collective bargaining became a pervasive phenomenon. When school boards agreed or were compelled to bargain with teachers and other employees, they surrendered some of their governing prerogatives. Even when the scope of bargaining was limited to wages, benefits, and working conditions, board and superintendent prerogatives were reduced significantly. Typically, 65 to 85 percent of the school budget supported salaries and fringe benefits. Decisions made through collective bargaining severely restricted other options that had financial implications. Moreover, not only did board members and superintendents have to deal with teachers in collective bargaining, but it was not uncommon for mediators, fact finders, arbitrators, attorneys, and even mayors and governors as well to become involved in resolving collective bargaining issues (Cresswell et al., 1980, p. 395).

Collective bargaining made teachers and other employee groups major contributors to the school governance process. In the face of rising teacher militancy, superintendents and principals came to realize the need to acquire skills in bargaining, grievance administration, mediation, contract administration, conflict resolution, and consensus building. Education writer Myron Lieberman, once a strong advocate of collective bargaining in education, now believes that teachers have gained too much power and dominate the decision-making process at the expense of board members, administrators, and ultimately the public (1981, pp. 232–234). Whether or not this is true, teachers are unlikely to give up the power and prerogatives they have won.

Career Patterns of Superintendents

The career ladder leading to the superintendency has been relatively long compared with many other professions, such as medicine, law, engineering, and architecture. Almost all superintendents began their professional life as teachers; after several years of teaching, they became school administrators. The career of Harold Spears, for example, who served as superintendent of the San Francisco School District from 1955 to 1967, was typical. He began his career as a teacher in Evansville, Indiana. Eventually, he was appointed principal and then curriculum director in Evansville. After earning his doctorate at Teachers College, Columbia University, he became superintendent of a small district in Illinois at age 39. Three years later he left Illinois to become head of the Department of Education at Montclair Teachers College in New Jersey. In 1947, he accepted the position of curriculum director in San Francisco. After two years, he was promoted to assistant superintendent for elementary schools and finally to superintendent in 1955. He was 53 years old at the time and remained in the position until retirement (Cuban, 1976, p. 59).

The superintendency has never been a career of great security and stability. Most superintendents were appointed by school board members for contract periods of from two to five years. School board members come and go, so that it was not uncommon for a superintendent to find, at the end of a first three-year term, that the majority membership of the school board had changed. The new majority might or might not have expectations similar to those of the earlier board. Moreover, conditions and circumstances in local school districts often changed rapidly. The leadership style of an incumbent superintendent might have been appropriate and effective in one set of circumstances but ineffective in a different set.

A case in point is the superintendency of Benjamin Willis in Chicago from 1953 to 1966. Historian Larry Cuban (1976, Chap. 1) traced Willis' career through those years of social change and upheaval. Willis arrived in Chicago during the relatively placid 1950s, when the major challenge facing the Chicago School District was a rapid increase in enrollment. He became a builder of schools par excellence. By 1962, he had directly supervised the building of over one hundred new schools and an equal number of additions representing over 126,000 new classroom stations. He had eliminated double shifts and reduced the average class size from 40 to 32. During those same years, the single salary schedule was instituted and teachers' salaries doubled. A number of important curriculum improvements were also achieved. Willis was praised widely for his prodigious accomplishments. In 1961, the budding civil rights movement began to manifest itself in the form of criticism of segregated schools in Chicago. For the next five years, Willis had a running battle with civil rights groups that grew in intensity until Willis resigned in 1966 under pressure from the school board. Willis was highly effective as a builder, but much less effective as a negotiator and mediator during the tumultuous civil rights era of the 1960s.

In recent years, superintendents have typically had short tenures, particularly in the troubled big cities. In 1982, the average tenure in one position for all superintendents was 5.6 years, and the average number of total years in the superintendency was 7 (Cunningham & Hentges, 1982, p. 55). Superintendents began their careers rather late and served relatively few years in individual superintendencies and in total years of service as a superintendent. In addition to social factors affecting the tenure of superintendents, Richard Carlson (1962) found that the nature of the appointment itself also affected tenure. Superintendents appointed from inside the organization sought less change than did superintendents recruited from outside the organization. "Insiders" also tended to have longer tenure than did "outsiders."

Traditionally, school superintendents have been predominately Caucasian males from rural, small town backgrounds. The percentage of women and minorities in the superintendency has been and continues to be very low.

Upgrading School Administrators

A major theme in many recent studies and reports on public education has been the critical need for effective leadership in public education at the building, district, and state levels. Such reports generally assumed that the quality of leadership in public schools is directly related to the improvement of education. Among recommendations for attracting and holding capable people in school administration were improved selection and preparation programs, economic incentives, and opportunities to exercise educational leadership.

Compared with teaching, school administration offers greater financial rewards. Historically, a large part of the advantage has been the opportunity for full-year rather than nine-month employment. Teachers who aspired to administration primarily because of the lure of a higher salary did not always have a high interest in or potential for administration. Yet, it was relatively easy for many of them to pursue graduate course work in administration on a part-time basis and eventually earn an administrative credential. This has been a common pattern in the past, which sometimes resulted in ineffectual administrative leadership.

Several trends stimulated by the recent reform movement appeared to hold promise for attracting more capable people to school administration. School districts, stimulated by the press and other forces for reform, became more careful about selecting administrators. In many cases, school districts established their own training programs for prospective administrators and insisted on successful completion of the training program for district employees as a prerequisite to consideration for an administrative appointment. Many districts that once considered only internal candidates for administrative appointments began advertising outside the district, with the commitment to hire the best available candidates.

The National Association of Secondary School Principals developed assessment procedures that some school districts and departments of educational administration used as a screening tool. In some instances,

school districts and schools of education became more collaborative in
jointly identifying critical skills associated with effective administration
and cooperatively planning preservice and inservice programs designed
to develop such skills.

RELATIONSHIP OF THOUGHT AND PRACTICE

The evolution of administrative positions in the public schools has been
noted, and a number of professional developments affecting school
administration have been considered. It is now possible to examine the
relationship between administrative thought and practice, and the
points in the past where the major views of administration have become embodied in administrative practices.

The task of describing how administrative ideologies are translated
into practice is made difficult by several factors. First, most practitioners do not keep a detailed written record of their day-to-day administrative work, which makes it difficult to discover the origins of their
ideas or to trace through their application. Also, there have been few
instances (particularly in the past) where trained observers have recorded the activities of individual school administrators (again, such
recording might assist in illustrating what prompts administrators to
behave in certain ways or implement certain practices). Added to this is
the fact that writings on administration have often been more prescriptive or exhortative than descriptive or analytical in character. Finally,
theorists have frequently advocated administrative changes without
describing the processes by which such changes could be brought
about.

Another difficulty encountered in determining the relationships
between thought and practice lies in the great variety of administrative
styles encountered. Some administrators emphasize organizational efficiency; others focus on human relations. Still others demonstrate
political astuteness, and some devote their attention to curriculum
improvement. These differences in administrative style and focus make
generalizations about the relationship between thought and practice
difficult to make and tenuous at best. However, notwithstanding such
factors, historical evidence can be used to illuminate, however imper-
fectly, the nature of this relationship. This evidence will now be used to
suggest to what extent four major views of administration discussed
earlier—scientific management, human relations, bureaucratic administration, and open systems—have been reflected, or have found expression, in administrative practices in the schools.

Scientific Management

Chapter 2 discussed the adoption of scientific management ideas by leading educators. It is now possible to look more closely at the translation of such ideas into practice.

As noted earlier, Superintendent Frank Spaulding's 1913 NEA address in Philadelphia represented one of the first attempts to apply Taylor's principles to school administration. Spaulding, of course, had used such concepts in administering his own district. Students in the Newton grammar schools had been tested for achievement in all school subjects; the results had led Spaulding (1913, p. 261) to conclude that such scientific testing provided "not a perfect nor a complete, but an exceedingly valuable comparative measure of the quality of education afforded by the . . . schools."

Scientific management ideas were also reflected around this time in the general testing movement. Two prominent members of the test construction business were S. A. Curtis, supervisor of research for the Detroit school system and Leonard Ayres of the Russell Sage Foundation. Arithmetic tests designed by Curtis in 1909 were widely used in schools at least until the time of the Great Depression. In one year, Curtis distributed more than 450,000 tests to schools in 42 states (Barr & Burton, 1926, p. 93). Ayres' 1913 study, "A Measuring Scale for Ability in Spelling," was also popular with school officials across the nation in the early decades of the twentieth century.

Closely allied with the testing programs was the advent of the school survey movement. Hollis Caswell, a graduate of Teachers College, Columbia University, examined the school survey movement and, after identifying 181 such studies of city school systems between 1910 and 1927 (and many more were conducted at state and rural levels), concluded:

> Once underway, the survey movement spread with great rapidity. This advance was due in no small measure to the great emphasis placed on educational measurements and standards in education at that time. Achievement and intelligence tests were being developed. Statistical methods were everywhere being applied to school problems. The survey movement supplemented this larger scientific movement and in a measure was carried forward by the widespread enthusiasm of the time. (1929, p. 104)

Once completed, these survey reports did not simply occupy shelf space; rather, they made a considerable difference to school practices.

Caswell (1929, pp. 72–74) examined specific changes growing out of surveys in fifty school systems and found that thirty-four of these school systems reported curriculum changes—half of which were a direct result of the surveys and an additional quarter of which were indirectly brought about by the surveys. Surveys prompted similar changes to long-term plant programs. As Caswell noted, the influence of surveys was more pervasive than this: "Standards and methods of measurement for administrative purposes, which have been developed through surveys, have vitally influenced all educational development" (1929, p. 106).

Still another reflection of scientific management in the schools was the creation and spread of the platoon school. William Wirt, school superintendent at Bluffton, Indiana, was an early pioneer of the platoon school idea. After eight years of experimentation with the platoon plan in his own school system, Wirt was employed by the Gary, Indiana school board to institute the platoon plan in that city.

Sometimes known as the "work-study-play" school, the platoon school invoked John Dewey's ideas about an activity pedagogy and attempted to provide a well-rounded educational program at the lowest possible cost by maximizing the use of the school plant. For example, in a simple platoon arrangement of eight groups of pupils, there would be four home rooms and four special rooms, often one each for art, music, physical education, and auditorium. Each group or platoon would spend one-half day in the home room, where the basic subjects were taught, and one-half day in the four special rooms, a 45-minute period in each. Each home room teacher had two groups, one in the morning and the other in the afternoon: the home rooms were utilized every minute of the school day. Each special teacher would meet eight groups during the day, so that each special room also was utilized every minute of the school day.

At the request of the U. S. Commissioner of Education, W. P. Burris examined the Gary schools in 1914 and had this to report:

> The superintendent and the board of education of the Gary schools have succeeded in working out plans for a more economic use of school funds, a fuller and more efficient use of the time of the children, a better adjustment of the work of the schools to the needs of the individual children, greater economy in supervision, better correlation of the so-called "regular work" and "special activities" of the school, and at a cost less nearly prohibitive than is usually found in public schools in cities of this country. (Case, 1931, p. 7)

With a report of this kind, it is little wonder that the practice spread. Whereas in 1914 there were only twenty school systems using the platoon plan, by 1929 Case reported that more than one thousand school systems had established such schools (1931, p. 27).

Not every school system used standardized tests extensively, employed outside consultants to conduct school surveys, or established platoon schools. But school administrators and their boards of education in many school districts generally relied on information provided by standardized tests for instructional organization and evaluation, used outside experts to examine all aspects of the program of the district—from curriculum to finance—in an effort to achieve greater efficiency, and adopted the platoon school organization or some version of it to maximize plant and staff use. While there may have been more advocacy than practice of scientific management in the schools, efficiency efforts were widespread during the early part of this century and administrative thought and practice tended to correspond.

Democratic Administration   *Human Relations*

The extent to which administrative practice in the 1930s, 1940s, and 1950s reflected democratic and human relations views about organization is more difficult to determine, largely because of the amorphous nature of these concepts. Neither democratic nor human relations approaches set out a strict plan to revise school practices; rather, such views were more exhortative in character. Nevertheless, in a number of ways it can be seen how democratic and human relations ideas about school management were translated into practice.

For instance, it is apparent that these ideas were much on the minds of practitioners as well as professors during the interwar era. For the three-year period 1939–1941, the *Education Index* lists forty-five journal articles (many of which were written by superintendents and principals) that contain the word "democracy" or one of its derivatives in their titles. This count does not include titles where such words as "cooperative" or "participative" were used to describe administrative approaches.

Practitioner interest in democratic administration can also be seen in the publications of professional associations. The American Association of School Administrators' 1955 Yearbook, *Staff Relations in School Administration*, stated that the Yearbook Commission (composed of four superintendents, among others) had been guided by the belief that "school administration must be a cooperative enterprise," and that "such convictions imply a leaning toward *democratic school administration* as opposed to the older concept of *control based on power, status and authority*" (AASA, 1955, p. 5).

Further illustration of practitioner interest in democratic management is found in the Department of Supervisors and Directors of Instruction 1938 Yearbook entitled *Cooperation: Principles and Practices.* This volume, half of which focused on cooperative practices, contained a report by O. S. Williams on a case study of a suburban community with a population of 20,000 where teacher participation was provided through a council that reported to the superintendent. After two years of experience with this approach to management, 74 percent of teachers indicated that they desired to participate in formulating administrative policies, and 98 percent indicated "that they were willing to accept the responsibility that is an integral part of group planning and thinking" (Department of Supervisors and Directors of Instruction, 1938, p. 138).

A second case pertained to a survey of cooperative practices in the schools; the survey was conducted by E. T. McSwain. Some 4,000 copies of a survey questionnaire were sent to teachers and administrators in 55 school systems located in 22 states. When asked about the participation of teachers in policy formation, the administrators reported the extent of teacher involvement in various areas as follows: preparing courses of study, 80 percent; preparing the budget, 74 percent; and evaluating personnel, 63 percent. Participation reported by teachers in these same areas was: courses of study, 75 percent; budget, 32 percent; and evaluating personnel, 35 percent. While differences in the perceptions of administrators and teachers were readily apparent, the results indicated that teachers were participating to some degree in the formulation of policy in these school systems.

On the eve of World War II, a more definitive study of teacher participation was conducted by Wilber E. Moser (1939, pp. 50–52). He differentiated among four types of participation ranging from complete cooperation (Type I) at one end of the scale and complete administration autonomy (Type IV) at the other. Moser asked teachers and administrators in over one hundred California school districts to rate levels of teacher participation in ten areas of decision making. Again, in actual study of practice, Moser found that although perceptions of teachers and administrators varied, democratic administration was being attempted in many school systems.

Inferential evidence also exists that suggests that ideas about democratic school management found their way into the world of the practitioner. As early as the depression years, graduate study programs for school administrators featured courses on cooperative and democratic decision making in work groups (Fleming, 1982, Chap. 6). In the 1930s and 1940s, various agencies for professional development, most notably the National Training Laboratory in the years after 1947, provided teachers, principals, and superintendents with short courses on cooperative decision making and problem solving and on how to work harmoniously with people of different ethnic, racial, religious, and economic backgrounds (Fleming, 1982, Chap. 6). Such developments clearly suggest that democratic and human relations ideas circulated widely and were used by more than professors of education. Although the links between thought and practice are not as pronounced as in the case of scientific management, it is equally evident that many school practitioners were trying to implement democratic ideas.

Bureaucracy

Evidence abounds that school systems and other educational agencies have been bureaucratically organized for some time, even though scholars did not begin to describe them as such until the 1960s and 1970s. In his volume, *Class, Bureaucracy, and Schools*, historian Michael Katz (1975, p. 59) observed that "between 1850 and 1876 the Boston school system became a full-scale bureaucracy," and that this change "illustrated a general process taking place in other aspects of American urban life" (1975, p. 65). Throughout the third quarter of the nineteenth century, Katz noted, the administrative offices of Boston's schools came to exhibit many bureaucratic characteristics, including centralized control and supervision, differentiated functions, special qualifications for services, and the imposition of new standards of objectivity, precision, consistency, and discretion.

In an article entitled, "Bureaucracy and the Common School: The Example of Portland, Oregon, 1851–1913," Stanford's David Tyack likewise concluded that in the years after the mid-nineteenth century, "most American urban school systems became bureaucracies" (1973, p. 164). This movement toward bureaucratization was made manifest in administrative efforts to design new organizational lines of control and to regulate more closely the behaviors of teachers and other staff.

Despite the fact that urban schools had been bureaucratic in their organization for several decades, it was not until the early 1960s that professors of educational administration began to study them from the perspective of Weber's model. Around this time, Gerald Moeller examined the relationships between bureaucracy in school systems and teachers' sense of power, using twenty school systems in the St. Louis metropolitan area for his study. Moeller (1964, p. 139) found, to his surprise, that teachers in more bureaucratized systems had a higher sense of power than those in less bureaucratized systems.

In an empirical study of nearly 900 teachers in urban school systems in and around Toronto, Ontario, Keith Punch (1969, p. 53) found that the schools in that area were bureaucratic organizations and that teachers in those schools were able to identify practices that were the essence of bureaucracy. James Anderson (1968) took a more direct approach to the identification of bureaucratic practices in schools in his attempt to determine to what extent bureaucratic practices were present in the junior high schools of Baltimore. Interestingly enough, Anderson reported that "contrary to expectations, rules appear to mediate authority conflict, making the imposition of hierarchical authority more tolerable to professionals" (1968, p. xi). He also found that "in education rules may be particularly necessary because of the lack of accepted performance measures, difficulty in effectively supervising instruction, and varying degrees of professional competence among teachers trained in the various disciplines" (1968, p. xi).

More recently, Robert Herriott and William Firestone tested two images of schools as organizations: rational bureaucracy and anarchy, or loosely coupled systems. These investigators studied 111 elementary and secondary schools in New Jersey and Pennsylvania. Two major variables, goal consensus and centralization of influence, were used to differentiate the two images, and teachers were asked to report their perceptions on items representing the two variables. What Herriott and Firestone learned was that:

> Schools can be arrayed into two distinct clusters: one with substantially higher goal consensus and centralization of influence than the other. Elementary schools fall almost exclusively into the first cluster and senior high schools in the second cluster, with junior high schools divided between the two. (1984, p. 53)

These findings suggest that elementary schools, even as late as the 1980s, are still reflecting at least some of the characteristics of bureaucracy.

In short, there has been little disagreement that many schools exhibit the characteristics of a bureaucracy or that teachers and administrators see themselves as parts of a bureaucratic system. As Harry Wolcott pointed out after observing an elementary school principal for a year: "Consider how Ed Bell occasionally epitomized the insensitivity

of the bureaucracy, at times ameliorated it, and at times
(usually unintentional) insensitivity and replaced it with a l
tivity of his own" (1978, p. 320). James March's (1978, p. ,
tion that "educational administration is hierarchical," and
systems "use conventional bureaucratic forms of organ
standard ideas of authority, administration, and control" has been well
established by both historians of education and students of educational
administration.

Open Systems

Rationality reconstructed, as found in the bureaucratic view of
administration, was not without its limitations. Flaws in the concept
seemed to be of two kinds: The bureaucratic view focused on organizational concerns and tended to ignore personal concerns; it also focused
on the organization as such and tended to ignore the environment of
the organization. In that sense, bureaucracy was essentially a closed
system, as were democratic administration and scientific management,
concepts that prevailed earlier. But closed systems were no longer
acceptable. Social changes, elaborated on in Chapter 5, impinged upon
organizations, particularly public organizations. The *Brown* decision,
civil rights legislation, the student revolt, and the women's rights movement had a direct and long-term impact on the schools. If thought was
to reflect reality, it became clear that environmental forces, or forces
external to the organization, as well as those internal to the organization had to be taken into account in any concept designed to explain
organizational behavior. Thus, with or without explicit recognition on
the part of many practitioners and scholars, the open-systems view of
administration became a prominent administrative framework in the
1970s. Clearly, administrators in schools and school districts were
forced to give increasing attention to members of their organizations
and to concerned people outside their organizations, a condition set
forth dramatically by Cuban in *Urban School Chiefs Under Fire* (1976),
discussed above.

While the nature and status of teachers' organizations varied
greatly among school districts, these organizations were recognized by
boards of education and teachers' concerns were heard (Johnson, 1983).
At the same time, in many school districts, parent participation was
more widespread and probably more influential than was once the case
(Malen & Ogawa, 1985). But social forces affecting the schools go far
beyond those exerted by teachers and parents. State legislatures and
state boards of education stepped up their concern about the operation

of schools. Michael Kirst, a careful observer of the scene, contends that "the most striking feature of state-local relations in the last 20 years has been the growth in the state control over education" (1984, p. 190). National control, supposedly reduced under the Reagan administration, has remained a force of consequence, as can be seen, for example, in the implementation of programs for the handicapped. Nor have schools escaped the attention of many and sundry interest groups. Some of these groups, such as ethnic and religious groups, often see the schools as key to their demands (Campbell et al., 1985, Chaps. 13–14).

Herriott and Firestone, as noted above, have provided some evidence to suggest that the bureaucratic image of schools is beginning, particularly in secondary schools, to be replaced by a more open image of schools. There is other evidence as well. When a national sample of school superintendents was questioned about the significant issues and challenges they faced in 1982, their first six responses were as follows: financing schools, planning and goal setting, assessing educational outcomes, accountability/credibility, staff and administrator evaluation, and administrator/board relations (Cunningham & Hentges, 1982, p. 38). Five of these challenges reflect conditions and/or expectations in the environment of the school. The evaluation issue reflects greater sensitivity to concerns of people in the organization. All of these responses mirror an open-systems concept.

Willower and Fraser interviewed fifty superintendents regarding their feelings about their work. Some of their responses are summarized below:

> . . . individuals dealing with a range of problems . . . and feeling the pressures of the job but ready to do it over again if they could. Finally, it seems to us that school superintendents are not quite as beleaguered as is sometimes claimed and when they are, they appear to have come to grips with it rather well, often with good humor. (1980, p. 4)

While this study did not focus on the view these superintendents held of administration, the perceptions they held of their work do lend some credence to the open-systems concept of administration. Although the superintendents reportedly coped rather well with the other forces in the environment, the forces were still there and the demands of government were in the background.

The presence of forces outside school organizations that make a difference to school organizations commanded the attention of Frederick Wirt and Michael Kirst in their treatment, *Schools in Conflict*. They rejected completely the once-held myth that schools were apolitical, and instead contend:

> We are not discussing *how* schools should be run. . . . Rather our focus is on *how the process of policy making in schools has characteristics that can be termed political.* We will show how the policy-making process is becoming increasingly and more openly politicized as a result of major changes in how state and local governments and citizens themselves relate to the school system. New definitions of school purposes, new claims on school resources, new efforts to make the schools responsive to certain groups and their values are all giving rise to a larger more weblike set of political relationships surrounding the local school. (1982, p. 2)

While the bureaucratic view of administration may still characterize the operation of many school systems, and the influence of earlier views of administration has not entirely disappeared, it seems clear that school administrators themselves and those who observe administrators recognize that a new formulation, often called open systems, has come onto the scene. On one side, this new view accords more influence to teachers and other members of the organization and may be characterized as "loosely coupled." On the other side, parents and interest group spokespeople as well as government at state and national levels, which are all part of the environment of schools, contend for more influence over the schools. Little wonder that school superintendents have found themselves cast into an advocacy role with patrons, their boards of education, and the state legislature. As principals have become major actors in the move to strengthen school site management, they too have had to give greater recognition to forces in the school environment. While some may regret that the schools have become politicized, most recognize that politics, in the best sense, has to do with the allocation of values and resources. School administrators have been thrust into this kind of political process.

SUMMARY

The history of public school administration in the United States, following a period of lay governance during most of the nineteenth century, has been reviewed here. The growth of city school districts and consolidated rural districts eventually resulted in the appointment of full-time professional administrators to assist lay boards in managing the schools. The struggle to delineate the roles and responsibilities of

school boards and superintendents and the emergence of the principalship and state and city superintendencies have also been noted. As school
districts became larger and more complex in organization and program
development, specialized administrative roles proliferated. Superintendents in larger districts became delegators and coordinators of administrative specialists.

The growth of collective bargaining in public schools gave teachers
and other school employees significant influence in school governance.
Administrators had to acquire specific skills in bargaining, mediating,
sharing power and influence with employee groups.

The relationship between administrative thought and administrative practice in the schools was also examined. A precise answer as to
the extent of congruence between thought and practice cannot be
given. Educational practice in the United States has been very much a
local phenomenon. There are thousands of school districts, and they
vary greatly in terms of size, cultural composition, financial resources,
and administrative outlook. In each of these districts there are from one
to hundreds of school attendance areas, and these also often vary in
many ways. These school and district variations have prevented the
formulation of any homogeneous administrative practice in American
education. Also, most practitioners, unlike most scholars, do not leave
descriptions of their practices, and those who do often have difficulty
being objective about such practices. Nonetheless, sample observations
of school practices were noted and the best inferences possible from
those samples were made. With respect to scientific management,
school administrators during the early part of the century were impressed by the movement, and many of them tried to make their
schools more efficient, particularly through the use of standardized
tests and school surveys. Regarding democratic administration, administrators perceived more participation in administration than did
teachers. Most of the case studies reporting successful democratic
practices were done in smaller, suburban districts, where interpersonal
relations were more easily maintained. Bureaucracy seems to have
crept into school systems much as it did in business and government: as
a convenient response to growth in organizational size and complexity.
While most schools exhibited elements of bureaucratic practice, the
conflict between such practice and the growing professionalism of
teachers required some modification of bureaucracy in schools. In open
systems, much as in bureaucracy, practice may have preceded theory.
The growing power of teachers internally and the increasing concern of
parents and others externally required that schools move from closed
to open systems, even though in some cases reluctantly.

ADMINISTRATIVE PRACTICES IN THE PUBLIC SCHOOLS

Theme

Thus, there has been some relationship between thought and practice. As each view of administration came to center stage, many school administrators reflected, explicitly or implicitly, such a view in their practice. There seem to be plausible reasons why there was not more congruence. Each view of administration has been limited and incomplete. Each view appears to have some relevance for particular problems, in particular places, with particular personnel, and for a particular stage of an organization's development. None of the views set forth depicts reality adequately. Perhaps the other side of this point is that administrators, by the very nature of their jobs, deal with practical problems, not with theoretical niceties.

8

COLLEGE AND UNIVERSITY GOVERNANCE

HIGHER EDUCATION AND PUBLIC EDUCATION have worked in surprising isolation from each other in America, despite their related missions and the fact that millions of students flow directly from one to the other each year. Attempts to link the efforts of those who set policy for and administer these two sectors of American education have come and gone, but their considerable independence from one another has continued due to differences in their origins, purposes, and organization. The field of educational administration, however, has bridged the two systems: In the simplest terms, its practice takes place in schools, and its scholars are housed in universities. Yet its practitioners are prepared in universities, and its scholars study organizational behavior in public education. Finally, of course, colleges and universities are themselves one of the educational arenas in which administration is practiced. For these reasons, the history, governance, and study of higher education are essential to an understanding of educational administration. This chapter traces the rise of the modern university, analyzes thought and scholarship about higher education, and reflects upon the practice of university governance.

There are over 450 doctoral-granting universities, nearly 1,500 baccalaureate institutions, and approximately 1,300 two-year colleges in the United States. These institutions of higher learning range in size from unique Deep Springs College in California, which has a student body of twenty, to campuses such as The Ohio State University or the University of Minnesota that enroll over 50,000 students, to multi-campus systems like the University of California and the State University of New York that far exceed 100,000 students. Further, the spectrum includes everything from local trade schools that grant no degrees, to centers of learning that bring together some of the world's most renowned scholars. Because major universities are the flagships of American higher education, setting standards by which other colleges and universities often measure their progress, the governance of doctoral-granting American universities, both public and private, is the focus of this chapter.

Evolution of Universities and Their Governance

European Beginnings

Universities are the most enduring secular institutions in Western civilization. A few European universities, such as Bologna, claim their beginnings in the twelfth century, and many others appeared in the thirteenth century. The University of Paris traces its origins to 1215, Salamanca to 1218, Padua to 1222, Oxford to 1249, and Cambridge to 1284. By the year 1400, the European landscape was dotted with at least fifty universities. Although they bore little resemblance to modern universities, many of the traditions and values they established have endured.

Many of these early universities originated as cathedral schools, established by Catholic bishops to educate the clergy. But scholarship and religion have seldom been at peace with one another; secular perspectives and values gradually prevailed and the early clerical schools metamorphosed into independent, or partially independent, universities. This process was aided by Pope Gregory IX's bull of 1231, which sanctioned the emerging autonomy of professors at the University of Paris, where the faculty had become a largely self-governing body. Faculty control over curricula and degrees has been stoutly defended ever since.

In the style of medieval guilds, students came from far and near to apprentice with master-scholars, usually conversing in Latin, the pan-European language of the learned. Phrases like *cum laude* still grace diplomas 700 years later; academic robes, doctoral hoods, mortar boards, and presidential medallions are other surviving medieval traditions. Ceremonial customs and academic processions notwithstanding, these early universities were loosely organized. Students were free to affiliate with instructors as they chose, campuses did not exist, and administrative functions such as admissions and registration were yet to be conceived. Licenses to teach, and exams to vouchsafe student progress, emerged very slowly. Further, even in the thirteenth century, universities were regarded by local communities as mixed blessings. Students offended local townspeople by entertaining heretical ideas and raising hell, yet the prestige of prominent thinkers and the excitement of new ideas were matters of enormous pride. When, on occasion, scholars and students made themselves unbearable to villagers, nearby towns clamored to give them a home.

American Colonial Colleges

Sixteen years after the Mayflower landed at Plymouth in 1620, the Massachusetts Colony General Court established Harvard College in Newtowne, later renamed Cambridge in an effort to acquire respect by association. Instruction began in the president's living room (he was the only professor) in 1638; the first nine bachelor of arts degrees were conferred in 1642. Several generations later, The College of William and Mary opened for instruction in Virginia in 1700, Connecticut chartered the Collegiate School (later Yale) in 1701, and the College of New Jersey (later Princeton) received its charter in 1746. These colonial colleges, and others that followed, were devoted to the education of freemen—those who held property sufficient to qualify them as voters. Like their European forebearers, American colonial colleges sought to prepare the sons of the elite for the company of the educated and the governance of the uneducated. They were staffed primarily by clergy, who taught classical languages, literature, rhetoric, geometry, mathematics, and natural and moral philosophy. In the tradition of distinguished British universities, the colonial college was residential, pastoral, and devoted to the aims of building character and nurturing civilized behavior. Educational leadership was exercised by respected clergymen-scholars; cultural advancement and social responsibility were the primary objectives of teaching. Prevailing religious orientations and values were to be served, not questioned.

The first serious attempts to democratize education came with the American revolution. Advocating the Northwest Land Ordinances of 1785 and 1787, Thomas Jefferson suggested that if Americans were to broaden the franchise, they must also broaden opportunities for education. As the proportion of citizens who participated in decision making increased, Jefferson believed, opportunities to understand the public interest must also expand. Although it is not generally known, the Ordinances made provision for higher education as well as public schools.

Rise of Modern Universities

In the latter half of the nineteenth century, one of the ideals of the European enlightenment and the American revolution, that of free inquiry, began to shape and be shaped by the American college. Two major events in the history of American higher education occurred in this period. The Morrill Act of 1862, sponsored by Senator Justin Morrill from Vermont, granted enormous tracts of land to states for the establishment of agricultural and mechanical colleges—most of which later became major research universities. The act was intended both to improve American agriculture by availing future farmers of new scientific knowledge and techniques and to provide America's scattered rural populations access to the refinements conferred by liberal education. The second Morrill Act (1890) and subsequent legislation linked the nation's economic welfare with higher education; America's public universities began to expand their student admissions to include not only the socially elite but also a broad spectrum of the intellectually gifted. Aristocracy began to give way to meritocracy in higher education.

The second major development that influenced the character of higher education in the late nineteenth century was the emergence of the modern German university. The "German model," as it was called, put research and theory at the heart of academe; graduate seminars and advanced study supplanted undergraduate teaching as the primary educational mission. Scholarly objectivity assumed new importance in these centers of experimental research, giving birth to the notion of *Lehrfreiheit*, the principle that grants professors the right to teach and investigate according to their own best judgment. In the closing decades of the nineteenth century and the early years of the twentieth, many of America's most promising young intellects steamed across the Atlantic for advanced study with German mentors in their laboratories and libraries.

The establishment of Johns Hopkins University in 1876, with its graduate school and scholars organized in departments based on the academic disciplines, marked the birth of the modern American university. In succeeding decades, the English model of undergraduate residential colleges, designed to educate citizens for broad service to society, faced stiff competition. American universities that chose to copy the German model grew in number, strength, and sophistication.

By 1915, the newly organized American Association of University Professors (AAUP) was leading the effort to define the values of the new universities. According to a 1915 AAUP statement, academic freedom involved (1) the professor's right to pursue knowledge wherever the quest might lead, coupled with the responsibility to report the results fully and accurately, (2) the right to teach without censorship of one's ideas or materials, provided one stayed within his or her area of acknowledged expertise, and (3) the right to speak without shackles in the public sphere, as long as one spoke as an individual rather than as an official representative of his or her university (AAUP, 1941, pp. 40–43). From that era forward, no other principles have rivaled these for a central place in the hearts and minds of American academicians. Academic tenure, including the elaborate procedures for awarding it to rising scholars, has been justified almost entirely by the need to protect academic freedom. Although the concept of tenure has often come under attack, generally from beyond the campus gates, and academic freedom is sometimes misunderstood even within the gates, both have proven remarkably resistant to change.

In higher education, the years between the two world wars were characterized by the consolidation of concepts and practices associated with the rise of universities. During these years, the proportion of high school graduates who went to college rose from 9 to 15 percent; the nation had 1.5 million college students by 1940. Due largely to their lower tuition, public universities grew much more rapidly than private ones. Even so, universities maintained relatively simple administrative structures. Corson (1975) characterized the typical university president of this period as a "scholar-statesman" who remained active in intellectual pursuits and glided serenely above the turmoil of institutional administration. Academic matters were usually orchestrated by a dean of faculties, and many of the administrative tasks later assumed by specialists—such as student advising and personal counseling—remained the responsibility of professors.

Academe Rises High: 1945 to 1965

Universities, like most social institutions, were transformed by the national emergency of World War II. Professors were asked to serve the public interest even more directly than in the past. Funds for defense-related research, which included organizational and psychological studies, poured into university laboratories. Further, classrooms were packed with aspiring military officers, engineers, and scientists needed to meet the national crisis.

At war's end, Congress enacted one of the most successful pieces of legislation ever devised—Public Law 346, better known as the G.I. Bill. To provide educational benefits to those who had loyally given their prime years to military service, generous allowances were granted to encourage these men and women to make up for lost time. As 16 million Americans laid down their arms, undergraduate enrollments mushroomed. Higher education reeled from the impact. Veterans of the Bataan Death March or the Battle of the Bulge refused to be treated like stripling youths; they brought new seriousness to campus life and challenged old traditions. Graduate enrollments burgeoned, too, as aspiring scholars in the arts and sciences clamored to capitalize on the huge demand for college teachers, and students in professional schools sought careers in arenas of public service that had been left wanting through the war years.

From 1945 to 1970, administrative adaptations were legion. The university presidents of this era tended to be builders rather than scholars. Often coming to academe with major experience in other large organizations, they devoted themselves especially to the tasks of raising money and constructing buildings. As a direct result of the shifting focus of presidential attention, the academic vice presidency emerged as a means to orchestrate educational policy and faculty affairs. The growth in size and specialization of faculties further decentralized administration as the scholarly disciplines became more distinct and academic departments became more autonomous.

A second change that had major implications for university administration occurred during the postwar era. As faculties focused more on research, some of their traditional duties lapsed. Teaching freshmen and sophomores was often farmed out to graduate students, academic and personal counseling gravitated increasingly to master's degree-holding psychologists, and student personnel administrators flocked to nurture the campus environment. Bureaucracy had its day as scores of specialists filled the vacuum created by the faculty's retreat into the laboratory or library. A dual authority structure became more evident in universities. One structure, concerned primarily with academic policy matters, was rooted in the faculty, decentralized, and generally collegial. From the work of departmental committees and faculty senates, to the appointment of chairpersons and deans, the tradition of the scholar-leader survived. The other structure, encompassing centralized and largely nonacademic management functions ranging from libraries to financial aid, and from spectator sports to student activities, became more hierarchical and bureaucratic. Although the academic structure has lost much of its collegiality, leadership within it has continued to pass periodically from professor to professor. By contrast, career administrators became the backbone of the nonacademic structure.

Fall From Grace: 1965 to the Present

Universities were to postwar America what government had been to the Great Depression era and what business had been at the turn of the century—the institution to which Americans turned to solve their most crucial problems. Riding this crest of public appreciation, faculty salaries increased rapidly and institutional prestige waxed strong. But such times never last. Protests associated with the war in Vietnam and the civil rights movement convulsed American campuses in the late 1960s. As college-age citizens died in the jungles of Asia, many who remained at home or returned safely raised serious questions about the purposes and morality of the war. The idealism and political activism of students in this era also did much to sustain the civil rights movement. These phenomena, coupled with the fact that military conscription forced many "involuntary students" into college, made most universities centers of social upheaval. As a result, the traditional gap in intergenerational understanding widened, and legislators and the public began to look askance at the professors from whom they had so recently sought advice.

Funding for higher education began to slacken in the early to mid-1970s. At about the same time, demographic trends caused a leveling off and eventual decline in the 18 to 24 year age group, providing legislators a concrete rationale for cutting higher education appropriations. The campus-builder presidents of the previous decades began to give way to a new type of leader—the mediator or crisis manager. Attorneys, psychologists, and others who possessed unusual skills in mediating conflicts among interest groups were much in demand by governing boards.

Driven by a combination of social idealism and pragmatic aims to bolster enrollments, American universities in the 1970s welcomed members of the new interest groups; minorities, women, the handicapped, and the disadvantaged entered college classrooms in unprecedented numbers (Soloman, 1985). The meritocratic university of the prewar era, which provided opportunities for the most able, became the democratic university of the late twentieth century. New administrative services sprang into being to provide support to these "new constituencies." The flood of federal legislation designed to fund campus programs and enforce regulations to aid the new students also contributed to the growth of bureaucracy in higher education.

The decline of faculty salaries relative to the cost of living in the 1970s stimulated new interest in collective bargaining. The National Labor Relations Board (NLRB) facilitated this movement by bringing nearly all private as well as public institutions under its jurisdiction in 1970. Half the states followed by granting bargaining rights to professors in public colleges and universities. Faculty unions caught on quickly in community colleges and edged up the ladder of institutions, reaching some major universities, especially in the Northeast, before the trend cooled. In general, however, faculties at research universities preferred to take their chances with merit pay and presidential advocacy, rather than relinquish their independent collegial customs. The tradition of the academic governance structure within universities and the instinctive independence of those who chose scholarly careers proved remarkably resistant to bargaining unity. Nor were chairpersons and deans, who were temporary appointees rather than career administrators, stereotypical managers.

Major readjustments in college and university governance began to appear in the 1980s because of declines in the 18 to 24 year age group and public resistance to taxation, illustrated best by California's 1978 passage of Proposition 13. Leadership in austere times is often without glory, and many universities found themselves pressed to attract the imaginative administrative leadership required to sustain their traditional missions. Administrative staffs had to be streamlined, and faculty (whose programs and even jobs were in jeopardy) frequently sought more influence in the bureaucratic structure. In addition, gains made by nontraditional or disadvantaged students in the 1970s, when universities adopted open enrollment policies, were imperiled when staffs were reduced and budgets cut back. The cost of remedial instruction, once accepted as an institutional responsibility, was increasingly shifted to special fees borne by the student.

In a time of retrenchment, power seems to gravitate to the center, yet the university presidents of the 1980s often found themselves able to do little more than mediate differences among contending parties, both internally and externally. Ironically, in public higher education the center often shifted to the state capitol. The creation of multi-campus university systems and state coordinating agencies contributed, along with departmental autonomy, interest group politics, and collective bargaining, to the impotence of presidential leadership. Power was more diffuse than ever and academic reform more difficult to achieve.

It is not surprising that the vast changes in colleges and universities after World War II, coupled with the emergence of new theories of organizational behavior and new methods to test those theories, provided the impetus for a new academic speciality—the field of higher education. The scholars and scholarship of higher education, and the organizational values and administrative practices scholars have sought to understand, are the focus of succeeding sections of this chapter.

STUDY AND PRACTICE IN HIGHER EDUCATION

It is important at the outset to distinguish between the general term higher education, which refers to that part of the educational system that begins where the high schools end, and the specific use of the term that defines the academic field devoted to the study of colleges and universities. Professors who hold appointments in the scholarly field of higher education have traditionally concerned themselves broadly with the philosophy and nature of colleges and universities, rather than focusing their attention primarily on organizational or administrative matters. This is one reason that the theoretical and empirical study of universities as organizations has flowered only recently.

Scholars of higher education have tended to take a broader view because professors hold much more authority in universities than do teachers in public schools. Since most academic administrators are themselves professors who agree to serve only fixed terms as a chairperson, dean, or academic vice president, it is difficult to study administrative affairs in higher education as though they were separate from faculty affairs and faculty values. When one reflects that the literature of higher education has been written primarily by professors who study about the people and institutions that make up their own profession, their perspective is quite understandable.

The history of thought and scholarship about higher education should be considered in light of the evolution of American universities described in the previous section. There are two salient considerations. First is the coexistence in universities of the two structures of authority: one that manages the supporting services, and the other that deals with the "production functions" of scholarship, teaching, and learning (Corson, 1960). This separation alone accounts for much of the confusion that surrounds both the study and the practice of administration in higher education. Second, the formal study of academic governance has come very late because of its bewildering complexity, the broader orientation of higher education professors, and the fact that any insights gained have been thought to lack applicability in other kinds of institutions.

Although most universities, unlike most schools or school systems, have maintained excellent archives, records of administrative behavior are scattered and historians have made comparatively little use of them. Much of the literature about higher education governance has been descriptive, however, thus providing an impressive accumulation of contemporary accounts of how universities have administered their affairs since the 1940s. Knowledge of practice and thought about higher education governance are therefore intertwined, and they are treated in relation to each other in the ensuing pages. To understand the emergence of the study of higher education, however, it is useful to go back more than a century and consider the origin of thought about universities.

The "Sacred Literature"

The literature of higher education can be said to begin with a series of eight discourses delivered by John Henry Newman "to the Catholics of Dublin." This former Anglican vicar who converted to Catholicism in 1845 was determined to establish a Catholic university in Ireland. His initial lectures were published in 1852, revised and reissued in 1859, and expanded with ten additional essays under the well-known title *The Idea of a University* in 1873 (Newman, 1947). Later elevated to Cardinal, Newman set out to reconcile the rising conflict between religion and science, between revealed truth and discovered truth. He articulated or anticipated most of the values that have become central to the universities of the Western world. Believing that ecclesiastical interference with the work of scholars, whether scientists or humanists, would deal a death blow to the idea of a university, Newman warned that "unless a scholar is at liberty to investigate on the basis, and according to the peculiarities, of his science, he cannot investigate at all" (p. 349).

While the notion of academic freedom was in its infancy, even in Germany, Newman's larger contributions were in defining the purposes of universities and of liberal learning:

> But a University . . . aims at raising the intellectual tone of society, at cultivating the public mind, at purifying the national taste, at supplying true principles to popular enthusiasm and fixed aims to popular aspiration, at giving enlargement and sobriety to the ideas of the age, at facilitating the exercise of political power, and refining the intercourse of private life. (1947, p. 157)

If universities were to provide this leaven for society, they would do it, according to Newman, by distinguishing between useful and liberal knowledge. "I am prepared to maintain," he said, "that there is a knowledge worth possessing for what it is, and not merely for what it does" (p. 101). In contrast to "commercial education," liberal education should develop "a habit of mind which lasts through life, of which the attributes are, freedom, equitableness, calmness, moderation, and wisdom." (p. 90)

The Idea of a University is the first and foremost example of what might be called the "sacred literature" of higher education. Though few presidents, deans, or professors may have read Newman, his notions, and even his phraseology, remain widely held academic articles of faith. Universities continue to pride themselves on resisting external pressures, whether from church or state, on prizing knowledge for its own sake (as well as for its application), and on enlarging on or criticizing the prevailing ideas of the societies in which they exist.

Several major works published during the first four decades of the twentieth century may also qualify as "sacred literature." Each of the authors devoted his attention to the goals of twentieth-century universities, reflecting or reacting to the influence of the German graduate schools. Thorstein Veblen's *The Higher Learning in America* was published in 1918. An economist and social critic, Veblen took the view that universities should focus singly on scientific and scholarly research. Aside from training advanced students, who would apprentice directly with scholars in their own area of research, Veblen contended that universities should take no responsibility for the education of the rising generation. Education for purposes other than research expertise, he said, was "necessarily of a different kind and is best done elsewhere" (p. 17).

Abraham Flexner's (1930) *Universities: American, English, German* stated the case that American education had become a "dumping ground" for everything from job training to spectator sports and asserted that universities must focus clearly on one central task: high-level study in the academic disciplines and learned professions. Departing from Veblen, however, Flexner believed that the rising devotion to research threatened the advanced teaching he regarded as essential to the common good.

In more direct contrast to Veblen's preoccupation with the German research paradigm, Alfred North Whitehead (1929), in *The Aims of Education*, examined the purpose and nature of university teaching. His concern was with the type of people that universities produce: "What we should aim at producing is men who possess both culture and expert knowledge in some special direction. Their expert knowledge will give them the ground to start from, and their culture will lead them as deep as philosophy and as high as art" (p. 13). Both general and special expertise are nurtured by imagination, Whitehead claimed, but he lamented that the young have imagination without experience and the old have experience without imagination. A college education, he said, should provide the wisdom of experience without stifling the imagination.

In *The Higher Learning in America*, Robert Maynard Hutchins (1936) also championed the integrative functions of teaching. He seemed, in fact, to have chosen the same title that Veblen used for his work (which was reissued in 1935) as a way of saying to Veblen: *This* is the real higher learning. Vexed by the "infinite splitting of subject matters," Hutchins, then president of the University of Chicago, lamented that academic people were losing the capacity to converse with each other across disciplinary boundaries or about problems of mutual concern. The flood of information arising from new research, he feared, would "submerge ideas" and impoverish public discourse. His solution was to involve faculty and students in a vital general education curriculum at the heart of the university. Hutchins' "Chicago Plan" aimed to keep great and enduring ideas at the center of intellectual and cultural life. Similar "great books" curricula were launched at Amherst, St. John's College, and the Experimental College at the University of Wisconsin. For years, John Dewey debated with Hutchins regarding the appropriateness of this neoclassical approach to liberal education.

Speaking to the Federation of Students at the University of Madrid in the 1930s, Ortega y Gasset (1966) later compiled his lectures as *Mission of the University*. Like Whitehead and Hutchins, Ortega took exception to the preoccupation of universities with research, suggesting that a university, "in the strict sense, is to mean that institution which teaches the ordinary student to be a cultured person and a good member of a profession" (p. 85). He believed that professors should be promoted, not because of scholarly achievements, "but on their talent for synthesis and their gift for teaching" (p. 85).

The contrasting arguments advanced in these works continue to shape discourse about the purposes of American universities. Depending on the academic administrator's own values and priorities, these "sacred works" are used selectively, much like religious texts, to authenticate one's own vision of the university.

A Predisposition for Democratic Administration

The literature of higher education administration began playfully with F. M. Cornford's satirical *Microcosmographia Academica*. This frequently reprinted pamphlet, "being a guide for the young academic politician," first appeared in 1908. A British philosopher of some consequence, Cornford provided a humorous taxonomy of faculty types, listed strategies of subterfuge and control indulged in by administrators, and wished the aspiring academic well. This spritely essay presaged the enduring impatience with bureaucracy and the strong preference for democratic administration in colleges and universities.

It was not until mid-century that administrative and policy matters in higher education were examined with any consistency. At about that time, a variety of forces converged to make the scholarly investigation of college and university governance an identifiable academic specialty. These forces included the burgeoning knowledge of leadership and human behavior in organizations that was stimulated by war-related research, the rising demands on colleges as enrollments soared, and a renewed national debate about the relative importance of the individual and social benefits of higher learning.

With the flowering of the social sciences during and after World War II, it was natural that some scholars would become curious about the institutions in which they worked. Logan Wilson (1942), in *The Academic Man*, provided the first substantial study of the academic profession as an occupational culture. Writing in part "to administrators who may have forgotten how institutional problems appear from the staff (faculty) perspective," Wilson traced much of the tension in universities to the contrast between professed aims and actual practices (p. 5). Attacking the ubiquitous legend of the "community of scholars," Wilson found universities saddled with hierarchies of several kinds. Differences between academic administrators and faculty, supposedly only functional, were frequently characterized by significant differences in power, prestige, and remuneration. Authority, he observed, was more centralized than collective, and those who had it used it.

The Academic Mind: Social Scientists in a Time of Crisis, a ponderous work based on Paul Lazarsfeld and Wagner Thielens' (1958) examination of social science professors in the decade following World War II, examined perceived threats to professorial autonomy caused by national security needs and public distrust. Several of the authors' conclusions related directly to administrative affairs. First, the larger and more prestigious a university, the more likely was its president to understand academic freedom and respect faculty authority. Second, in cases where administrators brought pressure to bear on social scientists, faculty often experienced a sense of powerlessness and, if forced to compromise, a sense of guilt. Lazarsfeld and Thielens asserted:

> A powerful administration need pay no attention to the convictions of its faculty. Thus numerous professors indicated both their strong belief that a presidential ban on the Red China debate would violate campus freedom of speech, and their certainty that a vigorous protest to the president over the issue would endanger their jobs. (1958, p. 229)

Another study of the academic profession was provided by Theodore Caplow and Reece McGee (1958/1965) in *The Academic Marketplace*. Dwelling particularly on what they called the faculty "vacancy-and-replacement" cycle, the authors examined the internal workings of ten major universities. Their recommendations, reported in a modest, readable volume, emphasized that "the order of seniority at each academic level be respected and strengthened," that "regular, orderly procedures be established for the selection of a new faculty member from a roster of candidates," and that "the personal and arbitrary control of administrative officers over members of the faculty be reduced as far as possible" (pp. 205, 213, 210). Caplow and McGee concluded that deans and department chairpersons often abused their trust by playing favorites when awarding salary increases, travel money, and sabbatical leaves. Established procedures, they said, ought "to include the proper safeguards to assure that these decisions are in fact not made whimsically" (p. 211). After three decades, *The Academic Marketplace* remains one of the most lucid and useful analyses of institutional life in American universities. The following passage foreshadowed much that later writers would build on:

> The university is a fascinating specimen of social organization, remarkably unlike any other. Its roots, and some of its rituals, go back to the Middle Ages and beyond, but its principal business is innovation. Its hierarchical arrangements are simple and standardized, but the academic hierarchy includes a greater range of skills and a greater diversity of tasks than any business or military organization. Above all, the university is remarkable for pursuing an intricate program with little agreement about fundamental purposes. (p. 1)

Clearly, the literature of higher education has not followed the same pattern of theoretical development that has characterized the study of educational administration. The works of Wilson, Lazarsfeld and Thielens, and Caplow and McGee were not preceded by tomes that extolled the virtues of scientific management in higher education. The specter of bureaucracy with which they all took issue probably revealed more about the extent to which authority is distrusted (and autonomy cherished) by academics than it did about scientific management and bureaucratic practices in American universities. By the time these scholars wrote their well-known works, however, war and postwar strains on higher education had pushed governing boards and university administrators further toward hierarchical decision making than most faculty members were willing to accept. Some, like the authors cited above, reflected long-held faculty values and democratic preferences, while others evidenced a fair amount of alienation.

Scientific Management and Bureaucracy

The history of scholarship concerning universities *as organizations* is one of constant oscillation between democratic and rational approaches. Indeed, the revolt against hierarchical patterns of governance in universities, articulated so clearly by the professors whose works were just examined, was soon countered by authors who felt other pressures and sensed other needs. These writers were often presidents or management experts who had experienced or observed the frustrations trying to provide direction for an institution of higher learning. One such person was Stanford's William H. Cowley, formerly president of Hamilton College, who completed a 520-page appraisal of American higher education in 1956—but never published it. Especially interested in comparing perceptions and realities and in defending the prerogatives of duly appointed academic officers, Cowley deflated such cherished academic myths as the decline of faculty autonomy and the increasing vulnerability of universities to outside influences, by showing that the halcyon days never existed. Professors, he demonstrated, had seldom enjoyed such independence as they did following World War II, and universities had always had to struggle mightily to protect their intellectual integrity. Cowley believed that administrative authority must be respected and exercised if universities were to be governable and if their values were to be defended from internal and external threats. Fortunately, in 1980 one of Cowley's former students compiled some of his most notable essays in a posthumous volume, *Presidents, Professors, and Trustees.*

Probably the first *bona fide* empirically based book devoted entirely to administration in higher education was John Corson's (1960) *Governance of Colleges and Universities.* A professor of business administration who maintained close contact with leading higher education scholars like Cowley and T. R. McConnell, Corson observed and analyzed administration and decision making in ten institutions of higher learning. He developed the notion of organizational dualism based on parallel structures in universities, brought the term governance into the parlance of higher education, and advocated greater cooperation among faculty, administrators, and trustees.

Corson's original book was out of date within a few years, due to the advent of student participation in governance, but he substantially revised the work in 1975. Building on the earlier edition, he compared university leadership with administration in business and government and illuminated important differences in institutional purposes, philosophies, and values. He advocated modernization of university administration and the adoption of advanced management techniques from business and government, so that presidents and trustees could regain "the power to act promptly and decisively" (p. 186).

The university presidency, the most visible and prestigious administrative position in higher education, received early and exhaustive scholarly examination. Beginning with Dodds' *The Academic President— Educator or Caretaker?* (1962), the prevailing theme has been the analysis of dilemmas faced by presidents, poised as they are on the fulcrum between the faculty and the community and between educational and administrative demands. As president Dodds reflected on the presidency, Robert Williams (1965) wrote about the deanship in *The Administration of Academic Affairs in Higher Education.* Williams was administrative dean at the University of Michigan, a position that in 1965 had not everywhere been recast as academic vice president. He dealt specifically with academic appointments, promotions, tenure, and salaries, and directed his attention to faculty teaching loads, instructional cost, budgets, and planning. This was a descriptive, not a theoretical work, and it examined the functions of a chief academic officer from the eyes of an incumbent. Similar in scholarly approach, but all-encompassing in scope, was Blackwell's (1966) *College and University Administration.*

Each of these works, like many others published in the 1970s, assumed a "yes, but" position on academic governance: Yes we must respect faculty prerogatives, but we must also organize our tasks and dispatch our work with greater efficiency. One embattled university administrator in this era even went so far as to propose, perhaps only partly in jest, that presidents adopt the most advanced management information systems available, but be prepared to deny their existence if faculty should inquire! Whatever the response to this advice, Secretary of Defense Robert McNamara's use of flowcharts and technical management schemes during the Vietnam War resulted in a national preoccupation with new scientific management tools. University faculty and administrators, tied in so many ways to the Department of Defense in the 1960s and early 1970s, decorated their laboratories and boardrooms with flowcharts and cluttered their conversations with the jargon of bureaucracy. With this trend came marked increases in the number of career administrators, especially in the institutional research and staff positions made necessary by government-mandated as well as self-imposed efforts to monitor programs and measure progress toward goals.

A Period of Transition

Until the 1970s, most of the higher education literature was written from the perspective of the authors' roles—with professors usually preferring democratic administration and presidents leaning toward more centralized, scientific management techniques. According to Marvin Peterson (1985), the *organizational* literature about higher education began in 1963. Algo Henderson (1963) and T. R. McConnell (1963) each published an article that urged theoretical development supported by empirical research concerning the governance of colleges and universities. Interesting as the debates of previous decades had been about rational versus democratic approaches to university administration, proponents of both views had substantiated their claims primarily by descriptive studies and ideological predispositions.

For a time, the struggle between rational and democratic ideologies was muted. Theories and methods from the social sciences were borrowed and tested in an effort to gauge more precisely how universities governed themselves. The scholars of this era assumed that universities were self-directing institutions functioning almost independent of external forces.

The open-systems approach to university governance was foreshadowed, however, by a landmark book published the same year as the Henderson and McConnell articles. University of California president Clark Kerr (1963) drew on what was by then a familiar tradition by delivering a series of papers (the Godkin Lectures at Harvard) and publishing them as *The Uses of the University*. This modest volume carried a powerful message: Cardinal Newman's idea of a university, enduring as it was, no longer fit the university of the late-twentieth century. Owing to a proliferation of societal demands, the disintegration of common aims and methods among professors, and the bewildering complexity of research institutions, Kerr suggested the term *multiversity*. With the Balkanization of universities, he said, "the president is mostly a mediator." Kerr was concerned, too, with the threat to university autonomy posed by the emergence of enormous federal grants and with the widening gap between the "federal grant universities" and other institutions that had less prestige and less success in winning grants. So well received was this little book that Kerr reissued it with new postscripts in 1972 and again in 1982.

An enduring contribution of the ensuing decade resulted from the empirical research of Victor Baldridge (1971a, 1971b) at New York University in the late 1960s. Baldridge suggested that there were two dominant images of university administration: One was the collegial "republic of scholars," long since dispatched by Cowley, and the other was the bureaucratic model seen as hierarchical, rational, and authoritarian. Based on his analysis of decision making at New York University, Baldridge proposed a third characterization of university administration which he called political. "This place is more like a political jungle, alive and screaming, than a rigid, quiet bureaucracy," Baldridge wrote, quoting a New York University professor (1971b, p. 9).

Based on his examination of practice, Baldridge (1971b) advanced six observations about university governance: (1) conflict is natural, (2) the academic community is fragmented into many power blocs, (3) small groups of political elites dominate most of the major decisions, (4) despite the elites, democratic tendencies continue to exist, (5) administrative authority is severely limited by political pressure and bargaining, and (6) external interest groups do influence internal policies. The political model of university administration, unquestionably accentuated by the campus conflicts of those years, represented a new view which was neither bureaucratic nor democratic. Indeed, Baldridge applied the Hegelian dialectic to come up with the political model, but his synthesis dealt primarily with the internal affairs of the university. It foreshadowed, but did not represent, an open-systems theory of administration in universities.

Open Systems and Beyond

In 1967 the Carnegie Commission on Higher Education began its work, chaired by former University of California president Clark Kerr. In twenty-one reports issued over its six-year life, the Commission underwrote the study of virtually every aspect of higher education in the United States. One of the Commission's important contributions was to bring social scientists together to examine policy issues in higher education. Perhaps the most widely cited of any work in this collection, Michael Cohen and James March's *Leadership and Ambiguity: The American College President* (1974) set forth an open-systems view of higher education administration, based on a thorough examination of presidential behavior, presidential careers, and the expectations others had of presidents.

Characterizing the American college or university as "an organized anarchy," the authors cited problematic goals, unclear technology, and fluid participation as some of the properties of university organizations. According to Cohen and March, institutional goals are loosely defined and constantly changing, administrative procedures are both highly complex and poorly understood, and those who participate in making a decision seldom remain in place until the issue surfaces again. They concluded:

> The logic of bureaucracy is the specification of objectives and technology. The logic of democracy is the organization of consent. The logic of collective bargaining is the discipline of conflict. The realities of higher education seem to be resistant to all three logics. (1974, p. 40)

168 THE EVOLUTION OF ADMINISTRATIVE PRACTICE

Given these anarchical conditions, Cohen and March recommended eight "rules" to help presidents enhance their leadership. Among them were (1) to invest large amounts of time and energy in the decision-making process, if for no other reason than to increase the "chance of being present when something important" comes up; (2) to persist—many successful decisions evaporate during the implementation stage; (3) to help adversaries participate in the decision-making process; (4) to provide "garbage cans"—or forums for faculty to expound on their pet concerns; and (5) to manage as unobtrusively as possible. The authors also suggested that presidents take an active part in interpreting the history of their institutions and be willing to suppress their own egos long enough and often enough to give others credit and recognition for institutional achievements.

Grappling with the same problems Cohen and March identified, Kenneth Mortimer and his senior colleague, T. R. McConnell, proposed decision-making processes that would involve varying patterns of participation based on legal, moral, and practical considerations. In *Sharing Authority Effectively* (1978), the authors refreshingly admitted the difficulty of assessing the effectiveness of decisions, owing to the impossibility of measuring the long-term effects of curricula on students, and the value of new scientific discoveries or scholarly achievements.

Based on extensive travel and research, George Keller (1983) reported major changes in the ways colleges and universities were administered in the early 1980s. With the widespread use of computers, scholarly work was being transformed and institutional planning and management were being revolutionized. Libraries struggled to keep up with new methods for storing and retrieving information, extension educators raced to serve remote students with new "interactive technologies," and computerized recordkeeping promised to liberate teaching and learning from slavish dependence on traditional academic cycles. While Keller provided useful information regarding developments in administrative practice and offered some thoughtful recommendations, his study, like Mortimer and McConnell's, was not designed to address unresolved theoretical and methodological issues in higher education.

Theory and research pertaining to the functions of colleges and universities, however, have mushroomed in recent years. Without question, the student movements of the late 1960s and early 1970s focused both public and scholarly attention on higher education. The rise of student participation in almost every phase of campus governance, the public impatience resulting in legislators' and trustees' thrusting themselves into governance issues previously left to faculty and administrators, and the rapid rise in popularity of faculty unions all pricked the curiosity of organizational theorists and other scholars. But the changes that had called forth the development of open-systems theory also suggested a complexity that demanded ideas of greater explanatory power. With more scholars looking at more variables and using more sophisticated methods, an inevitable splintering occurred in the field of higher education. Peterson (1985) noted that the open-systems approach had significant competitors, representing both adaptations of and expansions on it. These included the environmental contingency model, the organizational life-cycle model, various strategic models, and other emergent social systems theories.

The idea of a loosely coupled organization, introduced by Weick in 1976, represents one of the more apt applications of a model from the larger literature of organizational theory. Both Bess (1983) and Cameron (1984), following Weick's idea of a loosely coupled organization, set out to make sense of this notion in their own way. Bess concerned himself primarily with understanding what can and cannot be explained by the array of available theories, while Cameron produced a taxonomy of emerging theories and evaluated the pros and cons of each. The conceptual confusion of the field, however, has yielded little to these efforts, partly because higher education has been in such flux that the half-life of information, and perhaps of theories, has been foreshortened. In recent years, a fundamental reassessment of the assumptions underpinning all four of the traditional schools of thought has begun to take place.

SUMMARY

This chapter focused on the evolution, study, and practice of administration in doctoral-granting American universities. The four conceptions of governance—scientific management, democratic administration, bureaucracy, and open systems—that have revealed themselves in thought and practice in public education also appear in the history of university governance. Owing to contrasting traditions, purposes, and faculty characteristics, however, the four views have not crested in the same sequence in higher education, nor have they taken identical form. Here, democratic administration came first and, despite the entry and exit of other approaches, it has never been relegated to the periphery.

College and university faculty enjoy a very high degree of autonomy in their professional lives, and they typically hold the same formal credentials (a doctoral degree) as those who occupy administrative positions within their institutions. Coupled with the faculty's traditional control over academic policy matters, ranging from curricular requirements to peer review for promotion and tenure, these factors give rise to an organizational culture unlike any other.

Observers often perceive greater status differences between junior and senior members of a faculty than between professors and academic administrators. This condition is reinforced by the fact that academic vice presidents and deans retain their professorships (and sometimes remain active as scholars and teachers) while holding administrative office. The great majority of them eventually "return to full-time teaching and research," to use the common phrase, without loss of status. Administrative processes, therefore, are characterized by a rather high degree of participatory decision making. No leader, regardless of his or her instincts, is likely to survive long with a blatantly authoritarian style.

If commitments to faculty autonomy have endured over centuries, however, changes in the nature of colleges and universities have altered the context of administration. Administrative functions have become vastly more complex with the growth in university size and the expansion of the constituencies served by higher education. As this has occurred, more nonacademic tasks have been delegated to a growing cadre of management specialists, student counselors, and program directors.

Of all the institutions in the contemporary world, only universities in free societies have no avowed aim to bring people to predetermined conclusions. No business, church, or government seeks such detachment. Universities hallow the methods of free inquiry and champion the unrestrained search for understanding and knowledge. Given such an ideal, political, religious, business, and other interest groups frequently find themselves at odds with universities and their professors. This inevitable tension has given a special character to the literature of higher education. From Cardinal Newman in the middle of the nineteenth century to many writers in the 1980s, higher education scholars and practitioners have been preoccupied with defining and defending the essential values of higher learning and making administration compatible with those values.

9

THE EDUCATION OF ADMINISTRATORS

Graduate programs in educational administration have constituted a crucial link between theoretical development and field application. It is through these university-based academic programs from master's through doctoral degrees that most members of the profession are selected, prepared, and launched or relaunched into their careers. This chapter describes the forces that have shaped graduate study in educational administration and analyzes the major ideas that have animated its development.

By the mid-1970s, nearly 150 universities offered doctoral degrees in educational administration, and over 300 offered master's degrees (Silver & Spuck, 1978, p. 6). When 100 or more sixth-year specialist programs were included, the total number of institutions offering advanced preparatory work was at least 375. These figures have changed little in the last decade. In 1982, American institutions of higher learning granted 1,464 Ph. D. and Ed. D. degrees in educational administration, and 651 in the study of higher education (National Research Council, 1983, p. 29). Together, they totaled nearly 7 percent of all earned doctorates that year.

Graduate programs in educational administration have oscillated between "preparing the person" and "preparing for the role." In the first case, the candidate is especially encouraged to develop his or her intellectual capacities, educational philosophy, and cultural awareness. Knowledge and self-understanding are primary. In the other case, the emphasis is on shaping the individual to fit the role or roles he or she is preparing to assume. Here the chief purpose is to help the student understand the job and the institution and to acquire the skills necessary to serve the institution and meet the requirements of the position. At no time in the history of preparation programs, and certainly in no specific program, has one of these views prevailed completely over the other. But the proportion of faculty and student effort devoted to these different approaches to graduate preparation has shifted over time, and various university programs in the mid-1980s attribute relatively different value to these two views.

Assumptions made about these differing goals of graduate study shape the perceptions of professors, practitioners, and students about the content and design of graduate programs. For instance, those who view the intellectual and personal development of the *person* as the essential element in preparing future leaders tend to prefer a broad historical and philosophical curriculum that emphasizes the role and nature of leadership, the centrality of a philosophy of education, and a broad understanding of societal issues and values. By contrast, those who see the *role* as the controlling idea find special merit in role theory and behavioral research derived from the social sciences. These professors rely heavily on competency development, role plays, simulations, and field work.

THE FIRST FORTY YEARS: 1905 TO 1945

Modern notions of the school principalship or district superintendency emerged gradually. At the turn of the century, for instance, propinquity ruled the selection process. Certain elementary school teachers were given administrative responsibility and promoted to principalships simply because they were available and had shown a talent for leadership. Like teachers of that day, some did not hold baccalaureate degrees and many, regardless of the extent of their education, had little or no experience in pedagogy or administration. In 1924, two-thirds of principals held bachelor's degrees, one-fifth had master's degrees, and barely one in a hundred held a doctorate. One principal in ten still held no college degree at all (Eikenberry, 1925).

As the superintendency became unified and the responsibilities associated with it became more complex, traditional pathways to the job, such as previous service on the board of education, a principalship, or occasionally a college or university position, proved inadequate (Reller, 1936). The emergence, therefore, of a literature of educational administration, a corps of professors interested in extending knowledge and teaching students, and the availability of university graduate programs in educational administration came in response to new developments in practice in the early decades of this century.

First Professors

At the turn of the century there were no departments of educational administration or professors in this academic field. The study of educational administration began, as so many other new fields have, as a speciality growing out of more established domains of inquiry. When Ellwood P. Cubberley and George D. Strayer received their doctorates from Teachers College, Columbia University, in 1905, they earned them in education, with an emphasis in administration. Cubberley was already an associate professor of education at Stanford when he went to Columbia to pursue his doctorate. The first professors of educational administration, therefore, were trained in more comprehensive fields, usually education, and then developed increasing expertise in the management of schools and school systems.

Although Strayer and Cubberley were products of Teachers College, they built their professorial careers—and laid the foundations of the academic field—on opposite edges of the continent; Strayer taught at his *alma mater* in New York, while Cubberley resumed his professorship, and later served as dean, at Stanford University. Graduate programs that took shape between 1910 and the early 1920s generally prepared students to become practitioners, but a few of these well-educated superintendents later assumed professorships. Movement directly from graduate study to a university faculty position seldom occurred in the formative decades.

The generation of professors that included John K. Norton (Columbia), Frank W. Hart (Berkeley), Frank E. Henzlik (Nebraska), Julian E. Butterworth (Cornell), Edgar L. Morphet (Berkeley), and Paul R. Mort (Columbia) was the first to be educated by others in educational administration. With the exception of Butterworth, they all took their doctorates at Teachers College, Columbia University. Through the years of depression and war (1929 to 1945), their numbers were few and the links among them remained tenuous and informal.

Prior to the close of World War II, there were no national associations explicitly for professors of educational administration and no scholarly meetings or academic journals to expedite their exchange of ideas. In the early 1940s, professors of educational administration still focused their work at the local and regional level; they taught and wrote primarily from their own experience. Other developments in the field, however, were hastening the flow of information and creating a national network.

School Surveys

No account of the early development of graduate programs in educational administration can ignore the school survey movement. Early school surveys were descriptive studies, limited by unsystematic techniques, that often focused only on certain elements of a school or school system. Surveys of school buildings and sites were most popular, but school organization, finance, curricula, and administrative policies also came under scrutiny (Sears, 1925, 1929).

As early as 1918, Bliss advocated "unified" survey reports, and Sears (1925) soon became a leading proponent of this view. But despite the great popularity of school surveys prior to World War II and of annual national meetings to discuss survey techniques and findings, such as the Cleveland Conference, serious analysis and integration of results remained rare. In his 1946 doctoral dissertation at the University of Chicago, Cooper revealed that fewer than one-seventh of the 5,764 recommendations made in the surveys he reviewed were based on objective evidence. His findings underscored the unscientific methods of most surveys—a painful paradox since the survey movement was a prominent manifestation of the era of scientific management.

The fragmented nature of school surveys and the sparsity of objective evidence to substantiate recommendations did not seem to limit their application. Eells' (1937) study of over 50 survey reports revealed that nearly half of the 5,000 recommendations he was able to trace were carried out in full, while another quarter were at least partially implemented. Regardless of the methodological limitations, the school survey movement represented the first broad effort to gather evidence on which to base school reforms.

The survey movement stimulated the development of graduate study in educational administration. Survey reports often identified the need for more knowledgeable, better trained administrative personnel. They also constituted the first descriptive research conducted on a large scale in the field of educational administration, thereby providing a large body of information to which graduate study might be anchored. Finally, school surveys offered field study opportunities for the growing number of students pursuing advanced work in school administration. Given the paucity of scholarly literature in the early years, school surveys were particularly important to professors and students as well as practitioners.

Certification and Students

Shortly after receiving his doctorate from Columbia University, Cubberley (1906) proposed that each state offer an administrative certificate for educators seeking appointment to leadership positions. Wisconsin had already piloted such a plan, but no other state had yet followed. Despite advocacy by Cubberley and others, the certification movement progressed only haltingly for several decades. The American

Association of School Administrators claimed in 1939 that thirty-three states issued certificates, but only nineteen considered them a condition for administrative appointment. Even where certificates were demanded, requirements were meager and work specifically in educational administration or supporting disciplines was minimal at best (Peterson, 1937). On the eve of World War II, therefore, graduate training in educational administration may have given an aspiring superintendent an advantage, but such preparation was seldom necessary. Even so, the certification movement began to exert a powerful influence on the number and type of students who entered graduate study, on the curriculum, and ultimately on the character of educational leadership. Certification was to be a mixed blessing, ushering in more uniform professional standards at the price of bureaucratic controls.

Of the students in graduate programs during the first four decades, in the early years, almost all were male and studied education with an emphasis on administration, mostly in the summers while on leave from school employment. Before 1920, comparatively few superintendents or principals availed themselves of this formal preparation, but those who did began to set a standard that others would follow (Stinnett, 1969). For many, the notion of an administrative career came only after years of teaching. Thus, graduate study in this field often initiated a *second* stage of professional development. Further, since programs were generally pursued on a part-time basis, master's and doctoral degrees were often received at or near mid-career.

With the growth of state certificates as a requirement for administrative appointment, professors noticed a critical shift in students' commitments and attitudes. Traditional voluntary students were engulfed by peers who came, often grudgingly, to "get the certificate." The phenomenon of the "involuntary student" has been a fact with which admissions committees, advisors, and seminar leaders have grappled ever since. It has remained a factor that influences the quality and motivation of those who pursue graduate work in this field. Educational administration has always attracted a reasonable share of committed students, but they and their professors have continued to deal with the realities of an academic subculture that also includes some who are less intent.

Pioneering Texts

With the exception of A. N. Raub's 1882 book entitled *School Management* and possibly William Payne's *Chapters on School Supervision* (1875), texts in the field did not emerge until after the turn of the century. According to Jesse Newlon (1934), however, seventeen other texts had been published by 1932. It should come as no surprise that Strayer (1912) and Cubberley (1922) each produced a widely used volume. But their mentors at Columbia, Dutton and Snedden (1909), had produced an earlier text, *The Administration of Public Education in the United States*, which probably reveals rather accurately what the first doctoral students in the field studied.

One finds in Dutton and Snedden's work an unmistakable urgency about the role education was expected to play in a rapidly industrializing American society flooded with immigrants. With the scope and responsibility of public education expanding, the authors argued for school efficiency and opined that under these conditions, "inspection becomes a large and important function of educational administration. . . ." (p. 47). Widespread state control and support of education had become necessary, according to Dutton and Snedden, because of the "relative incapacity and unwillingness of individuals to meet the burden" (p. 46). If states were to assume responsibility to fund and supervise schools, then the job must be done well. This 600-page text left nothing unexamined. Headings and subheadings ranged from "Factors Favoring the Advance of Education" and "The National Government and Education" to "Corridors," "Blackboards," and "Basement and Attic."

The assumptions of scientific management are evident throughout the book. "Problems of active interest" were described as: (a) the centralization of administrative functions; (b) the determination of the most effective areas of local administration, according to type of education under consideration; (c) the most effective distributions of functions between lay and ex-officio administrators, on the one hand, and experts, on the other; (d) supervision of instruction in non-urban areas; (e) and the development of new agencies of control for new types of educational activity (p. 97).

Some sections of the book seem surprisingly current, while other passages are quaint and moralistic, but Dutton and Snedden's work is illustrative of pioneering textbook writing in several respects. A veritable catalogue of available knowledge and information pertaining to educational policy and administration, it encompassed everything from grand notions about schooling in a free society to the daily trivia of schoolhouse management. The following passage provides evidence of the detail of the authors' recommendations and the extent to which times have changed:

It has long since been ascertained that the sanitary facilities of a schoolhouse can be secured without objectionable results no matter where they are located. It is simply a matter of plumbing and ventilation. If placed in the building, there should be the most approved appointments. The same is true if located, as is often done, in separate buildings connected by a close passage. In both instances the very best appliances that the plumber's art can devise are none too good, considering the requirement of a large school. (1909, p. 184)

The audience is not at all specific; while the volume was intended as a textbook for students of educational administration, parts of it would be applicable to everyone from state legislators to school janitors. This 1909 volume is based on the broad experience and keen observational powers of the authors, but it benefits little from systematic investigation. While the book's philosophy was democratic, its pronouncements exemplified scientific management.

The third edition of Cubberley's *Public School Administration* (1929a), published on the eve of the stock market crash, illustrates important changes that were occurring in preparatory programs. Scientific management had begun to give way to the human relations movement. In the preface to that edition, the author noted that the book had been completely rewritten since the publication of the 1922 edition. Such was not the case between 1916 and 1922. To explain the shift, Cubberley observed that professors could no longer "cover the field in one course" (p. vi). While he still envisioned this book as a general introduction, the author recommended other texts to colleagues who taught the new specialized courses—namely his *State School Administration* (1929b) and his then forthcoming *City School Administration* (which never came to fruition).

Jesse H. Newlon's 1934 *Educational Administration as Social Policy* was not a textbook, but it said much about the state of knowledge and preparation in educational administration at the time. Like Dutton and Snedden, Newlon was a professor of education at Teachers College, Columbia University, when he wrote the book. He had earlier served as superintendent of schools in Denver. Newlon focused his attention almost exclusively at the policy level, believing "that the control of education is one of the major social problems of our times and that educational administration is, in the broadest sense, essentially a branch of politics, an applied social science" (p. 8). He went on to suggest that educational leaders could work effectively to shape schooling only if they possessed broad backgrounds in "educational and social history" and were keen observers and actors in the changing American culture.

In a final chapter on "The Education of School Executives," Newlon renewed his case for a socially aware, intellectually alive superintendent and laid a foundation for the development of theory. Education, like engineering, must draw upon "many sciences," he claimed. "It is not hostile to the scientific method as such but, on the contrary, is very congenial to it" (p. 263). He stressed, however, that educational administration must look to the emerging social sciences, not to the physical sciences, for its methods of inquiry. He concluded his treatise with a bow to the human relations movement:

> The task set is not an impossible one for the administrator who conceives his major responsibility as the releasing and co-ordinating of leadership inside and outside the school. He will eagerly seek wisdom and knowledge in every direction, invite the assistance of all who can aid him, and bring to their suggestions a trained, informed, and judicial mind. (1934, p. 270)

Newlon exemplified the growing sophistication of the field, recognized the prevailing environment within it, and, at the same time, foreshadowed things to come.

Two textbooks that appeared at the end of this era are also worthy of special note. Arthur Moehlman published *School Administration* in 1940, and Ward Reeder came out with *The Fundamentals of Public School Administration* in 1941. Complementing Newlon's concern with broad educational policy, Moehlman stated in his opening sentence that the "thesis of this book rests upon the simple but frequently neglected principle that instruction is the supreme purpose of the schools and that all activities essential to the successful operation and improvement of instruction must be considered as purely contributory in character" (p. v). Both Moehlman and Reeder began their texts with chapters on education in a democracy—reflecting not only the larger democratic administration movement, but also the immediate threat to free societies posed by the rise of Nazi military power.

Following their similar initial chapters, Moehlman and Reeder moved in different directions. Reeder emphasized the administration of schools and schooling *per se*, while Moehlman directed more of his attention to state and federal policy. Reeder concluded his volume with chapters on school accounting and efficiency in office management, while Moehlman's final sections dealt with the federal interest in public education and federal/state relationships. These different approaches may be attributable to the fact that Reeder's first edition was released in 1930. His 1941 edition, though it was billed as "revised and enlarged," still reflected an earlier view. Moehlman's giant (nearly 950-page) text, on the other hand, revealed more authentically the accumulating sophistication, the wider perspective, and the democratic values of the early 1940s. Moehlman did not ignore the daily tasks at the schoolhouse, but his interest was clearly at a higher, more philosophical level.

While the works of Dutton and Snedden and of Moehlman were both estimable for their times, the thirty-two years of development in the profession that separated the two were quite evident. Moehlman's text not only illustrated the shift from scientific management to democratic administration, but it also built on the considerable work of a growing number of scholars in educational administration. Still, Moehlman and even Newlon drew their information and ideas primarily from within the field of education.

The Prescriptive Era Ends

Conscious attention to the theory and practice of educational administration, like the production of automobiles and schoolhouses, was held in abeyance during the global war in the early 1940s. But in 1946, under the auspices of the National Society for the Study of Education (NSSE), leading figures in the field cooperated in putting together NSSE's Forty-Fifth Yearbook (Part II), *Changing Conceptions in Educational Administration* (Henry, 1946). The remarkable thing about this volume was how little the authors' notions had changed. The Forty-Fifth Yearbook revealed a continuing isolation from larger streams of scholarship about administration and human behavior and a persisting preoccupation with democratic administration. Reflecting a major concern of that era, one of eight sections was devoted to "Providing Appropriate Housing for Schools." But a final chapter on graduate programs in educational administration advanced several observations and recommendations that are worthy of note. A one-year internship in an administrative position was suggested, and Alonzo Grace, Commissioner of Education for Connecticut, recommended that state certification guidelines be relaxed to eliminate the mindless perpetuation of traditional courses and requirements.

The scale and character of doctoral study during the early years reveals much about the field. In 1934, Newlon identified fewer than 300 doctoral dissertations that had been completed in educational administration in the previous 23 years (p. 260). That average of 13 a year contrasted sharply with more than 2,000 a year in the late 1970s and early 1980s. Of the dissertations before 1934, five addressed administrative organization, four examined boards of education, and three analyzed educational organization. On the other hand, nineteen concerned buildings and equipment, thirty-four focused on business administration, and fifty-five examined fiscal administration. These figures reveal dramatically the focus of professorial and student interest in the early decades. It also seems clear that tension existed between two views of preparatory programs. From Dutton and Snedden to Reeder, there was strong concern with the performance of administrative tasks. By contrast, the works of Newlon and Moehlman stressed the importance of helping future leaders develop ethical sensitivity, intellectual acumen, and societal understanding. Cubberley's approach seemed to span the two schools of thought.

Finally, it is worth noting that over half (155) of all dissertations completed before 1934 were done at Teachers College, Columbia University. The University of Iowa ranked a distant second (16), with the University of Chicago third (15) and the University of California at Berkeley fourth (10) (Newlon, pp. 271–290). A historical study of Teachers College characterized Columbia as the temple of educational administration in the pre-World War II era (Cremin, Shannon, & Townsend, 1954). The common professional parlance for the leading professors associated with the Columbia program, however, was less ethereal. They were known as the "Columbia barons." By whatever name, George Strayer, Paul Mort, and Nicolaus Engelhardt were masterful talent brokers who moved their former students into key positions around the country with apparent ease. As Tyack and Hansot (1982) pointed out, however, "canny graduates emulate their sponsors"; the University of Chicago, Ohio State, and other institutions soon had barons of their own (p. 142). These webs of mentors and their former students, whatever their other merits and shortcomings, provided vital connections among scholars scattered across the continent—linking those who studied administration with those who practiced it. These informal networks played an important part in the early development of educational administration.

THE SECOND FORTY YEARS: 1945 TO 1985

The evolution of graduate programs following World War II was bound closely to the theory movement. Since the movement has been described and discussed in earlier chapters, this treatment will deal primarily with its implications for graduate programs. Preparatory programs since the 1940s have been studied by other scholars such as Robin Farquhar (1977), Paula Silver and Dennis Spuck (1978), and Erwin Miklos (1983). In general, however, their theses differ from ours. The theory movement may have been something of a revolution in ideas, but its manifestations in graduate programs were not so dramatic. The years prior to World War II have often been viewed as a kind of dark age in which nothing very important happened in educational administration, whereas the period following 1945 is frequently characterized as a great awakening. As already shown, much notable progress was achieved prior to 1945, and progress since that time has often been exaggerated.

Even so, the rechanneling of human resources following World War II, coupled with the magnitude of educational problems that had long begged for attention (and were destined to get worse with postwar readjustments), brought an introspective mood among professors of educational administration. Their efforts to reexamine the field, the knowledge base, and even their own teaching initiated several decades of change in preparatory programs.

Professors and Their Associations

The isolation of professors of educational administration from one another and from their counterparts in related disciplines ended in the years immediately following World War II. Led by *School Executive* editor Walter Cocking, fifty-six professors and practitioners gathered at the International Business Machines Homestead in Endicott, New York in the summer of 1947 to consider the status of the field. This gathering initiated what later became known as the National Conference of Professors of Educational Administration (NCPEA) (Moore, 1957, pp. 3–4). The Endicott conversations met a commonly felt need to share concerns and ideas and reconsider the nature of the field. In succeeding years, moving the site of the annual summer meeting from one part of the country to another and expanding the number of participants enabled NCPEA to create a network through which new ideas concerning preparatory programs were generated and disseminated. While NCPEA was to remain a rather informal professional association, it represented an important first step in linking educational administration scholars from across North America (Flesher & Knoblauch, 1957).

A highly significant early achievement of NCPEA was the role it played in convincing the W. K. Kellogg Foundation to give nearly $3,400,000 over a five-year period to fund regional efforts to improve the study and practice of educational administration (Moore, 1957, p. 18). Through what became known as the Cooperative Project in Educational Administration (CPEA), nine universities in the United States and Canada were eventually chosen to host Kellogg centers. They were located at George Peabody College for Teachers; Harvard University; The Ohio State University; Stanford University; Teachers College, Columbia University; the University of Chicago; the University of Oregon; the University of Texas; and later the University of Alberta in Canada. Over 300 publications emanated directly from these centers, and many other manuscripts were published by regional and national associations, including NCPEA. In the judgment of Hollis Moore (1957) and others, CPEA projects also attracted significant new talent to the field of educational administration, built new bridges between study and practice, and stimulated the growth of inservice training.

On the strength of CPEA's successes and in light of the Kellogg Foundation's desire to wean the maturing centers, representatives of CPEA universities and about twenty-five others gathered in 1956 to form a consortium of universities that had leading departments of educational administration. The headquarters of the University Council for Educational Administration (UCEA) was located at Teachers College, Columbia University, until 1959, at which time The Ohio State University became the host institution and Jack A. Culbertson, then an assistant professor from the University of Oregon, assumed the Executive Directorship. He led UCEA for over twenty years, leaving an indelible mark on the field.

The primary purpose of the consortium was to improve graduate programs in educational administration through the stimulation and coordination of research, the publication and distribution of literature growing out of research and training activities, and the exchange of ideas. Inspired by this significant development, the Kellogg Foundation provided additional resources to help get UCEA underway. With foundation backing and an executive committee that included many prominent scholars in the field, UCEA became the dominant force in shaping the study and teaching of educational administration in the 1960s and 1970s.

Part of UCEA's influence over preparatory programs came through the setting of standards for institutional membership. At its height in 1970, nearly sixty of the most prestigious departments of educational administration in the United States and Canada held membership in the consortium. For most professors in member universities, UCEA became the professional association with which they identified and through which they forged professional ties with colleagues.

The strength and elite nature of UCEA, while serving well those whose institutions belonged to the organization, probably constituted a mixed blessing for the field. With much of the best talent and energy siphoned off to UCEA projects, NCPEA remained a relatively informal and ineffective force. It did not, for instance, develop a refereed journal and national convention like many professional associations did during the era following World War II. About two-fifths of the professors in the field were associated with UCEA-member universities, leaving the majority with diminished stimulation and sparse support for their professional development.

UCEA's leadership was expressed particularly through the initiation and sponsorship of the *Educational Administration Quarterly* (1965) and *Educational Administration Abstracts* (1966) and through annual or semi-annual career development seminars for professors and graduate students, case study series, school district simulation projects, and many commission reports or publications. Through these projects, standards were set, ideas generated, and innovations disseminated. During its first decade and a half, UCEA became a major force in the advancement of preparatory programs.

In the 1970s, however, some of the forces that had enabled UCEA to make its distinctive contributions began to ebb. The purposes of the consortium multiplied with the fostering of major projects in special education administration, international scholarly exchange, and the inclusion of selected school systems in the UCEA partnership. But a more vital factor seemed to be the fragmentation of scholarship in the field itself. By 1970, research in educational administration had become firmly rooted in a variety of academic disciplines—particularly the social sciences. Many scholars in the field, therefore, began to affiliate with specialized professional associations and to subscribe to journals related to such research interests as school law, public policy, administrative theory, and the social-psychology of leadership. Neither UCEA nor NCPEA could meet the needs of all.

Just as this splintering assumed major proportions, federal grants became harder to win and UCEA dues increased, factors that limited the range of cooperative projects and eventually placed UCEA in competition with its own member institutions. Universities such as Harvard, the University of California at Berkeley, and UCLA dropped their memberships, and institutions of lesser influence began to take their places. After a decade of drift and introspection, the consortium showed signs of renewal. A new generation of faculty leadership emerged in the Executive Committee, the central office was moved to Arizona State University in 1984, and another rising young scholar, Patrick Forsyth, accepted the Executive Directorship. By the end of

1985, UCEA had secured grants from Danforth and several other foundations to underwrite an ambitious effort to reassess and redirect the field; the recommendations of the National Commission on Excellence in Educational Administration were released in 1987.

The professional activities and values of professors have been examined in several studies. An initial survey conducted by Jean Hills was reported in the first issue of the *Educational Administration Quarterly* in 1965. Curious about the extent to which the scholarly values of the theory movement had permeated the thinking and teaching of professors, Hills selected and polled a random sample of 150 NCPEA members. In the two decades since the theory movement began, he concluded, actual changes in teaching and research were more myth than reality. He found professors so overwhelmed with teaching, advising, field work, and university administration that they had little time or energy to invest in scholarly activity. In light of his findings, Hills urged the establishment of research professorships, the funding of summer programs for professional renewal, and the establishment of a national or international institute "at which professors of administration might spend at least a year in the study of theory, research methods, and relevant social science literature." Hills concluded: "Whether that study results in improved teaching, in publication, or in both, seems irrelevant, but there can be no scholarship without study" (p. 66).

Campbell and Newell (1973) conducted a comprehensive study of professors of educational administration and higher education in 1972. They sent questionnaires to nearly 2,000 professors and found most of them occupied with a range of duties that precluded serious and sustained scholarship. At the same time, the researchers noted a significant expression of interest by professors in doing more scholarly work. Campbell and Newell also found three distinct role orientations within the professoriate—a group of cosmopolitans who had a national reference group and high interest in theory and research, a second group with primarily loyalty to their own universities and to the teaching and advising of graduate students, and a third group consisting of faculty members whose primary interests and identity were with practitioners. Those professors who were most loyal to and involved in the life of their own universities were not the locals. Instead, cosmopolitans seemed to have a special sense of dedication to the *idea* of a university and to the notion of free inquiry. Apparently these shared values propelled many top scholars to the center of their institutions' affairs.

Newell and Morgan (1983) replicated the earlier study in 1980 and identified some notable trends. The proportion of time that the average professor reported spending in scholarly activity increased from 14 to 24 percent in UCEA universities and at least as dramatically (although the totals were not as great) among faculty located at other institutions. Similarly, the percentage of faculty who believed that quality teaching and research were interdependent increased from 75 percent to 90 percent. During the eight-year period, the number of professors who agreed with the statement that "scholars with specialized training in a related discipline make the best professors" increased from a little over a quarter to a little over half (p. 76).

Clearly, professors of educational administration were spending more time in scholarly pursuits by 1980, and their publication records reflected the change. The average number of scholarly articles published during the previous five years increased significantly, as did the satisfaction most professors reported from their production of books and ideas (Morgan & Newell, 1982; Newell & Morgan, 1983).

It may be that the dream precedes the fact when major movements are afoot; although the professoriate was not surfeited with scholars in the mid-1980s, there was reason for more optimism than Hills found in 1965 or than Campbell and Newell observed in 1973. When Halpin and Hayes (1977) and others lamented the failure of the theory movement, they may simply have judged too quickly or too narrowly.

Willower ably articulated the critical values and ideas of the professorship on several occasions. In *The Professorship in Educational Administration* (1964), he, Culbertson, Campbell, and others analyzed the evolving nature of the professorship and philosophized about what ought to be. Campbell (1964) argued that the grooming of a first-rate professor was largely a socialization process that brings young scholars more and more to a temperament of inquiry and places a high value on ideas and their creation. Willower reflected on professors' responsibility to link theories and general knowledge to practice and particular events. He also emphasized the importance of reflective scholarship and the essential role that educational philosophy should play in a professorial career.

If Willower's 1964 concern was with the inadequacies of theory and theoretical development in the field, he was sobered in 1983 by the plenitude of extant theories, each with a small coterie of devotees. But if the antidote to sparse and inadequate theories in 1964 was open and searching minds, by 1983 Willower believed that this same prescription would serve to improve the field and save it from its new problems. Faculty members who are beholden to certain theories are inadequate professors, Willower contended. He called for scholars who could dispassionately evaluate the strengths and weaknesses of all applicable theories and build sturdy syntheses from competing explanations of the same phenomenon. Willower's analysis of the professoriate in educational administration is a reminder not only of how far the academic field had come, but of how far it still had to go. He described the ideal professor as an "explorer, creator, critic, and deliberate user of theories and methods, not as an unthinking devotee of one [theory or method]" (1983, p. 189).

Changing Origins
and Characteristics of Students

Other important facets of preparatory programs include admissions criteria and processes. The number of students seeking master's degrees, certification, and doctorates in educational administration is higher than in almost any other field in American higher education. While professors and their universities grappled with changing and expanding notions of research and scholarship, they were also making enormous changes in the scale of their programs. The massive influx of students in the decades following World War II was a function of the widespread imposition of state certification requirements, the G.I. Bill, which provided educational benefits for veterans, the expansion of schools and schooling generally to accommodate the postwar "baby boomers," and the general escalation of educational expectations. Whatever the reasons, the expansion immediately after World War II occurred primarily among middle class, Caucasian, male students. According to Farquhar (1977), the typical student in the 1950s was probably in his mid- to late-thirties, possessed an established record as an administrator, received little or no support from assistantships or fellowships, and needed no full-time residency as a part of his doctoral program. Evenings, weekends, and summers were sufficient to squeeze advanced study around a full-time career position.

By the mid-1960s, Farquhar contended, most states required seventy hours of graduate study or a completed doctorate for appointment to a superintendency. Again, applications increased. By then, however, the typical student had to quit his or her job or take a sabbatical to meet a requirement for one full academic year on campus. Students in this era were significantly younger than their predecessors had been, but they were still overwhelmingly middle class and male. The environment in which the students studied was one of excitement and promise—the bloom was on the rose and social science knowledge was expected to lead to administrative progress.

By the mid-1970s, admissions committees were becoming painfully aware that white principals were almost everywhere managing schools in black, Hispanic, and Native American communities. Further, affirmative action guidelines were in place, and the doctoral student cohort at many universities soon included a number of blacks and a few women. The condition of America's schools and universities, threatened by a curious mix of student idealism and cynicism associated variously with racism and war, brought an air of sober reality to doctoral study. But fellowships and scholarships were reasonably plentiful, as federal policies channeled money to education as a means of achieving President Lyndon Johnson's Great Society.

Further changes were apparent by the mid-1980s. Economic troubles, tax crises, and the decline in school populations made graduate study more expensive and more difficult. Fewer practicing or prospective administrators were able to leave their positions to pursue doctoral work, giving rise to two important changes. The proportion of part-time students rose significantly, and the proportion of women in doctoral programs rose dramatically. The women's movement had helped to raise aspirations and furnish opportunities; many who had been teachers before bearing children and raising their families returned at mid-career to seek doctorates in administration. Thus, women constituted a third to half of the student cohort in many educational administration programs. This academic field was at the forefront of an important social movement.

Because graduate study in educational administration seldom comes immediately after undergraduate study, but rather follows a period of teaching or entry-level administration, doctoral students are frequently older than their counterparts in other graduate programs. Although the women's movement has helped, attracting a higher proportion of truly able students to doctoral study will remain a severe problem until elementary and secondary education programs at the undergraduate level are able to attract a larger proportion of gifted undergraduates (Sykes, 1983).

Design and Content of Programs

As noted earlier, the design and content of graduate programs changed more slowly in response to the theory movement than was commonly believed a decade or two ago. Theory-based research came gradually into the classroom, and "reality-based" teaching methods competed for time and resources. Willower and Campbell may have been calling for a more questioning climate of inquiry in the 1960s, but others were busy "simulating" entire schools and school systems by such methods as devising typical "in basket" materials for different administrative roles, filming critical incidents, and staging personal confrontations. Technology continued to open new possibilities for training of this kind through videotapes of actual or simulated administrative situations and computer models of budgetary, personnel, or demographic problems.

The Thirty-Eighth Yearbook of the American Association of School Administrators, published in 1960, was entitled *Professional Administrators for America's Schools*. In a chapter that analyzed the condition of master's, sixth-year, and doctoral programs in educational administration at the close of the 1950s, the authors found little cause for satisfaction and a great deal of room for improvement. They remarked that "admission" was a more honest term than "selection" for the process of inducting students into graduate programs. In all but a few cases, a student needed simply to present evidence of a baccalaureate degree, a teaching certificate, and minimal experience in the classroom. Full-time students were so few that concentrated study was a rarity, and the only program strengths about which there was any agreement were field experiences and internships. As for content, courses in organization and administration were offered and required at most institutions, while supervision courses and classes on curriculum appeared somewhat less frequently. Distant by comparison were courses that dealt with research methodology, school finance, and school law. Courses in federal, state, and local relations were almost nonexistent. Mincing no words, the report concluded: "The professional preparation of school superintendents is badly in need of overhauling" (p. 84).

A later chapter in the same volume was entitled "A Proposed Program of Preparation." Recommendations included at least two years of full-time graduate study, following "strong undergraduate foundations in the social sciences, the natural and physical sciences, the communication arts, philosophy, and one or more of the fine arts," content emphasis on research and theory, and a core curriculum demanding enough to "weed out" as many as one-quarter of the students admitted.

In the early 1960s, UCEA sponsored a series of reports and position papers that analyzed learning needs, examined program content, and recommended changes. Van Miller and his associates published a position paper in 1963 entitled "Common and Specialized Learnings for Educational Administrators." They argued that the increasing complexity and growing size of school systems was giving birth to more specialized administrative jobs. The performance of such tasks required more focused preparation, but, ironically, also demanded more enlightened perception of the purposes and nature of educational institutions as a whole. Thus, Miller concluded, graduate programs must be at once more specialized and more generic. The common learnings were to be concentrated in the initial year of study, while specialized education would be offered at the advanced graduate level. Ideally, according to Miller, "staff positions could normally be filled by specialists in the task areas, while the line positions of principal and superintendent would be filled by persons with a more general orientation" (p. 10).

Reflecting the theoretical and social science trends of the 1950s and 1960s, Keith Goldhammer (1963) produced a UCEA booklet entitled "The Social Sciences and the Preparation of Educational Administrators." The theory movement was over a decade old when this volume appeared, and Goldhammer suggested that "all of the social sciences are pertinent, but there is no sure basis for knowing what particular dosages of each to prescribe" (p. 39). He recommended that each student be given an overview of each of the social science disciplines, as well as a chance to choose and concentrate on the one most appropriate to his or her intended career specialization. Further, students should not be told about the social sciences, but should be given experience in using social scientific methodology "in actual research and field operations" (p. 41). Goldhammer concluded the monograph by recommending a tripartite balance in program content among the social sciences, the humanities, and technical management skills.

The romance with social science content proceeded rapidly in the 1960s, particularly in the more prestigious educational administration departments. By the end of the decade, some were beginning to wonder if the pendulum had swung too far. In fact, by 1970 it was difficult to find humanities content in curricula at all. There had not been much for decades, but the omnipresent social sciences now made the absence of the humanities more conspicuous. One of the first scholars to respond to this was the Canadian Robin Farquhar, who published a little monograph in 1970 entitled "The Humanities in Preparing Educational Administrators." The preoccupation of the social sciences with fact and theory, Farquhar argued, left students unable to think imaginatively about the future. No vital social institution, he asserted, could expect to remain healthy in times of change unless its leaders were able "to consider carefully the 'oughts's' as well as the 'is's'" (p. 3).

Farquhar's monograph foreshadowed a frontal attack on the theory movement, launched by Thomas Greenfield (1975) at the Ontario Institute for Studies in Education. Farquhar had argued for the complementarity of social science research and humanities content, but Greenfield attacked the assumptions of social science research and the applicability of scientific theory to human organizations. The challenge to the traditional social science research paradigm presented originally by

Greenfield, and later joined by others, was countered most directly by Daniel Griffiths (1979). The ensuing methodological debate has continued to enliven sessions at professional meetings and conversations in the halls of academe. Christopher Hodgkinson, of the University of Victoria, published two books, *Towards a Philosophy of Administration* (1978) and *The Philosophy of Leadership* (1983), that dealt ably with humanities content and value questions in administrative work. Again, however, there appeared to be a lag of a decade or more between the emergence of new ideas in educational administration and their general application in graduate study.

Graduate programs in educational administration continued to deal with several forms of fragmentation: on the one hand, the atomization brought on by increased task and scholarly specialization, and the bifurcation that resulted from the rising use of reality-based or competency training materials, and on the other, the enduring, reflective, socially conscious aims of leadership education. By the mid-1980s, neither of these dilemmas had been resolved, but it seemed that the debate was closer to equilibrium than in previous decades. The limitations of logical positivism and the empirical method were more apparent and more widely discussed, while philosophical and qualitative inquiry again rose in respectability. The debate between advocates of quantitative and qualitative research, long muted by the overwhelming dominance of the former, again became a lively issue among educational administration faculty and students (Bates, 1985). Although specialized seminars generally replaced survey courses, and monographs and scholarly articles largely superseded general textbooks, there was a new concern with the integration of knowledge and the articulation of the values that should animate the work of practitioners and professors.

Doctoral Study in Higher Education

Universities that offered doctoral study in higher education typically organized their programs in one of two ways. Some established separate academic units such as departments of higher education or centers for the study of higher education. Departments have usually been staffed by three to six full-time professors, supplemented by an array of part-time faculty who jointly hold administrative positions within the university or the state system. By contrast, centers have tended to be interdisciplinary units in which several higher education professors and a variety of scholars from the academic disciplines join together to conduct research. Usually funded by government or foundation grants in the 1960s and early 1970s, centers often employed full-time research associates without professorial rank. Since departments of higher education were usually organized for purposes of graduate instruction, and centers typically focused only on research, some leading institutions like the University of California at Berkeley and Pennsylvania State University spawned both departments and centers—and some scholar-teachers held appointments in both units. Departments of higher education have always been located within colleges of education, but centers and institutes, being interdisciplinary in nature, have spanned college boundaries.

Another form taken by doctoral programs in higher education was their existence within departments of educational administration; these were commonly known as "combined" programs. Depending on the degree to which professors were organized in departmental subdivisions, the doctoral degree either was granted in higher education or it was considered an emphasis within educational administration. Higher education programs located in departments of educational administration have often been severely understaffed and have depended on part-time teaching by administrators—many of whom have made no pretense of active scholarship. However, some of the larger and more highly developed combined programs have had significant faculty strength in higher education, including some faculty who shared their time between educational administration and higher education. While the leadership of the Association for the Study of Higher Education (ASHE) and other professional associations has generally come from scholars in higher education centers and departments, a number of distinguished contributors to the literature have been located in combined departments or have held their professorships in one of the academic disciplines.

Before leaving this overview of degree programs in higher education, the complexity and variety of departmental organization deserve mention. Higher education departments have often included adult and continuing education programs, while educational administration departments sometimes encompass larger faculty groupings under such names as educational policy studies. Because higher education doctoral programs have been relatively few and their history has been rather brief, they have often waxed and waned, depending on the sympathies of a particular president or academic vice president. In the 1970s and early 1980s, therefore, some well-known departments or centers suffered attrition or merged with educational administration departments, while a few combined programs achieved status as independent departments of higher education. Severe cutbacks both in federal and foundation funding for research in higher education and in university budgets generally took their toll, especially on centers. Virtually all were scaled down during this period and some disappeared altogether.

The academic fields of higher education and educational administration have reflected the separate traditions of the institutions studied, as well as the contrasting histories and philosophies that characterize schools and colleges. Higher education has been a less specialized academic field than educational administration, maintaining a more consciously encompassing view of its mission. Although cooperation between higher education and educational administration faculties has increased, the distinctive traditions and values of those connected with the two fields of study have persisted.

SUMMARY

Educational administrators, including both scholars and practitioners, constitute a professional group roughly comparable in size to law or medicine. By contrast, however, educational administration is a very young field, emerging only in this century as a distinct professional specialization. Partly for this reason, there has been more variation in the quality of graduate preparation programs and even in practice than is the case with the older professions. The boundaries of this professional group have been less distinct, entrance requirements have generally been less rigorous, and the field has been characterized by a high degree of public involvement and visibility. Educational administrators work in the public domain and make decisions in highly visible situations.

Since the early decades of this century, proponents of contrasting philosophical views have sought to shape the graduate experience. One view has placed administrative roles at the center of thought and teaching—and has organized instruction to develop skills necessary to perform certain administrative tasks. The other view has emphasized the centrality of ethical and intellectual qualities essential to leadership in the larger public domain and within schools and school systems themselves.

As for the post-World War II theory movement, preparatory programs in the 1960s and even the 1970s exposed students to far less of the new knowledge and theory than those immersed in the events had believed and hoped. Some claimed that the theory movement had aborted. Evidence from the late 1970s and early 1980s, however, suggests increasing research output on the part of professors, more sophisticated research by students, and curricular changes of a substantial nature.

Ironically, just as social scientific methods in research were having their day in preparatory programs, the implications of these methods and their application to graduate study were being called seriously into question for the first time. If this history demonstrates anything, it is that preparatory programs have often lagged as much as a generation in their adoption of emerging scholarly ideas and educational philosophies. In many respects, however, the theory movement probably produced more heat than light during its first decade or two, spurred on by those who felt its excitement but failed to see its then fledgling substance.

By the late 1980s, it appeared that most preparatory programs imbued students with knowledge of all four views of administration and reflected a conscious balance among several enduring dichotomies: Should graduate study emphasize the role or the person? practical skills or societal understandings? knowledge of "what is" or some wisdom concerning "what ought to be"?

Know for
Final

10

CONCLUSION:
CHARACTER OF THOUGHT AND PRACTICE

THE PRECEDING CHAPTERS have traced developments in educational administration as a field of thought and practice. To conclude this work, it seems appropriate to reflect on the evolution of these developments and to suggest the current status of the field.

EVOLUTION OF THOUGHT AND PRACTICE

Professions develop in response to their environments. The emergence of educational administration in the United States has been shaped by vast changes in the nation itself, immense increases in the size and complexity of the educational establishment, and the growth of academic disciplines that are devoted to the expansion of knowledge about organizational behavior. Those who have practiced and studied educational leadership in this century have borrowed heavily from ideas arising from the work of sociologists and psychologists, for example, as well as from business and public administration. But educational administration has also contributed to the expansion of knowledge in these areas. In both regards, the era following World II deserves special mention.

Entry of the Social Sciences

During the 1950s and early 1960s, the social science disciplines came into wide use in the study of educational administration. At the 1954 meeting of the National Conference of Professors of Educational Administration (NCPEA), held in Denver, Jacob Getzels of the University of Chicago, Arthur Coladarci of Stanford University, and Andrew Halpin of the Ohio State University argued that the social sciences had much to offer those who sought theoretical understandings of educational administration. Within a few years following that meeting, Coladarci and Getzels (1955) published *The Use of Theory in Educational Administration*; Campbell and Gregg (1957) edited the NCPEA-sponsored book, *Administrative Behavior in Education*; UCEA sponsored a seminar that led to the publication of *Administrative Theory in Education*, edited by Halpin (1958); and Griffiths (1964) edited the 1964 NSSE Yearbook, *Behavioral Science and Educational Administration*. These documents, written by social scientists and by professors of educational administration, related emerging concepts from the social and behavioral sciences to the applied field of educational administration.

In a more recent study of prominent research in educational administration during the 1950s and 1960s, Griffiths (1983) focused on four major pieces of research. First, social-psychologists Jacob Getzels and Egon Guba developed a social systems model that brought fresh insight to relationships between individuals and organizations. Second, Neal Gross and his associates in sociology conducted an empirical study of role theory as applied to the school superintendency. Third, psychologist Andrew Halpin developed and tested two instruments—the Leader Behavior Description Questionnaire (LBDQ) and the Organizational Climate Description Questionnaire (OCDQ). Fourth, Griffiths himself and psychologists John Hemphill and Norman Fredricksen sought to determine relationships between administrative performance and certain personality variables. Significantly, six of the seven notable researchers named by Griffiths were social scientists.

A still more forthright recognition of the place of the social sciences in educational administration was the publication in 1973, under the auspices of UCEA and edited by Jack Culbertson and associates, of *Social Science Content for Preparing Educational Leaders*. From the preface came the following:

> During the last two decades the use of the social sciences in programs to prepare school leaders has become a visible and clearly recognized movement. However, the movement has presented new problems to professors, students, and practitioners of educational administration, a central and basic one being the question: of all the social science content available, what is more and what is less relevant to the study and practice of educational administration? A related question is: what criteria can be used to determine the content which is most and least relevant to the preparation of students and practitioners of educational administration? (p. iii)

The book presented essays on the core content of five of the social sciences, provided respectively by a psychologist, a sociologist, an anthropologist, a political scientist, and an economist. The balance of the volume, written by professors of educational administration, dealt with the application of social science concepts to training and research programs in the field.

Educational administration not only borrowed from the social science or behavioral disciplines, but it also drew from applied fields such as business. Chapter 2 dealt with the influence of business practices and the business culture early in this century on school organization and operation. It was the business culture of the country that provided Frederick Taylor such a responsive environment for scientific management. The doctrine of scientific management, espoused for business, was avidly adopted by scholars and practitioners in education. Later, as shown in Chapter 3, Elton Mayo and others forged a new doctrine of human relations for business. The notion of democratic administration, born in education itself, made management by consensus attractive to educators. Still later, the elements of bureaucracy, such as division of labor, hierarchical structure, and rules and regulations, first set forth by Max Weber, became a way to describe large government, business, and educational organizations.

Understandably, educational administration has borrowed from business and the behavioral disciplines, and this borrowing has sometimes been indiscriminate. For instance, Maslow's (1954) hierarchy of needs and Hunter's (1953) community power structure found ready takers. Historically, it appears that professors and practitioners in educational administration did not always examine with care ideas found elsewhere, and they were sometimes negligent in testing adequately such concepts in education. For a time, professors of educational administration seemed to be overly impressed with administration *qua* administration, that is, generic approaches to leadership; they assumed that a concept or practice developed in one setting would work equally well in another. Despite some early warning on this matter, only in recent years have scholars in educational administration come to recognize that the field has some unique as well as some common elements with administration in other settings. Indeed, scholars outside of educational administration, such as Richard Scott (1981), provided ways of thinking about organizations that recognized both the unique and common elements.

The inadequate responses of educational administration to theory and research, as suggested above, help explain the widespread disenchantment in the field. Halpin (1970) characterized this as "The Fumbled Torch" and later, with Andrew Hayes (1977), wrote of "The Broken Ikon." If educational administration professors and practitioners borrowed too readily at first, these scholars also seemed to conclude too readily that theory was dead. Only recently has the critical examination of administrative theory, including testing in school settings, begun to receive serious attention.

Quality of Scholarship

Professors have shown mounting interest in the quality and nature of scholarship in educational administration. Some, such as Halpin and Greenfield, suggest that the theory movement fell short or was misguided. Others have taken a longer view of the field and point to evidence of improved scholarship. Charters (1975), a veteran scholar, insisted that scholarship in educational administration was markedly better than it was when he first began his work in 1950. He noted the development of several professional journals, the level of discourse at Division A presentations at the annual meetings of AERA, and the number of research articles and monographs on his "must read" list. "Quality research is waxing not waning," Charters concluded.

At the request of the editor of the *Educational Administration Quarterly* (*EAQ*), Campbell (1979) appraised all forty-two issues of the journal from its inception in 1965 through 1978. This examination provided strong evidence that the initial purpose of *EAQ*, to publish conceptual, empirical, and analytical manuscripts, had been largely achieved. Significantly, prior to 1965 no such outlet for scholarly work existed within educational administration. As all new journals do, *EAQ* encountered a number of problems, chiefly that of securing high quality manuscripts in sufficient number to justify regular publication. After examining Volumes I through XIV using a carefully developed set of criteria, Campbell concluded that most of the articles were sound in quality and some were superior. He found *EAQ* articles as well researched and clearly written as many of those that appeared in established scholarly journals in the disciplines. While this was a positive judgment in the main, ways of improving the journal were recognized and recommended.

Cecil Miskel and Terry Sandlin (1981) examined survey research in educational administration from 1972 to 1979. Their study was limited to the methodological rigor of survey studies, but their inquiry included articles appearing in the Australian *Journal of Educational Administration* (*JEA*) as well as those in *EAQ*. Judged by their criteria, journal articles were not improving. They (1981, pp. 17–18) concluded that "the topics, program definitions, and use of conceptual models are better in more recent volumes of *EAQ* and *JEA* but the sampling and measurement criteria of quality show wide fluctuations and demonstrate no discernable trends." These analyses by professors in the field, printed in journals devoted to its research, may themselves suggest a positive movement.

A comprehensive survey of the field undertaken by W. L. Boyd and

R. L. Crowson (1981), "The Changing Conception and Practice of Public School Administration," made reference to 238 books, monographs, and journal articles. The documents can be divided into two categories: those oriented essentially to education, which numbered 129, and those oriented essentially to the academic disciplines, which numbered 109. These proportions contrast sharply with the inbreeding so evident in the 1946 NSSE Yearbook, *Changing Conceptions in Educational Administration*, which testified to the insularity of the field in the 1940s. Clearly, scholars in economics, history, political science, and sociology had something to say about educational administration. Moreover, many scholars in educational administration felt confident using research methods derived from the supporting disciplines.

Open-Systems Challenge

Over most of its history, educational administration, like administration generally, reflected a closed and "top-down" concept of organizations. While the major views of administration—scientific management, human relations, and bureaucracy—differed in some rather fundamental ways, they were all premised on the assumption that organizations were self-contained entities. Organizational behavior was to be understood within institutions alone. With the advent of social activism in the 1960s, the organization's environment became a major component in understanding administrative behavior. These changes came as a shock and a challenge to both practitioners and scholars. Principals and superintendents, accustomed to viewing their organizations as closed systems, interpreted the demands of emerging interest groups, increasing state regulations, and more extensive federal intervention, particularly on the part of the federal judiciary, as aberrations that would disappear. Such has not been the case, nor is it ever likely to be the case again. Since its formulation, the open-systems concept has helped explain external forces at local, state, and national levels that attempt to influence policy and practice in public schools and other educational organizations.

The open-systems view emphasizes the complexity of the job of school administrators. This work is now seen to involve not only retaining a focus on teaching and learning but also coping with the external forces that may enhance, thwart, modify, or limit the purposes and programs of the schools. Administrators have been placed in a political as well as an educational role, a condition with obvious consequences for their selection, training, and work.

For the scholar, an open-systems view of organizations gave explicit recognition to the legitimacy of inquiry concerning the culture surrounding the school or college. Psychology and sociology had long been the chief wellsprings for concepts concerning learning and organizational behavior, but these time-honored areas had to move over and make room for studies based on concepts with their origins in law, economics, and political science. This expansion of the related disciplines resulted in what some describe as the fragmentation of the field. Some scholars have found refuge in the study of educational law; others have found satisfaction in applying economic concepts to school finance; still others have been concerned with the quest to examine schools and colleges as political systems.

Some students of the field have accepted as given the fragmentation to which the open-systems view seems to contribute. If educational administration ever had a central core or intellectual cohesion, that era seems to be past. Professors of educational administration now work from highly diverse academic orientations and face sharply contrasting problems within—and beyond—the school or college. But some contend that there is an alternative way of looking at these changes. Fragmentation may be a misnomer; extension of the field might be a more appropriate term. Educational law, educational finance, and the politics of education can be seen as increasing the comprehensiveness of the field. All of these extensions may be related to the central core of the field itself, organizational behavior. It now seems clear that the behavior of educational organizations can be explained adequately only when factors both external and internal to the organization are taken into account.

Changing Public Perceptions

Changing public perceptions about education and educational institutions have resulted in sharp alterations in educational administration. David Tyack and Elisabeth Hansot, in their *Managers of Virtue* (1982), expressed the belief that 1954 was a watershed year. They described the period 1890 to 1954 as "schooling by design in a corporate society." It was a time when the "educational trust" or the administrative progressives took charge. Public education was, in a sense, our secular religion. The high priests of that religion were those who possessed training in educational administration, and most people felt secure with and grateful for such a priesthood. The progressive revolution in politics, early in the century, which aimed initially at cleaning up corruption in municipal government, also supported the notion that school governance should be taken away from private citizens, who were thought to be especially vulnerable to patronage and other self-interests, and given to experts, who were thought to be less vulnerable and more impartial.

Tyack and Hansot described the period after 1954 as a time of "dreams deferred." School administrators, once secure, even complacent, within their well-ordered institutions and with their special training, often became confused functionaries amidst the many new social activists seeking racial justice, political influence, and economic opportunity. Many groups raised questions about the purposes and practices of the public schools and expressed doubt that school administrators any longer gave significant leadership to their institutions. Tyack and Hansot expressed hope that out of all this ferment would emerge a new, yet undefined consensus.

In the wake of the Soviet satellite Sputnik and the Vietnam War, public officials increasingly expected economic and national security benefits from the education sector. The loss of idealism among youth, associated not only with the protracted Asian war but also with the inflation and economic turmoil of the late 1970s and early 1980s, turned students themselves overwhelmingly toward the competitive advantages education might confer. As many became unmindful of—or even disdained—education as a *social* good, new questions arose about the public's financial support of education. People with no children in school increasingly questioned whether they should be taxed for education. With the reduction in the number of children per family, the proportion of the population with no children in school continued to grow. More significantly, as it became increasingly clear that for many there was no direct relationship between years of schooling and economic return, support for schooling further waned. As the essential social functions of education in a free society, such as the need to prepare the young for self-governance and public service, were devalued both by policy makers and students, the foundations of public support may have suffered serious damage.

The actual administration of schools has always involved a struggle between lay and professional forces. In the first half of this century, the balance shifted somewhat from lay boards to professional administrators. Perhaps no scholar documented the continuing conflict between lay boards and professional superintendents more clearly than Neal Gross. As reported in *Who Runs Our Schools?*, Gross and associates (1958) interviewed 105 superintendents and 508 school board members, a random sample of all such officials in Massachusetts. From these interviews, Gross concluded that "superintendents and school board members frequently disagree over their respective rights and obligations" (1958, p. 139). With the rising militancy of teacher organizations in the 1960s and 1970s, professional administrators found that they also had to cope with this new force within the education family itself. Many citizens, on the other hand, became disenchanted with administrator and teacher organizations. This disenchantment led to demands for more citizen involvement in education and gave credence to the family control movement in education, supported cogently by John Coons and Stephen Sugarman (1978).

The continuing argument over school control highlighted the difference between public and private sectors. School administrators and teacher organizations frequently invoked comparisons with the medical profession. Education spokespeople pointed out that citizens do not tell doctors how to remove an appendix; thus why should they tell teachers how to teach reading? While this argument seemed to have some validity, it overlooked the point that the practice of medicine is essentially a private matter while the practice of education is decidedly a public matter. In a democratic society, any *public* concern, whether public education, higher education, public health, public safety, control of public resources, or foreign policy, will seldom be left to the experts alone.

With the dominance of professional control in the first half of this century, school administrators were inclined to eschew political control. They contended that the schools were apolitical, that there was no such thing as Democratic or Republican arithmetic. Politics were seen as partisan politics. Obviously, politics and political decisions were not limited to issues involving political parties. As Harold Lasswell (1936) suggested long ago, politics has to do with "who gets what, when, and how." In this broader sense, there has always been political influence in education. Frequently, that influence has been exerted by dominant or elite groups in our society, with little regard to minority groups and their wishes. School board members have come from these elite groups and have exerted their political influence without being fully aware of how potent and exclusive it was. Social and moral insensitivity of this kind was found in many of the early conflicts over school desegregation.

Political influence in education, always present but often denied or unrecognized, has been made explicit in recent decades. Any major decision in education, whether involving financial support, changes in the school curriculum, the certification of teachers, or the closing of schools, has affected many social groups—and spokespeople for these groups have emerged and insisted on having a voice in such decisions. When these voices have not been heard by local boards of education, problems have been "bucked up" to state legislatures, or even to Congress. Now there are many actors, both in and out of education, who help determine policies for schooling.

Public Education and Higher Education

Public school administration, both its practice and its thought, has been the chief arena in which the development of educational administration has taken place. But the field has also come to encompass concerns about the administration of colleges and universities and other institutions where educational programs are organized and directed. Although the administration of public schools and the administration of higher education have some common elements, for many, both among practitioners and scholars, this has been a difficult alliance. There have been some unique elements in the administration of higher education, as noted in Chapter 8, and some continuing differentiations between administration of the public schools and higher education.

One major difference between school and college administration is the autonomy of faculty. In higher education, a long tradition exists that regards the faculty and even the institutions in which they work as a community of scholars. While this tradition has been called into question (Baldridge, 1971a), college and university faculty members, particularly as represented through the departmental structure, have had a major and often a controlling voice in the appointment, promotion, and tenure of their colleagues. Moreover, seldom did anyone in a college or university tell professors what or how they should teach. While college administrators have sometimes imposed budget sanctions on individual faculty members and even on whole departments, most chairpersons, deans, and vice presidents have found faculty recommendations rather persuasive.

There has been no corresponding tradition of teacher influence in the public schools. Teachers have had little, if any, voice in the selection, promotion, and tenure of their colleagues. While personnel decisions sometimes reflected consultation with teachers, such decisions have usually been made by administrative personnel. Nor have public school teachers had much control over what they teach. What and how they teach have been governed by state law, local school district policy, or, sometimes, the direction of principals or supervisors. Despite these overt external controls, teachers have managed to retain some autonomy within their micro-environment—when they closed the classroom door (Lortie, 1975). But this degree of autonomy has been far less than that exercised by college professors.

In recent decades, administrative decisions with respect to public school personnel have been constrained by another development: the advent of teacher unions. In terms of salaries and benefits, unions have exerted strong influence, but other matters, such as employment and lay-off policies, have also become part of the bargaining agenda between the union and the school district. However, neither union activity nor individual discretion exercised by some teachers has equated personnel decisions in public schools with those in higher education.

There have also been differences in the preparation and career patterns of chief administrators in higher education and public schools. In higher education, most department chairpersons and deans have been selected from among the professors within a given area, and they have been seen as occupying their administrative posts temporarily— for one or two fixed terms of three to five years each. Some of these administrators have become presidents and vice presidents and have completed their careers in such positions. College administrators have usually held earned doctoral degrees in one of the disciplines, not in educational administration. Significantly, these college officials often continued to think of themselves as professors.

The preparation and career patterns of public school administrators have contrasted sharply with those of college administrators. Most principals and superintendents were once teachers, more frequently in secondary than in elementary schools. Thus, at the baccalaureate and sometimes at the master's level, they had a teaching major in one of the disciplines. At the graduate level, however, their majors were usually in education or educational administration, often culminating in a doctoral degree. In 1982, about one-third of school superintendents had doctoral degrees (Cunningham & Hentges, 1982). In terms of experience as well as training, their socialization has been toward administration rather than teaching. Most superintendents have followed a career ladder that included teacher, principal, and central office positions prior to their assuming the superintendency.

Public schools and higher education have had overlapping purposes; both have been concerned with teaching and learning. In addition, however, universities have devoted much of their effort to research and service functions. While applied research has frequently been done by industry and governmental agencies, most basic research has been done by university professors. These professors have represented a pool of expertise found nowhere else. Many of them, therefore, have been called on to serve as consultants to public and private agencies. This consultation or service function of universities was given great impetus by the establishment of the land grant colleges during the last century; such service, in those institutions and many others, later spread far beyond the field of agriculture to include almost every field of human endeavor.

Teaching at the advanced level, extending knowledge through research, and disseminating knowledge to those able to use it for myriad purposes have led many universities to stress scholarship as the chief criterion for faculty selection, promotion, and remuneration. In higher education, scholarship has often counted more than acclaim in teaching or supportive relationships with students. In public schools, on the other hand, inspired teaching and caring about students has represented the chief expectation held for teachers. Thus, the different purposes of public education and higher education constitute still another reason why many have seen the administration of the two levels of education as quite distinct.

Other Settings

While not treated here because of space limitations, readers should note that educational administrators have found places not only in schools and colleges but in a number of other settings. These settings include government at both state and national levels, quasi-public organizations such as foundations and research organizations, industry, and the military. For instance, in the 1950s, Harold Clark and Harold Sloan (1958) noted that the educational budgets of many corporations rivaled those of good-sized colleges. As another example, Thomas Carr in the 1970s (1978, p. 416) suggested that the military "will assume an even larger part of the role once dominated by the family, the church, and the schools, and the civilian work setting" in socializing the young.

In all of these other institutions, as well as in schools and colleges, what has come to be called educational administration has been studied and practiced. Particularly in government and in the quasi-public organizations has educational policy been considered. Often, too, through allocation of governmental funds and through foundation grants, programs designed to implement policy directions were supported. Research organizations frequently engaged in studies of educational policy in terms of the policy-making process and of the policy provisions themselves. Industry and the military have conducted far-reaching programs in training and education. In each case, they made use of people with administrative insights and skills to help establish, operate, and supervise their educational programs.

Departments of educational administration and similar academic units on university campuses have discovered that many of their graduates secure employment in government, quasi-private organizations, industry, and the military. Indeed, some people find places in these organizations before they apply for advanced administrative training. These conditions suggest that educational administration, both in terms of policy issues and program implementation, may be broadly conceived and that study may be oriented to a wide range of institutions.

CURRENT STATUS OF THE FIELD

As the evolution of thought and practice in educational administration was characterized above, some elements of the current status of the field were suggested. At this point, more specific attention to current conditions in educational administration is noted.

Diverse Purposes of Schools

One characteristic of the present scene is the diversity of purposes of schools. In the first place, seldom is a distinction made between the purposes of education and the purposes of schooling. Clearly, the purposes of education are broad and are shared by many institutions, including the home, the church, and the marketplace, as well as the school and the college. The purposes of schooling, on the other hand, would seem to be more restricted in scope and to deal with what the school can reasonably be expected to achieve. Even in defining the more limited purposes of schooling, problems remain. There seems to be a growing willingness, however, to distinguish between purposes for which the schools can be seen as having *primary* responsibility and those for which they may have only *shared* or secondary responsibility. For instance, the school may have primary responsibility for teaching reading and shared responsibility in the development of mental health.

There is also the problem of dealing with the formal and the informal curriculum of the school. The formal curriculum encompasses what is deliberately planned and often set forth in curriculum guides or statements of educational mission. The informal curriculum has to do with the climate of the school, the daily regimen, and relationships among students, among faculty, and between students and faculty. The climate may be caring or not caring, reflect high or low expectations for students, and be supportive or not supportive of intellectual skills.

Students probably learn as much from *how* they live and learn in the schoolhouse as they do from the formal curriculum.

Perhaps at no other time have the purposes and programs of schooling received more attention. Spearheaded by *A Nation At Risk* (National Commission on Excellence in Education, 1983), in the early 1980s there were no fewer than seven major reports suggesting reforms. These reports were undertaken by foundations, professional associations, individuals (with foundation and government support), the Education Commission of the States, and the federal government itself. The reports varied in terms of methodology and scope. A few were based on data generated by the studies themselves, but most made use of existing data. All, however, made explicit recommendations for reform, particularly of the high school. Individually and collectively, the reports presented a genuine challenge to the education profession, particularly to those who occupy positions of leadership in the profession and have major roles to play in determining the purposes and directions of schools.

Fragmentation

Perhaps the ambiguity of school purposes has contributed to the real or perceived fragmentation of the field of educational administration, a condition noted earlier. For instance, some scholars in school finance seem to have more in common with colleagues in economics than with those who examine fiscal policy and behavior in school organizations. Similar estrangement seems to exist for some scholars in school law, the politics of education, and other areas.

All of the subfields in educational administration can be seen as important in their own right, but they may become more significant when their relationships to school organization and operation are maintained. For many, these relationships are not maintained and do not even seem maintainable. This disenchantment with the field takes several directions. For some, there is no longer a definition of the field or a core literature in the field. For those who have given up on a core literature, there seems to be a disposition to ignore the general journals in the field, such as *Educational Administration Quarterly* and *Journal of Educational Administration*, and support specialized journals that focus on such areas as school finance, school law, and educational policy. Some would characterize the field as rich in analysis, poor in synthesis— narrowly expert but clearly not integrated.

Another factor contributing to fragmentation of the field probably can be found in the professorial review processes in major universities.

The promotion and tenuring of professors of educational administration is orchestrated in part by professors in the academic disciplines; review committees at college- and university-wide levels play a vital role in these career-shaping decisions. From a disciplinary perspective, specialization is valued and field service is devalued. Basic research or attempts to extend knowledge are often seen as more significant than applied research. With such attitudes prevalent on most campuses, many professors of educational administration seem to have learned how to play the academic game.

Whatever the causes, the profession is confronted with fragmentation; the challenge facing the field is how to deal with it. Some professors are beginning to recognize that the subfields take on additional meaning when they continually relate to school-wide operation. Some university communities are beginning to see the differences between the basic disciplines and the applied fields, whether in engineering, medicine, or education.

Administrative Behavior and School Outcomes

A few years ago, the Georgia State Department of Education faced the task of revising standards for the public schools of the state. Instead of merely drawing on the conventional wisdom of the profession, as Herbert Walberg (1982) reports, the department decided that research findings would be assessed as a basis for establishing new standards in each of twelve areas. A recognized scholar in each of these areas was asked to assess the research and suggest implications for the standards. One of the areas was "management strategies." Stephen Knezevich, an experienced professor and dean, assessed the research in educational administration "to explore the question of whether there is evidence garnered through carefully controlled research to document the impact of management on learning" (Walberg, p. 133).

Knezevich began his report by expressing doubt that research could provide direct guidance for the revision of state standards and, in large part, his doubts were confirmed. Despite the paucity of evidence and the inherent difficulty of procuring data, the question posed in Georgia was basic and is being asked with greater frequency. Can research inform administrative practice? More specifically, is there any relationship, direct or indirect, between administrative behavior and student learning? Can administrators make a difference in the growth of individual students?

Such questions have prompted a number of investigators to observe how administrators actually spend their time. For instance, Martin and Willower (1981) observed five high school principals, each for a period of twenty-five days. They found the principals engaged in many activities; about one-third of their time was devoted to maintenance tasks, one-quarter to pupil control tasks, and one-sixth to the academic program. These findings caused many to conclude that with instructional concerns so low among the priorities of administrators, it is unreasonable to expect administrative behavior to make any difference in student learning. Others concluded that some of the so-called maintenance activities may indeed affect, indirectly at least, the instructional program. Even if that more supportive view of administration is accepted, there seems to be little research evidence to back it up.

In contrast with this bleak picture are many of the reports on effective schools. As some have pointed out, recent studies conclude that principals in "effective" schools are strong programmatic leaders who know about learning problems and allocate resources wisely. But the ray of hope provided by those studies may be dimmed on further consideration. In the first place, most of the studies are correlational in nature and do not get at basic causes. Second, there are some contradictions in the characteristics reported for effective schools. For instance, effective schools are seen as places where teachers have substantial instructional autonomy and principals, as strong programmatic leaders, give much direction to the instructional program—conditions that appear to be somewhat at odds. The most serious inadequacy of the effective schools literature, useful as it may be, seems to be its failure to recognize how many variables may be involved and how carefully they must be defined.

It is to this last problem that Bossert and his associates (1982) have addressed themselves. Their framework for examining instructional management suggests that the management behavior of principals is affected by personal characteristics, district characteristics, and external characteristics. Moreover, principals' behavior affects both the school climate and the instructional organization. With such a framework in mind, studies can be devised to test each of the variables named. Research of this magnitude is no overnight task, but such research may eventually clarify the relationships between administrative behavior and student learning.

A Paradigm Shift?

In terms of the study of administration, the current scene is not a tranquil one. A number of scholars in the field have called for a reassessment of theory and research methodology. As early as the mid-1960s, Jean Hills (1965) suggested that the field was in transition. About a decade later, Donald Erickson (1977, p. 125) contended that "we need intense work on causal models linking process and structure to student behavior and long-term accomplishment." As Jack Culbertson (1987) noted, it remained for Thomas Greenfield to fire "a shot at the theory movement which was heard around the world." Greenfield (1975) challenged many of the assumptions held by people in the field. His paper, "Theory About Organization: A New Perspective and Its Implications for Schools," was presented to an international audience in 1974. Greenfield argued "an alternative view which sees organizations not as structures subject to universal laws but as cultural artifacts dependent upon the specific meaning and intention of people within them" (1975, p. 74). Instead of the scientific paradigm, borrowed from the physical sciences, he advocated a phenomenological approach to the study of organizations. Instead of quantitative studies, Greenfield contended that "the case study and comparative and historical methods become the preferred means of analysis" (1975, p. 85). Daniel Griffiths (1979) challenged Greenfield's interpretation of the matter, but suggested that there was "intellectual turmoil in educational administration." Christopher Hodgkinson noted "a certain philosophical-ethical thrust integral to the Canadian endeavour in educational administration which . . . is unparalleled in the United States" (1982, p. 66). Moreover, it seems significant that Culbertson (1987), in his careful historical treatment of the field, should entitle the last section of his paper, "Administrative Science as an Embattled Concept: 1967–1984."

The debate has not ended in chaos. Norman Boyan (1981, p. 12) in his survey of research in the field found no "new, single paradigm to guide research across the entire territory or even within any of the several specializations." Donald Willower (1982), after surveying a number of developments in the field, concluded that "positivism is an inadequate philosophy, but it has some key strengths including its emphasis on meaning." One of the more succinct and reasonable treatments of the matter has been offered by Egon Guba and Yvonna Lincoln (1981, p. 77), who suggest that the two paradigms can be complementary: "There is no reason why both camps should not exploit both quantitative and qualitative techniques, should not be concerned with relevance and rigor . . . grounded theory as well as flashes of insight . . . verification and discovery. . . ." Instead of a paradigm shift, a paradigm enlargement appears to be emerging in educational administration.

Summary

Both thought and practice in educational administration were focused, to begin with, on the schools; later these concerns were extended to higher education and to a number of other settings. Predominant views of administration—scientific management, democratic administration, and bureaucracy—were essentially closed systems. Only with the emergence of the open-systems view was the environment as related to the organization given significant attention. The social sciences, particularly psychology and sociology, became supporting disciplines as the theory movement developed in the 1950s and 1960s. With the open-systems view, concepts in economics, political science, and anthropology also became pertinent to an understanding of educational administration.

Currently, the field struggles with ambiguity of purpose in education, fragmentation among its scholars, and a public expectation that administrative behavior should help improve instructional outcomes. These and other difficulties have motivated some scholars to seek a new paradigm—naturalistic as opposed to scientific—but other scholars insist that both paradigms are pertinent to thought and practice in the field.

EPILOGUE

WE HAVE HAD A STIMULATING EXPERIENCE as scholars in attempting to understand and depict what the documents say about the history of thought and practice in educational administration. Now, as actors in the field, it seems appropriate that we reveal some of our own convictions about it.

Educational administration is a complex arena. It is concerned with both thought and practice. As an applied field, it deals with both extending knowledge and improving practice. In terms of thought, many supporting disciplines provide concepts, models, and research methodologies that may have relevance. But this array of ideas must be considered with respect to its usefulness in examining problems in the field, not in the disciplines. In terms of practice, there are a wide variety of institutions—schools, colleges, and others—where administrators work. In many of these institutions, there are many kinds and levels of administrative positions. Great variations in size of institutions add still another complexity to the field. For each institution, regardless of size, level, or type of administrative position, there is an environment more or less unique to that organization.

Educational administration performs a crucial social service. Whether in a rural hamlet, an urban high school, a research university, a government agency, or a major industry, those who help determine educational needs, organize and direct programs to meet those needs, and seek public support for those programs perform one of the most essential services in our society. There is the problem not only of helping induct the young into society, but also of helping young and old to think more critically and more humanely.

Those who study and practice educational administration have embarked on a demanding career. In addition to the complexity of the field and societal expectations, noted above, changes in the field itself must be taken into account. For instance, it seems that educational services in the future will be delivered from a greater diversity of institutions, both public and private. It also appears that educational policies will be framed less by educational bodies and more by governmental actions. Related to these matters, it should be kept in mind that

211

educational administrators must always respond to two forces: one, public pressure for efficiency and accountability, and two, pressure for participation in school policy and decision making on the part of constituencies both in and out of their institutions.

There is a need for better selection and preparation of educational administrators. At present, it seems clear that many administrators fall short of the expectations suggested above. While perfection in this field is no more possible than in other professions, improvements can and must be made. The selection pool, now mainly the teacher corps, should be broadened to include other work groups and those doing graduate work in supporting disciplines. In addition to test data often used in the selection process, more effective use can be made of evidence available from prior work and academic experience of candidates. Complementing rigorous courses in administration and supporting disciplines, clinical programs in the field must also be improved.

Often studied as a science and practiced as an art, educational administration invariably draws on talents for synthesis and integration. Its scholars must be skilled at gleaning ideas and information from various disciplines and applying them wisely to the study of governance in schools and colleges. Its practitioners must exercise comparable intelligence in blending theoretical knowledge with their own values and experiences to forge a compelling leadership style. Both must constantly reconcile the demands of educational organizations with the needs of individuals, the purposes of education with the pressures of expediency, and the perspective offered by their chosen niche with an awareness of the field—and the society—as a whole. Indeed, in an era of specialists, those who study and practice administration must be, at least in some respects, a breed of generalists.

We have more hope than despair. Two sets of conditions will influence future directions of the field; one is social and external to the profession and the other is internal to the profession itself. On the external side, if our society devotes most of its natural and human resources to defense, if poverty at home and in many Third World nations is ignored, if natural resources are not conserved, if the well-being of all people is not sought, if some consensus about the purpose and nature of education is not achieved, then prospects for the schools and colleges of the future are indeed dark. But even if these calamities are avoided, the profession must recognize emerging social and economic conditions. If those in the profession insist on business as usual, if training programs do not reflect the new realities, if research does not focus on the most critical problems in the profession, if administrators themselves remain inflexible, then prospects for the future are still dreary.

On the other hand, external and internal conditions can be more favorable. Russia and the United States may learn to coexist, a way to reduce arms may be found, industrialized nations may find the will to provide necessary assistance to poor countries, conservation of natural and human resources may increasingly be realized, and a consensus may be achieved regarding the crucial role schools and colleges play in the development of the understandings, attitudes, and skills needed in a changing, interdependent world. Even with movement in these directions, there will be a need for internal movement in the profession itself. We think it likely that the profession will come to grips with the social and economic changes in society, that the study and practice of educational administration will respond imaginatively, if unevenly, to those changes, that there is more reason for hope than for despair. But there is much work to do.

REFERENCES

Abbott, M. G. (1960). "Values and Value Perceptions of School Superintendents and Board Members." Ph. D. dissertation, University of Chicago.

Abbott, M. G. (1969). "Hierarchical Impediments to Innovation in Educational Organizations." In F. D. Carver & T. J. Sergiovanni (Eds.), *Organizations and Human Behavior*. New York: McGraw-Hill.

American Association of School Administrators. (1939). *Standards for Superintendents of Schools, A Preliminary Report*. Washington, D. C.: American Association of School Administrators.

American Association of School Administrators. (1951). *The American School Superintendency*. Thirtieth Yearbook. Washington, D. C.: American Association of School Administrators.

American Association of School Administrators. (1955). *Staff Relations in School Administration*. Thirty-Third Yearbook. Washington, D. C.: American Association of School Administrators.

American Association of School Administrators. (1960). *Professional Administrators for America's Schools*. Thirty-Eighth Yearbook. Washington, D. C.: American Association of School Administrators.

American Association of University Professors. (1941). "Academic Freedom and Tenure: 1940 Statement of Principles." *Bulletin of American Association of University Professors, 17*, 40–43.

Anderson, J. G. (1968). *Bureaucracy in Education*. Baltimore, Md: Johns Hopkins University Press.

Anderson, R. C. (1963). "Learning in Discussions: A Resume of the Authoritarian-Democratic Studies." In W. W. Charters, Jr. & N. L. Gage (Eds.), *Readings in the Social Psychology of Education*. Boston: Allyn and Bacon.

Argyris, C. (1957). *Personality and Organization*. New York: Harper & Row.

Argyris, C. (1964). *Integrating the Individual and the Organization*. New York: John Wiley & Sons.

Ayres, L. (1913). *Laggards in Our Schools*. New York: Russell Sage Foundation.

Bailey, S. K., et al. (1977). *Simple Justice*. New York: Vintage Books.

Baldridge, J. V. (1971a). *Power and Conflict in the University*. New York: John Wiley & Sons.

Baldridge, J. V. (Ed.). (1971b). *Academic Governance*. Berkeley, Calif.: McCutchan.

Baritz, L. (1960). *The Servants of Power*. Middletown, Conn.: Wesleyan University Press.

215

Barnard, C. I. (1938). *The Functions of the Executive.* Cambridge: Harvard University Press.

Barr, A. S. & Burton, W. A. (1926). *The Supervision of Instruction.* New York: Appleton-Century.

Bartky, J. A. (1953). *Supervision as Human Relations.* Boston: D. C. Heath.

Bates, R. J. (1982). "Toward a Critical Practice of Educational Administration." *Studies in Educational Administration,* 27 (September 1982).

Bates, R. J. (1985). "Administration of Education: Towards a Critical Practice. In T. Hugen & T. N. Postlethwaik (Eds.), *The International Encyclopedia of Education,* Vol. 1, pp. 63–73. Oxford: Pergamon Press. (Original work published 1982.)

Becker, C. L. (1935). *Everyman His Own Historian: Essays on History and Politics.* New York: F. S. Crofts & Co.

Bell, D. (1956). *Work and Its Discontents.* Boston: Beacon Press.

Bell, D. (1976). *The Cultural Contradictions of Capitalism.* New York: Basic Books.

Bendix, R. (1956). *Work and Authority in Industry: Ideologies of Management in the Course of Industrialization.* New York: John Wiley & Sons.

Bendix, R. (1960). *Max Weber: An Intellectual Portrait.* Garden City, N.Y.: Doubleday.

Berman, B. (1983, Fall). "Business Efficiency, American Schooling, and the Public School Superintendency: A Reconsideration of the Callahan Thesis." *History of Education Quarterly,* 23, 297–321.

Bess, J. (1983). "Maps and Gaps in the Study of College and University Organization." *Review of Higher Education,* 6, 239–251.

Bestor, A. E. (1953). *Educational Wastelands.* Urbana, Ill.: University of Illinois Press.

Bidwell, C. E. (1965). "The School as a Formal Organization." In J. G. March (Ed.), *Handbook of Organizations.* Chicago: Rand McNally.

Blau, P. (1955). *The Dynamics of Bureaucracy.* Chicago: University of Chicago Press.

Blau, P. & Meyer, M. W. (1971). *Bureaucracy in Modern Society.* New York: Random House.

Bliss, D. C. (1918). *Methods and Standards for Local School Surveys.* Boston: D. C. Heath.

Bobbitt, F. (1913). "Some General Principles of Management Applied to the Problems of City School Systems." In S. C. Parker (Ed.), *The Supervision of City Schools:* Twelfth Yearbook of the National Society for the Study of Education. Part I. Bloomington, Ill.: Public School Publishing Company.

Bossert, S. T., Dwyer, D. C., Rowan, B., & Lee, G. (1982). "The Instructional Management Role of the Principal." *Educational Administration Quarterly,* 18(3), 34–64.

Boyan, N. J. (1981). "Follow the Leader: Commentary on Research in Educational Administration." *Educational Researcher,* 10 (February 1981), 6–13, 21.

Boyan, N. J. (1987). *The Handbook of Research on Educational Administration.* White Plains, N.Y.: Longman, Inc.

Boyd, W. L. & Crowson, R. L. (1981). "The Changing Conception and Practice of Public School Administration." In D. C. Berliner (Ed.), *Review of Research in Education*, Vol. 9, pp. 311–373. Washington, D. C.: American Educational Research Association.

Brennan, B. (1973, October). "Principals as Bureaucrats." *The Journal of Educational Administration*, XI, 171–178.

Brown et al. v. Board of Education of Topeka et al., 347 U.S. 483 (1954).

Brubacher, J. S. (1966). *A History of the Problems of Education*. (2nd Ed.). New York: McGraw-Hill.

Callahan, R. E. (1962). *Education and the Cult of Efficiency*. Chicago: University of Chicago Press.

Callahan, R. E. (1966). *The Superintendent of Schools: An Historical Analysis*. Final Report of Project S–212, Cooperative Research Branch, Washington, D. C.: U. S. Office of Education, Department of Health, Education and Welfare.

Callahan, R. E. (1975). "The American Board of Education, 1789–1960." In Peter J. Cistone (Ed.), *Understanding School Boards*. Lexington, Mass.: D. C. Heath.

Cameron, K. (1984). "Organizational Adaptation and Higher Education. *Journal of Higher Education*, 55(2), 122–144.

Campbell, C. M. (1955). "Human Relations Techniques Useful in School Administration." *American School Board Journal*, 130 (June 1955), 32.

Campbell, R. F. (1964). "The Professorship in Education Administration: Preparation." In J. D. Willower & J. Culbertson (Eds.), *The Professorship in Educational Administration*, pp. 15–28. Columbus, Ohio: University Council for Educational Administration, and University Park, Pa.: The Pennsylvania State University.

Campbell, R. F. (1979). "A Critique of the Educational Administration Quarterly." *Educational Administration Quarterly*, 15 (Fall, 1979), 1–19.

Campbell, R. F. & Gregg, R. T. (Eds.). (1957). *Administrative Behavior in Education*. New York: Harper and Bros.

Campbell, R. F., Bridges, E., Corbally, J. E., Nystrand, R. O., & Ramseyer, J. (1971). *Introduction to Educational Administration* (fourth edition). Boston: Allyn and Bacon.

Campbell, R. F. & Newell, L. J. (1973). *A Study of Professors of Educational Administration: Problems and Prospects of an Applied Academic Field*. Columbus, Ohio: University Council for Educational Administration.

Campbell, R. F., Corbally, J. E., & Nystrand, R. O. (1983). *Introduction to Educational Administration*. (6th Ed.). Boston: Allyn and Bacon.

Campbell, R. F., Cunningham, L., Nystrand, R. O., & Usdan, M. (1985). *The Organization and Control of American Schools* (5th Ed.). Columbus, Ohio: Merrill Publishing Co.

Caplow, T., & McGee, R. J. (1965). *The Academic Marketplace*. New York: Anchor Books, Doubleday. (Originally published in 1958)

Carey, A. (1967). "The Hawthorne Studies: A Radical Criticism." *American Sociological Review*, 32 (June 1967), 403–416.

Carlson, R. O. (1962). *Executive Succession and Organizational Change*. Chicago: Midwest Administration Center, University of Chicago.

Carr, T. W. (1978). "Education in the Military: A Look Into the Future." In Franklin D. Margiotta, *The Changing World of the American Military.* Chap. 24. Boulder, Colo.: Westview Press.

Cartwright, D. & Zander, A. (1953). *Group Dynamics Research and Theory.* Evanston, Ill.: Row Peterson and Co.

Case, R. D. (1931). *The Platoon School in America.* Stanford, Calif.: Stanford University Press.

Caswell, H. L. (1929). *City School Surveys.* New York: Bureau of Publications, Teachers College, Columbia University.

Center for the Study of Public Policy (1970). *Education Vouchers.* Cambridge, Mass.: Harvard University.

Chandler, A. D. (1962). *Strategy and Structure: Chapters in the History of Industrial Enterprise.* Cambridge, Mass.: Massachusetts Institute of Technology Press.

Charters, W. W., Jr. (1963). "The Social Background of Teaching." In N. L. Gage (Ed.), *Handbook of Research on Teaching.* Chicago: Rand McNally.

Charters, W. W., Jr. (1977). "The Future (and a Bit of the Past) of Research and Theory." In Luvern L. Cunningham et al., *Educational Administration: The Developing Decades,* pp. 362–375. Berkeley, Calif.: McCutchan.

Chase, S. (1941). "What Makes the Worker Want to Work?" *Reader's Digest, 38* (February 1941), 15–20.

Clark, H. F. & Sloan, H. S. (1958). *Classrooms in the Factories.* New York: New York University Press.

Cohen, S. (1976). "The History of American Education, 1900–1976." *Harvard Educational Review,* 46 (August 1976), 298–330.

Cohen, M. D. & March, J. G. (1974). *Leadership and Ambiguity: The American College President.* New York: McGraw-Hill.

Coladarci, A. P. & Getzels, J. W. (1955). *The Use of Theory in Educational Administration.* Stanford, Calif.: School of Education, Stanford University.

Committee on the Objectives of General Education in a Free Society. (1945). *General Education in a Free Society.* Cambridge, Mass.: Harvard University Press.

Cook, L. & Cook, E. (1957). *School Problems in Human Relations.* New York: McGraw-Hill.

Coons, J. E. & Sugarman, S. D. (1978). *Education by Choice.* Berkeley, Calif.: University of California Press.

Cooper, D. H. (1946). *The City School Survey as an Instrument for Educational Planning.* Unpublished Ph. D. thesis, University of Chicago.

Cornford, F. M. (1908). *Microcosmographia Academica: Being a Guide for the Young Academic Politician.* London: Bowes & Bowes.

Corson, J. J. (1960). *Governance of Colleges and Universities.* New York: McGraw-Hill.

Corson, J. J. (1975). *The Governance of Colleges and Universities: Modernizing Structure and Processes.* (Rev. Ed.). New York: McGraw-Hill.

Corwin, R. (1969). "Professional Persons in Public Organizations." In F. D. Carver & T. J. Sergiovanni (Eds.), *Organizations and Human Behavior.* New York: McGraw-Hill.

Courtis, S. A. (1916). "Courtis Tests in Arithmetic: Value to Superintendents and Teachers." In G. M. Whipple (Ed.), *Standards and Tests for the Measurement of the Efficiency of Schools and School Systems*: Fifteenth Yearbook, National Society for the Study of Education. Chicago: University of Chicago Press.

Cowley, W. H. (1956). *An Appraisal of American Higher Education*. Unpublished, Stanford University, Palo Alto.

Cowley, W. H. (1980). *Presidents, Professors, and Trustees: The Evolution of American Academic Government*. (D. T. Williams, Jr., Ed.). San Francisco: Jossey-Bass.

Cox, H., & Wood, J. R. (1980, October). "Organizational Structure and Professional Alienation: The Case of Public School Teachers." *Peabody Journal of Education, 58*, 1–6.

Cremin, L. A. (1961). *The Transformation of the School: Progressivism in American Education, 1876–1957*. New York: Random House, Vintage Books.

Cremin, L. A. (1964). *The Wonderful World of Ellwood Patterson Cubberley*. New York: Teachers College, Columbia University.

Cremin, L. A., Shannon, D. A., & Townsend, M. E. (1954). *A History of Teachers College, Columbia University*. New York: Columbia University Press.

Cresswell, A. M., & Murphy, M. J. (1976). *Education and Collective Bargaining*. Berkeley, Calif.: McCutchan.

Cresswell, A. M., Murphy, M. J., & Herschner, C. T. (1980). *Teachers Unions and Collective Bargaining in Public Education*. Berkeley, Calif.: McCutchan.

Cuban, Larry (1976). *Urban School Chiefs Under Fire*. Chicago, Ill.: University of Chicago Press.

Cubberley, E. P. (1906). *The Certification of Teachers: A Consideration of Present Conditions with Suggestions as to Future Improvement* (Yearbook of the National Society for the Scientific Study of Education, Vol. 5, Part 2). Chicago, Ill.: University of Chicago Press.

Cubberley, E. P. (1916). "Uses of Standard Tests at Salt Lake City, Utah." In G. M. Whipple (Ed.), *Standards and Tests for the Measurement of the Efficiency of Schools and School Systems: Fifteenth Yearbook of the National Society for the Study of Education*. Part I. Bloomington, Ill.: Public School Publishing Company.

Cubberley, E. P. (1919). *Public Education in the United States*. Boston: Houghton Mifflin.

Cubberley, E. P. (1922). *Public School Administration* (Rev. Ed.). Boston: Houghton Mifflin.

Cubberley, E. P. (1924). "Public School Administration." In I. L. Kandel (Ed.), *Twenty-Five Years of American Education*. Freeport, N.Y.: Books for Libraries Press.

Cubberley, E. P. (1928). *Public School Administration*. New York: Houghton Mifflin.

Cubberley, E. P. (1929a). *Public School Administration*. (3rd Ed.). San Francisco: Houghton Mifflin.

Cubberley, E. P. (1929b). *State School Administration*. Boston: Houghton Mifflin.

Culbertson, J. (1987). "A Century's Quest for a Knowledge Base." In Norman J. Boyan (Ed.), *The Handbook of Research on Educational Administration*. White Plains, N.Y.: Longman's Inc.

Culbertson, J., Farquhar, R. H., Fogarty, B. M., & Shibles, M. R. (Eds.). (1973). *Social Science Content for Preparing Educational Leaders.* Columbus, Ohio: Charles E. Merrill Publishing Co.

Cunningham, L. L., Hack, W. G., & Nystrand, R. O. (Eds.). (1977). *Educational Administration: The Developing Decades.* Berkeley, Calif.: McCutchan.

Cunningham, L. L. & Hentges, J. J. (1982). *The American School Superintendency, 1982—A Summary Report.* Washington, D. C.: American Association of School Administrators.

Curti, M. (1959). *The Social Ideas of American Educators.* Totowa, N.J.: Littlefield, Adams.

Davies, D. (Ed.). (1981). *Communities and Their Schools.* New York: McGraw-Hill.

Department of Supervisors and Directors of Instruction. (1938). *Cooperation: Principles and Practices.* Washington, D. C.: National Educational Association.

Derber, M. (1970). *The American Idea of Industrial Democracy.* Urbana, Ill.: University of Illinois Press.

Dewey, J. (1916). *Democracy and Education.* New York: Macmillan & The Free Press.

Dewey, J. (1946). *Problems of Men.* New York: Philosophical Library.

Dodds, H. W. (1962). *The Academic President—Educator or Caretaker?* San Francisco: McGraw-Hill.

Dutton, S. T. & Snedden, D. (1909). *The Administration of Public Education in the United States.* New York: Macmillan.

Easton, D. (1965). *A Framework for Political Analysis.* New York: Prentice-Hall.

Eddy, W. P. (1970, March). "The Relationship of Role Orientation of Teachers to Organization of Schools." *Alberta Journal of Educational Research, XVI,* 13–21.

Educational Policies Commission. (1938). *The Purposes of Education in American Democracy.* Washington, D. C.: Educational Policies Commission, National Education Association and American Association of School Administrators.

Educational Policies Commission. (1940). *Learning the Ways of Democracy.* Washington, D. C.: National Education Association.

Educational Policies Commission. (1943). *Education and the People's Peace.* Washington, D. C.: National Education Association.

Education Times. "Tuition Tax Credits." July 26, 1982, p. 2.

Eells, W. C. (1937). *Surveys of American Higher Education.* New York: Carnegie Foundation for the Advancement of Teaching.

Eikenberry, D. H. (1925). *Status of the High School Principal* (Bulletin No. 24). U. S. Bureau of Education. Washington, D. C.: Government Printing Office.

Engelhardt, N. L., Reeves, C. E., & Womrath, G. F. (1932). *Survey Data Book for Public School Janitorial-Engineering Service.* New York: Teachers College, Columbia University.

Erickson, D. A. (1977). "An Overdue Paradigm Shift in Educational Administration." In L. L. Cunningham, W. G. Hack, & R. O. Nystrand (Eds.), *Educational Administration: The Developing Decades,* Chap. 7. Berkeley, Calif.: McCutchan.

Etzioni, A. (1964). *Modern Organizations*. Englewood Cliffs, N.J.: Prentice-Hall.

Farquhar, R. H. (1970). "The Humanities in Preparing Educational Administrators" (State-of-the-Knowledge Series, No. Seven). University of Oregon: The ERIC Clearinghouse on Educational Administration.

Farquhar, R. H. (1977). "Preparatory Programs in Educational Administration, 1954–1974." In L. L. Cunningham, W. G. Hack, & R. O. Nystrand (Eds.), *Educational Administration: The Developing Decades*, pp. 329–357. Berkeley, Calif.: McCutchan.

Ferris, A. L. (1969). *Indicators of Trends in American Education*. New York: Russell Sage Foundation.

Fleming, T. (1982). "Management by Consensus: Democratic Administration and Human Relations, 1929–1954." Unpublished Ph. D. dissertation, University of Oregon.

Flesher, W. R. & Knoblauch, A. L. (1957). *A Decade of Development in Educational Leadership: The First Ten Years of NCPEA, 1947–1956*. (n.p.). The National Conference of Professors of Education Administration.

Flexner, A. (1930). *Universities: American, English, and German*. New York: Oxford University Press.

Follett, M. P. (1920). *The New State*. London: Longman's, Green and Company.

Follett, M. P. (1930). *Creative Experience*. London: Longman's, Green and Company.

Friedman, M. (1955). "The Role of Government in Education." In Robert A. Salo (Ed.), *Economics and the Public Interest*. New Brunswick, N.J.: Rutgers University Press.

Froebel, F. (1887). *Menschenerziehung* (English trans., *The Education of Man*) (W. N. Hailmann, Trans.). New York: D. Appleton & Co. (Original work published 1826.)

Gerth, H. H. & Mills, C. W. (1948). *From Max Weber: Essays in Sociology*. London: Routledge and Kegan Paul.

Getzels, J. W. (1952). "A Psycho-Sociological Framework for the Study of Educational Administration." *Harvard Educational Review*, 22 (Fall 1952), 235–246.

Getzels, J. W. (1958). "Administration as a Social Process." In Andrew W. Halpin (Ed.), *Administrative Theory in Education*, Chap. 7. Chicago: Midwest Administration Center, University of Chicago.

Getzels, J. W. (1977). "Educational Administration Twenty Years Later, 1954–1974." In L. L. Cunningham, W. G. Hack, & R. O. Nystrand (Eds.), *Educational Administration: The Developing Decades*. Berkeley, Calif.: McCutchan.

Getzels, J. W. (1978). "The Communities of Education." *Teachers College Record*, 79 (May 1978), 659–682.

Getzels, J. W. & Guba, E. G. (1957). "Social Behavior and the Administrative Process." *School Review*, 65 (Winter 1957), 423–441.

Getzels, J. W., Lipham, J. M., & Campbell, R. F. (1968). *Educational Administration as a Social Process*. New York: Harper & Row.

Gilland, T. M. (1935). *The Origin and Development of the Power and Duties of City School Superintendents*. Chicago: University of Chicago Press.

Goldhammer, K. (1963). "The Social Sciences and the Preparation of Educational Administrators." Columbus, Ohio: Division of Educational Administration, University of Alberta and The University Council for Education Administration.

Goldman, E. (1960). *Crucial Decade—and After: America 1945-60.* New York: Random House.

Gosine, M. & Keith, M. V. (1970). "Bureaucracy, Teacher Personality Needs and Teacher Satisfaction." *The Canadian Administrator, 10,* 1-5.

Gouldner, A. (1954). *Patterns of Industrial Bureaucracy.* Glencoe, Ill.: Free Press.

Greenfield, T. B. (1975). "Theory about Organization: A New Perspective and Its Implications for Schools." In M. Hughes (Ed.), *Administering Education: International Challenge.* London: The Athlone Press.

Greenfield, T. B. (1979). "Ideas versus Data: How Can the Data Speak for Themselves?" In G. L. Immegart and W. L. Boyd (Eds.), *Problem Finding in Educational Administration.* Lexington, Mass.: D. C. Heath.

Greenfield, T. B. (1980). "The Man Who Comes Through the Door in the Wall: Discovering Truth, Discovering Self, Discovering Organizations." *Educational Administration Quarterly, 16* (Fall 1980), 25-59.

Griffiths, D. E. (1956). *Human Relations in School Administration.* New York: Appleton-Century-Crofts.

Griffiths, D. E. (Ed.). (1964). *Behavioral Science and Educational Administration.* Sixty-Third Yearbook of the National Society for the Study of Education, Part II. Chicago: University of Chicago Press.

Griffiths, D. E. (1966). *The School Superintendent.* New York: Center for Applied Research in Education.

Griffiths, D. E. (1979). "Intellectual Turmoil in Educational Administration." *Educational Administration Quarterly, 15* (Fall 1979), 43-65.

Griffiths, D. E. (1983). "Evolution in Research and Theory: A Study of Prominent Researchers." *Educational Administration Quarterly, 19* (Summer 1983), 201-221.

Gronn, P. C. (1982). "Neo-Taylorism in Educational Administration." *Educational Administration Quarterly, 18* (Fall 1982), 17-35.

Gross, Neal (1958). *Who Runs Our Schools?* New York: John Wiley & Sons.

Guba, E. G. & Lincoln, Y. S. (1981). *Effective Evaluation.* San Francisco: Jossey-Bass.

Gulick, L. & Urwick, L. (1937). *Papers on the Science of Administration.* New York: Institute of Public Administration.

Halpin, A. W. (1956). *The Leadership Behavior of School Superintendents.* SCDS Monograph No. 4. Columbus, Ohio: College of Education, The Ohio State University.

Halpin, A. W. (Ed.). (1958). *Administrative Theory in Education.* Chicago: Midwest Administration Center, University of Chicago.

Halpin, A. W. (1970). "Administrative Theory: The Fumbled Torch." In A. M. Kroll, *Issues in American Education,* pp. 156-183. New York: Oxford University Press.

Halpin, A. W. & Winer, B. J. (1952). *The Leadership Behavior of the Airplane Command-ers*. Columbus, Ohio: The Ohio University Research Foundation.

Halpin, A. W. & Hayes, A. E. (1977). "The Broken Ikon, Or, Whatever Happened to Theory?". In Luvern L. Cunningham et al. (Eds.), *Educational Administration: The Developing Decades*, pp. 261–297. Berkeley, Calif.: McCutchan.

Hansot, E. M. (1975, Autumn). "The Modern Educational Bureaucracy and the Process of Change." *Educational Administration Quarterly, 11*, 21–36.

Harris, C. W. (Ed.). (1960). *Encyclopedia of Educational Research*. (3rd ed.). New York: Macmillan.

Henderson, A. (1963). "Improving Decision-Making Through Research." In G. Smith (Ed.), *Current Issues in Higher Education*. Washington, D. C.: American Association for Higher Education.

Henderson, A. M. & Parsons, T. (1947). *Max Weber: The Theory of Social and Economic Organization*. New York: Oxford University Press.

Henry, N. B. (Ed.). (1946). *Changing Conceptions in Educational Administration*. Forty-Fifth Yearbook of the National Society for the Study of Education, Part II. Chicago: University of Chicago Press.

Henry, N. B. (Ed.). (1954). *Citizen Co-Operation to Better Public Schools*. Fifty-Third Yearbook of the National Society for the Study of Education, Part I. Chicago: University of Chicago Press.

Herriott, R. E. & Firestone, W. A. (1984). "Two Images of Schools as Organizations: A Refinement and Elaboration." *Educational Administration Quarterly, 20* (Fall 1984), 41–57.

Hill, H. (1947). *Personnel Problems in American Education."* In *American Association of School Administrators Official Report, 1946*. Washington, D. C.: National Education Association.

Hills, J. (1965). "Educational Administration: A Field in Transition." *Educational Administration Quarterly, 1* (Winter 1965), 58–66.

Hitch, C. J. & McKean, R. N. (1960). *The Economics of Defense in the Nuclear Age*. Cambridge: Harvard University Press.

Hodgkinson, C. (1978). *Towards a Philosphy of Administration*. Oxford, England: Basil Blackwell.

Hodgkinson, C. (1982). "Educational Administration in Canada: A Conspectus." *School Organization and Management Abstracts*, Vol. 1, No. 2.

Hodgkinson, C. (1983). *The Philosophy of Leadership*. New York: St. Martin's Press.

Hoy, W. K. (1982). "Recent Developments in Theory and Research in Educational Administration." *Educational Administration Quarterly, 18* (Summer, 1982), 1–11.

Hoy, W. K. & Miskel, C. G. (1987). *Educational Administration: Theory, Research, and Practice*. (3rd ed.). New York: Random House.

Hunter, F. (1953). *Community Power Structure*. Chapel Hill, N.C.: University of North Carolina Press.

Hutchins, R. M. (1936). *The Higher Learning in America*. New Haven: Yale University Press.

Immegart, G. L. & Boyd, W. L. (Eds.). (1979). *Problem-Finding in Educational Administration.* Lexington, Mass.: D. C. Heath.

Isherwood, G. B. & Hoy, W. K. (1972, Fall). "Bureaucratic Structure Reconsidered." *The Journal of Experimental Education, 41,* 47–50.

Isherwood, G. B. & Hoy, W. K. (1973, May). "Bureaucracy, Powerlessness, and Teacher Work Values." *The Journal of Educational Administration, XI,* 124–138.

James, H. T. (1969). *The New Cult of Educational Efficiency.* Pittsburgh: The University of Pittsburgh Press.

Johnson, S. M. (1983). "Teacher Unions in Schools: Authority and Accommodation." *Harvard Educational Review, 53* (August 1983), 309–326.

Katz, M. B. (1975). *Class, Bureaucracy, and Schools.* New York: Praeger.

Keller, G. (1983). *Academic Strategy: The Management Revolution.* Baltimore, Md.: Johns Hopkins University Press.

Kerr, C. (1953). "What Became of the Independent Spirit?" *Fortune, 48* (July 1953), 110–111.

Kerr, C. (1963). *The Uses of the University.* New York: Harper Torchbooks, Harper & Row.

Kerr, C. (1972). *The Uses of the University.* (2nd Ed.). Cambridge, Mass.: Harvard University Press.

Kilpatrick, W. H. (Ed.). (1933). *The Educational Frontier: Twenty-first Yearbook of the National Society of College Teachers of Education.* Chicago: University of Chicago Press.

Kimbrough, R. B. & Nunnery, M. Y. (1983). *Educational Administration: An Introduction* (2nd Ed.). New York: Macmillan.

Kirst, M. W. (1984). "The Changing Balance in State and Local Power to Control Education." *Phi Delta Kappan, 66* (November 1984), 190.

Kluger, R. (1977). *Simple Justice.* New York: Vintage Books.

Knezevich, S. J. (1973). *Program Budgeting.* Berkeley, Calif.: McCutchan.

Knezevich, S. J. (1982). *Management Strategies.* In H. J. Walberg (Ed.), *Improving Educational Standards and Productivity.* Berkeley, Calif.: McCutchan.

Koerner, J. D. (1959). *The Case for Basic Education.* Boston: Little, Brown.

Koerner, J. D. (1968). *Who Controls American Education?* Boston: Beacon Press.

Lasswell, H. (1936). *Who Gets What, When, How.* New York: McGraw-Hill.

Lawrence, P. R. & Lorsch, J. W. (1967). *Organization and Environment.* Homewood, Ill.: Richard D. Irwin.

Lazarsfeld, P. F. & Thielens, W., Jr. (1958). *The Academic Mind: Social Scientists in a Time of Crisis.* Glencoe, Ill.: The Free Press.

Leithwood, K. A. & Montgomery, D. J. (1982). "The Role of the Elementary School Principal in Program Improvement." *Review of Educational Research, 52*(3), 309–339.

Levine, D. U. (1976, April). "Social Change and the Job of the Teacher." *Clearing House, 41,* 502–504.

Levine, D. U. & Havighurst, R. J. (Eds.). (1971). *Farewell to Schools.* Worthington, Ohio: Charles A. Jones Publishing Co.

Lieberman, M. (1981). "Teacher Bargaining: An Autopsy." *Phi Delta Kappan, 63*(4).

Link, A. S. & Catton, W. B. (1967). *American Epoch: A History of the United States Since the 1890s.* New York: Alfred A. Knopf.

Lortie, D. C. (1975). *School Teacher.* Chicago: University of Chicago Press.

Lynd, A. (1953). *Quackery in the Public Schools.* Boston: Little, Brown.

Malen, B. & Ogawa, R. T. (1985). "The Implementation of the Salt Lake School Districts Shared Governance Policy: A Study of School Site Councils." Report to Salt Lake City, Utah Board of Education, 40 pages.

March, J. G. & Simon, H. A. (1958). *Organizations.* New York: John Wiley & Sons.

March, J. G. (1978). "American Public School Administration: A Short Analysis." *School Review, 86* (February 1978), 217-250.

Marrow, A. J. (1956). *The Practical Theorist: The Life and Work of Kurt Lewin.* New York: Basic Books.

Martin, W. J. & Willower, D. J. (1981). "The Managerial Behavior of High School Principals." *Educational Administration Quarterly, 17* (Winter 1981), 69-90.

Martin, W. B. W. (1975). "The School Organization: Arenas and Social Power." *Administrator's Notebook.* XXIII(5), 1-4.

Maslow, A. (1954). *Motivation and Personality.* New York: Harper and Bros.

Mayo, E. (1923). "The Irrational Factor in Human Behavior: The 'Night Mind' in Industry." *The Annals of the American Academy, 110* (November 1923), 117-130.

Mayo, E. (1933). *The Human Problems of an Industrial Civilization.* New York: Macmillan.

Mayo, E. (1945). *The Social Problems of an Industrial Civilization.* Boston: Division of Research, Harvard University.

McConnell, T. R. (1963). "Needed: Research in College and University Organization and Administration." In T. Lunsford (Ed.), *Study of Academic Organizations.* Boulder, Colo.: Western Institute Commission on Higher Education.

McGregor, D. (1960). *The Human Side of Enterprise.* New York: McGraw-Hill.

McPherson, R. B. (1983). "The Evolution of the Getzels Model." Unpublished paper, 23 pp.

Merton, R. (1959). *Social Theory and Social Structure.* Glencoe, Ill.: Free Press.

Metcalf, H. C. & Urwick, L. (Eds.). (1940). *Dynamic Administration: The Collected Papers of Mary Parker Follett.* New York: Harper & Row.

Michaelsen, J. B. (1981). "The Political Economy of School District Administration." *Educational Administration Quarterly, 17* (Summer 1981), 98-113.

Miklos, E. (1983). "Evolution in Administrator Preparation Programs." *Educational Administration Quarterly, 19*(3), 153-177.

Miller, V. (1963). *Common and Specialized Learnings for Educational Administrators* (UCEA position paper). Columbus, Ohio: The University Council for Educational Administration.

Miller, V., Madden, G., & Kincheloe, J. (1972). *The Public Administration of American School Systems.* New York: Macmillan.

Miller, W. (1942). *Democracy in Educational Administration.* New York: Bureau of Publications, Teachers College, Columbia University.

Milstein, M. M. & Belasco, J. A. (1973). *Educational Administration and the Behavioral Sciences*. Boston: Allyn and Bacon.

Mintzberg, H. (1973). *The Nature of Administrative Work*. New York: Harper & Row.

Miskel, C. & Gerhardt, E. (1974, May). "Perceived Bureaucracy, Teacher Conflict, Central Life Interests, Voluntarism, and Job Satisfaction." *The Journal of Educational Administration, XII*, 84–97.

Miskel, C. & Sandlin, T. (1981). "Survey Research in Educational Administration." *Educational Administration Quarterly, 17* (Fall 1981), 1–20.

Moehlman, A. B. (1940). *School Administration*. Boston: Houghton Mifflin.

Moeller, G. H. (1964). "Bureaucracy and Teachers' Sense of Power." *School Review, 72* (Summer 1964), 137–157.

Monroe, W. S. (Ed.). (1950). *Encyclopedia of Educational Research*. New York: Macmillan.

Montgomery, D. (1976). "Workers' Control of Machine Production in the Nineteenth Century." *Labor History, 17*, 485–509.

Moore, H. A., Jr. (1957). *Studies in School Administration: A Report on the CPEA*. Washington, D. C.: American Association of School Administrators.

Morgan, D. A. & Newell, L. J. (1982). "Professors of Community College Education: Changes in Theoretical and Professional Orientations." *Community/Junior College Quarterly, 7*, 15–29.

Morphet, E. L., Johns, R. L., & Reller, T. L. (1967). *Educational Organization and Administration*. Englewood Cliffs, N.J.: Prentice-Hall.

Mort, P. R. & Ross, D. H. (1957). *Principles of School Administration: A Synthesis of Basic Concepts*. New York: McGraw-Hill.

Mortimer, K. P. & McConnell, T. R. (1978). *Sharing Authority Effectively*. San Francisco: Jossey-Bass.

Moser, W. E. (1939). "Do Teachers Help Run the Schools?" *The Nation's Schools, 23* (January 1939), 50–52.

Mouzelis, N. P. (1968). *Organization and Bureaucracy: An Analysis of Modern Theories*. Chicago: Aldine Publishing.

Munsterberg, H. (1913). *Psychology and Industrial Efficiency*. Boston: Houghton Mifflin.

Myrdal, G., Sterner, R., & Rose, A. (1944). *An American Dilemma: The Negro Problem & Modern Democracy*. New York: Harper & Bros.

National Commission on Excellence in Education. (1983). *A Nation At Risk*. Washington, D. C.: U. S. Department of Education.

National Commission on School District Reorganization. (1948). *Your School District*. Washington, D. C.: Department of Rural Education.

National Education Association. (1928). *Seventh Yearbook, Bulletin of the Department of Elementary School Principals*. Washington, D. C.: National Education Association.

National Education Association, Department of Superintendence and Directors of Instruction. (1943). *Leadership at Work*. Washington, D. C.: National Education Association.

National Education Association, Department of Elementary School Principals.

(1943). *Elementary Schools: The Frontline of Democracy.* Washington, D. C.: National Education Association.

National Education Association. (1944). *Morale for a Free World America and Not America Only: Twenty-Second Yearbook of the American Association of School Administrators.* Washington, D. C.: National Education Association.

National Education Association. (1955). *Staff Relations in School Administration: Thirty-Third Yearbook of the American Association of School Administrators.* Washington, D. C.: National Education Association.

National Research Council. (1983). *Doctorate Recipients from United States Universities.* (Summary Report 1982). Washington, D. C.: National Academy Press.

National Society for the Study of Education. (1946). *Changing Conceptions in Educational Administration: Forty-Fifth Yearbook of the National Society for the Study of Education.* Part II. Chicago: University of Chicago Press.

Nelson, D. (1980). *Frederick W. Taylor and the Rise of Scientific Management.* Madison, Wisc.: University of Wisconsin Press.

Newell, L. J. & Morgan, D. A. (1983). "The Evolving Higher Education Professoriate: Implications for ASHE." *Review of Higher Education,* 7(1), 67–83.

Newlon, J. H. (1934). *Educational Administration as Social Policy* (Report of the Commission on the Social Studies, Part VIII). San Francisco: Charles Scribner's Sons.

Newman, Cardinal J. H. (1947). *The Idea of a University* (New Ed.). New York: Longman's, Green and Co.

New York Times, 16 December 1940, 6–7.

Noble, D. F. (1977). *America by Design: Science, Technology and the Rise of Corporate Capitalism.* New York: Alfred A. Knopf.

Ortega y Gasset, J. (1966). *Mission of the University* (H. L. Nostrand, Trans.). New York: W. W. Norton & Company, Inc.

Ouchi, W. G. (1981). *Theory Z.* New York: Avon Books.

Page, C. H. (1951). "Bureaucracy and Higher Education." *Journal of General Education,* V (2), 91–100.

Parsons, T. (1958). "Some Ingredients of a General Theory of Formal Organization." In Andrew W. Halpin (Ed.), *Administrative Theory in Education,* pp. 40–72. Chicago: Midwest Administration Center, University of Chicago.

Parsons, T. (1960). *Structure and Process in Modern Societies.* New York: Free Press.

Payne, W. H. (1875). *Chapters on School Supervision.* New York: Wilson, Hinkle and Co.

Person, H. S. (1928). "Scientific Management: An Analysis with Particular Emphasis on Its Attitude Towards Human Relations in Industry." *Bulletin of the Taylor Society,* 13 (October 1928), 199–205.

Peters, T. J. & Waterman, R. H., Jr. (1982). *In Search of Excellence.* New York: Harper & Row.

Peterson, B. H. (1937). "Certification of School Administrators in the United States." *School and Society,* 45, 784–786.

Peterson, M. W. (1985). "Emerging Developments in Postsecondary Organization Theory and Research: Fragmentation or Integration." *Educational Researcher,* 14(3), 5–12.

Pfeffer, J. (1981). *Power in Organizations.* Marshfield, Mass.: Pitman Publishing, Inc.

Pierce, P. R. (1935). *The Origin and Development of the Public School Principalship.* Chicago: University of Chicago Press.

Potter, D. (1962). "The Quest for the National Character." In J. Higham (Ed.), *The Reconstruction of American History,* pp. 197–220. New York: Harper & Row.

Pugh, D. S., Hickson, D. J., & Hinings, C. R. (1964). *Writers on Organizations.* London: Hutchinson and Company.

Punch, K. F. (1969). "Bureaucratic Structure in Schools: Toward Redefinition and Measurement." *Educational Administration Quarterly,* 5 (Spring 1969), 43–57.

Punch, K. F. (1970, October). "Interschool Variation in Bureaucratization." *The Journal of Educational Administration, VIII,* 124–134.

Raub, A. N. (1882). *School Management.* New York: Raub and Co.

Ravitch, D. (1983). *The Troubled Crusade.* New York: Basic Books.

Reeder, W. G. (1930). *The Fundamentals of Public School Administration.* New York: Macmillan.

Reeder, W. G. (1941). *The Fundamentals of Public School Administration.* (Rev. & Enl. Ed.). New York: Macmillan.

Reller, T. L. (1936a). "Executive Responsibility in City School Administration." *American School Board Journal, 93,* 19–20.

Reller, T. L. (1936b). "The Historical Development of School Administration in the United States." In Clyde Milton Hill (Ed.), *Educational Progress and School Administration.* New Haven: Yale University Press.

Rice, J. M. (1893). *The Public School System of the United States.* New York: The Century Company.

Rickover, H. G. (1959). *Education and Freedom.* New York: E. P. Dutton.

Roethlisberger, F. J. (1941). *Management and Morale.* Cambridge, Mass.: Harvard University Press.

Roethlisberger, F. J. & Dickson, W. J. (1939). *Management and the Worker.* Cambridge, Mass.: Harvard University Press.

Rousseau, J. J. (1979). *Emile* (A. Bloom, Trans.). New York: Basic Books. (Original work published 1762.)

Sandler, B. (1977). "Title IX: Antisexism's Big Legal Stick." *American Education, 13* (May 1977), 6–9.

Schlesinger, A. M., Sr. (1933). *The Rise of the City, 1878–1898.* New York: Macmillan.

Schlesinger, A. M., Sr. (1941). *Political and Social Growth of the American People, 1865–1940.* New York: Macmillan.

Scott, W. D. (1912). *The Psychology of Advertising.* Boston: Small, Maynard and Company.

Scott, W. R. (1981). *Organizations: Rational, Natural, and Open Systems.* Englewood Cliffs, N.J.: Prentice-Hall.

Sears, J. B. (1924). "Development of Tests and Measurements." In I. L. Kandel

(Ed.), *Twenty-Five Years of American Education*. Freeport, N.Y.: Books for Libraries Press.

Sears, J. B. (1925). *The School Survey: A Textbook on the Use of School Surveying in the Administration of Public Schooling*. New York: Houghton Mifflin.

Sears, J. B. (1929). "The Survey Movement in School Administration." *Education Outlook, 3,* 202–216.

Sears, J. B. & Henderson, A. D. (1957). *Cubberley of Stanford and His Contributions to American Education*. Stanford, Calif.: Stanford University Press.

Selznick, P. (1948, February). "Foundations of the Theory of Organization." *American Sociological Review, 13,* 25–35.

Selznick, P. (1957). *Leadership in Administration*. New York: Harper & Row.

Sennet, R. (1979). "The Boss's New Clothes." *The New York Review, 26* (February 1979), 42–46.

Shartle, C. L. (1956). *Executive Performance and Leadership*. Englewood Cliffs, N. J.: Prentice-Hall.

Shine, E. H. (1985). *Organizational Culture and Leadership*. San Francisco: Jossey-Bass.

Silver, P. F. & Spuck, D. W. (Eds.). (1978). *Preparatory Programs for Educational Administrators in the United States*. Columbus, Ohio: The University Council for Educational Administration.

Smith, M. (1949). *And Madly Teach: A Layman Looks at Public School Education*. Chicago: Henry Regnery.

Smith, T. (1964). "Review." *History of Education Quarterly, 44,* 76–77.

Soloman, B. M. (1985). *In the Company of Educated Women: A History of Women and Higher Education in America*. New Haven, Conn.: Yale University Press.

Sousa, D. A. & Hoy, W. K. (1981, Fall). "Bureaucratic Structure in Schools: A Refinement and Synthesis in Measurement" *Educational Administration Quarterly, 17,* 21–39.

Spaulding, F. E. (1913). "The Application of the Principles of Scientific Management." In *Journal of Proceedings and Addresses*, National Educational Association, 51st Annual Meeting, pp. 259–279.

Spriegel, W. R. (Ed.). (1953). *The Writings of the Gilbreths*. Homewood, Ill.: Richard D. Irwin.

Stinnett, T. M. (1969). *Professional Problems of Teachers*. (3rd Ed.). London: Macmillan.

Strayer, G. D. & Thorndike, E. L. (1912). *Educational Administration*. New York: Macmillan.

Swift, D. W. (1971). *Ideology and Change in the Public Schools*. Columbus, Ohio: Merrill Publishing Co.

Sykes, G. (1983, March). *Teacher Preparation and the Teacher Workforce: Problems and Prospects for the 80s*. *American Education, 9*(12), 23–29.

Taylor, F. W. (1911). *The Principles of Scientific Management*. New York: Harper and Bros.

Taylor, F. W. (1967). *The Principles of Scientific Management*. New York: W. W. Norton.

Tead, O. (1946, May). "Review of Mayo's Social Problems of an Industrial Civilization." *Survey Graphic, 35,* 179–180.

Thorndike, E. L. (1904). *An Introduction to the Theory of Mental and Social Measurements.* New York: Science Press.

Thorndike, E. L. (1907). *The Elimination of Pupils from Schools.* Bulletin No. 4. Washington, D. C.: United States Bureau of Education.

Turner, F. J. (1947). *The Frontier in American History.* New York: Henry Holt and Company.

Tyack, D. B. (1973). "Bureaucracy and the Common School: The Example of Portland, Oregon, 1851–1913." In M. B. Katz (Ed.), *Education in American History,* pp. 164–181. New York: Praeger.

Tyack, D. B. (1974), *The One Best System.* Cambridge, Mass.: Harvard University Press.

Tyack, D. B. (1976). "Pilgrim's Progress: Toward a Social History of the School Superintendency, 1860–1960." *History of Education Quarterly, 16,* 257–300.

Tyack, D. B. & Hansot, E. (1981). "Conflict and Consensus in American Public Education." *Daedalus: Journal of the American Academy of Arts and Sciences, 110*(3), 1–25.

Tyack, D. B. & Hansot, E. (1982). *Managers of Virtue: Public School Leadership in America, 1820–1980.* New York: Basic Books.

Tyler, R. T. (1941). "Educational Adjustments Necessitated by Changing Ideological Concepts." In W. C. Reavis (Ed.), *Administrative Adjustments Required by Socio-Economic Change: Proceedings of the Tenth Annual Conference of Administrative Officers of Public and Private Schools.* Chicago: University of Chicago Press.

Veblen, T. (1935). *The Higher Learning in America: A Memorandum on the Conduct of Universities by Business Men.* New York: B. W. Huebsch.

Walberg, H. J. (Ed.). (1982). *Improving Educational Standards and Productivity.* Berkeley: McCutchan.

Warren, J. (1976). "Alum Rock Voucher Project." *Educational Researcher, 5* (March 1976), 13–15.

Weick, K. E. (1976). "Educational Organizations as Loosely Coupled Systems." *Administrative Science Quarterly, 2* (March 1976), 1–19.

White, T. H. (1982). *America in Search of Itself.* New York: Harper & Row.

Whitehead, A. N. (1929). *The Aims of Education.* New York: Macmillan.

Williams, R. L. (1965). *The Administration of Academic Affairs in Higher Education.* Ann Arbor: The University of Michigan Press.

Willower, D. J. (1964). "The Professorship in Educational Administration: A rationale." In D. J. Willower & J. Culbertson (Eds.), *The Professorship in Educational Administration,* pp. 87–105. Columbus, Ohio: University Council for Educational Administration, and University Park, Pa.: The Pennsylvania State University.

Willower, D. J. (1982a). "Some 'Yes, Buts' and Educational Administration." Unpublished paper, UCEA Conference, University of Texas at Austin, May 1982, 45 pp.

Willower, D. J. (1982b). "School Organizations: Perspectives in Juxtaposition." *Educational Administration Quarterly, 18* (Summer 1982), 89–110.

Willower, D. J. (1983). "Evolution in the Professorship: Past, Philosophy, Future." *Educational Administration Quarterly, 19*(3), 179–200.

Willower, D. J. & Fraser, H. W. (1980). "School Superintendents on Their Work." *Administrator's Notebook, 28* (1979–80), No. 5.

Wilson, L. (1942). *The Academic Man: A Study in the Sociology of a Profession.* London: Oxford University Press.

Wirt, F. M. & Kirst, M. W. (1982). *Schools in Conflict.* Berkeley, Calif.: McCutchan.

Wolcott, H. F. (1978). *The Man in the Principal's Office.* New York: Holt, Rinehart & Winston.

Yauch, W. (1949). *Improving Human Relations in School Administration.* New York: Harper and Bros.

INDEX

ABOUT THE AUTHORS

ROALD F. CAMPBELL completed a doctoral program in educational administration at Stanford University. He began his career as a teacher, a principal, and a superintendent in the Idaho public schools, and has held endowed chairs in Educational Administration at the University of Chicago and The Ohio State University. At Chicago, Dr. Campbell also served as Dean of the Graduate School of Education. Author and coauthor of numerous articles, monographs, and books in his field, he is currently an adjunct professor at the University of Utah.

THOMAS FLEMING is an historian of education who earned a Ph.D. degree at the University of Oregon. His research interests are in the intellectual and social history of educational administration. Dr. Fleming has published articles on the history of school inspectors and superintendents, provincial policy making in education, higher education, and educational thought. He is presently an assistant professor at the University of Victoria, British Columbia.

L. JACKSON NEWELL earned a Ph.D. in higher education administration at The Ohio State University, and an M.A. in American history at Duke University. His scholarly interests span the history of American universities and the philosophy of administration. He is editor of *The Review of Higher Education*, coauthor of *A Study of Professors of Educational Administration*, and author of numerous articles and a research report entitled *Among the Few: A Study of Deep Springs College, 1917–1980*. Dr. Newell is currently Professor of Higher Education and Dean of Liberal Education at the University of Utah.

JOHN W. BENNION received B.S. and M.A. degrees with majors in history and philosophy from the University of Utah, and a Ph.D. in educational administration from The Ohio State University. He was a public school teacher in Utah and later an assistant professor in educational administration at Indiana University. He served as superintendent of schools in Brighton, New York; Bloomington, Minnesota; and Provo, Utah. Currently, Dr. Bennion is superintendent of schools in Salt Lake City, Utah.